It's another Quality Book from CGP

This book is for anyone doing GCSE Mathematics at Intermediate Level.

Whatever subject you're doing it's the same
old story — there are lots of facts and you've just got
to learn them. KS4 Maths is no different.

Happily this CGP book gives you all that important
information as clearly and concisely as possible.

It's also got some daft bits in to try and make the whole
experience at least vaguely entertaining for you.

What CGP is all about

Our sole aim here at CGP is to produce the highest quality
books — carefully written, immaculately presented and
dangerously close to being funny.

Then we work our socks off to get them out to you
— at the cheapest possible prices.

Contents

Section One — Numbers Mostly

Special Number Sequences 1
Multiples, Factors and Prime Factors 2
LCM and HCF 3
Prime Numbers 4
Fractions, Decimals And Percentages 5
Rounding Off 6
Accuracy and Estimating 8
Conversion Factors 10
Metric and Imperial Units 11
Fractions Without the Calculator 12
More Fractions 13
Percentages 14
Calculator Buttons 16
Number Patterns 20
Finding the nth Term 21
Revision Summary for Section One 22

Section Two — Shapes

Regular Polygons 23
Symmetry 24
The Shapes You Need to Know 26
Areas 27
Circle Questions 28
Perimeters And Areas 29
Volume or Capacity 30
Solids and Nets 31
Length, Area And Volume 32
Enlargements — The 4 Key Features: 33
The Four Transformations 34
Combinations of Transformations 35
Geometry 36
Circle Geometry 38
Three-letter Angle Notation 40
Projections, Congruence and Similarity 41
Revision Summary for Section Two 43

Section Three — Bits and Bobs

Bearings 43
Vectors 44
Pythagoras' Theorem 45
Trigonometry — SIN, COS, TAN 46
Loci and Constructions 48
Ratios 50
Formula Triangles 52
Density and Speed 53
Two Hints When Using Formulas 54
Revision Summary for Section Three 55

Section Four — Statistics

Probability 56
Tree Diagrams 57
Graphs And Charts 58
Stem & Leaf Diagrams and Distribution 60
Mean, Median, Mode and Range 61
Frequency Tables 62
Grouped Frequency Tables 63
Cumulative Frequency Tables 64
The Cumulative Frequency Curve 65
Time Series 66
Revision Summary for Section Four 67

Section Five — Graphs

X, Y and Z Coordinates 68
Easy Graphs You should Know 69
Four Graphs You Should Recognise 70
Finding The Gradient of a Line 72
Plotting Straight Line Graphs 73
Straight Line Graphs: "y = mx + c" 74
Typical Graph Questions 75
Revision Summary for Section Five 77

Section Six — Algebra Mostly

Negative Numbers and Letters 78
Standard Index Form 79
Powers (or "Indices") 81
Square Roots and Cube Roots 82
Substituting Values into Formulas 83
Basic Algebra 84
Quadratics 86
Trial and Improvement 87
Solving Equations The Easy Way 88
Solving Equations 89
Rearranging Formulas 90
Compound Growth and Decay 91
Simultaneous Equations 92
Simultaneous Equations With Graphs 93
Solving Equations Using Graphs 94
Travel Graphs 95
Inequalities 96
Graphical Inequalities 97
Revision Summary for Section Six 98

Answers 99
Index 101

Published by Coordination Group Publications Ltd.
Written by Richard Parsons
Updated by: Claire Thompson,
Iain Nash and Simon Little

ISBN 1 84146 021 4
Groovy website: www.cgpbooks.co.uk
With thanks to Colin Wells for the proof-reading
Printed by Elanders Hindson, Newcastle upon Tyne.

Special Number Sequences

1) EVEN NUMBERS ...all Divide by 2

2 4 6 8 10 12 14 16 18 20 ...

All *EVEN* numbers END in 0, 2, 4, 6 or 8
e.g. 200, 342, 576, 94

2) ODD NUMBERS ...DON'T divide by 2

1 3 5 7 9 11 13 15 17 19 21 ...

All *ODD* numbers END in 1, 3, 5, 7 or 9
e.g. 301, 95, 807, 43

---

3) SQUARE NUMBERS:

They're called *SQUARE NUMBERS* because they're like the *areas* of this pattern of squares:

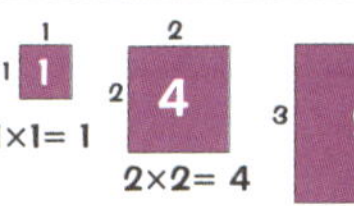

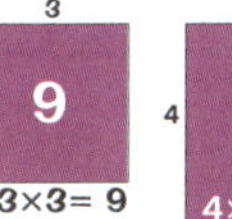

(1×1) (2×2) (3×3) (4×4) (5×5) (6×6) (7×7) (8×8) (9×9) (10×10) (11×11) (12×12) (13×13) (14×14) (15×15)

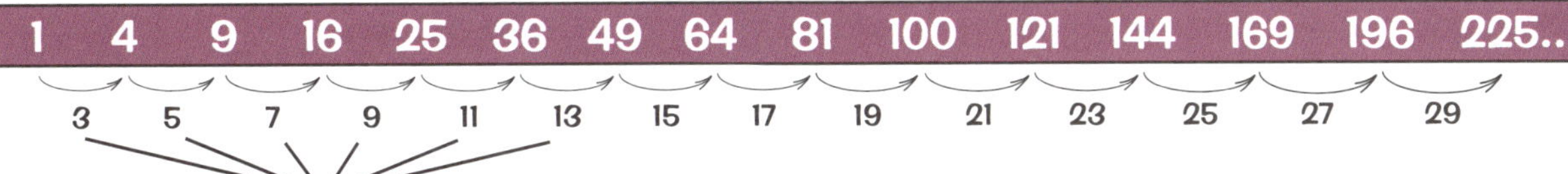

1   4   9   16   25   36   49   64   81   100   121   144   169   196   225...

3   5   7   9   11   13   15   17   19   21   23   25   27   29

Note that the DIFFERENCES between the square numbers are all the ODD numbers.

---

4) CUBE NUMBERS:

They're called *CUBE NUMBERS* because they're like the *volumes* of this pattern of cubes.

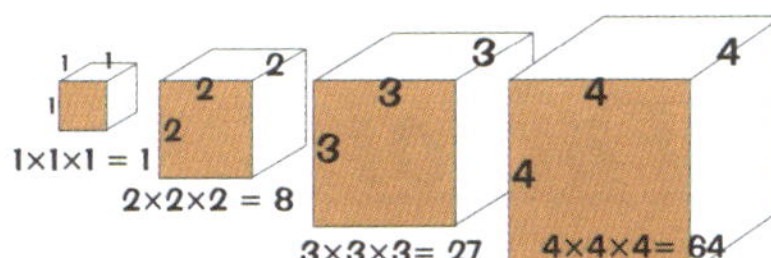

(1x1x1) (2x2x2) (3x3x3) (4x4x4) (5x5x5) (6x6x6) (7x7x7) (8x8x8) (9x9x9) (10x10x10)...

1   8   27   64   125   216   343   512   729   1000...

Admit it, you never knew maths could be this exciting did you!

---

5) POWERS:

Powers are "numbers *multiplied by themselves* so many times".
"*Two to the power three*" = $2^3 = 2 \times 2 \times 2 = 8$

Here's the first few *POWERS OF 2*:

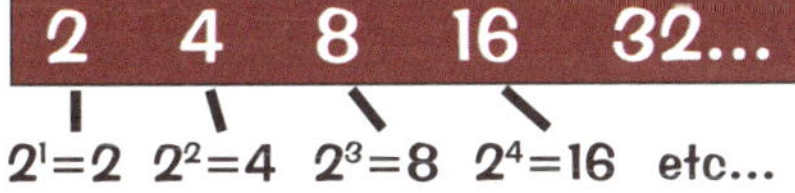

2   4   8   16   32...

$2^1=2$ $2^2=4$ $2^3=8$ $2^4=16$ etc...

... and the first *POWERS OF 10* (even easier):

10   100   1000   10 000   100 000...

$10^1=10$ $10^2=100$ $10^3=1000$ etc...

---

6) TRIANGLE NUMBERS:

To remember the triangle numbers you have to picture in your mind this *increasing pattern of triangles*, where each new row has *one more blob* than the previous row.

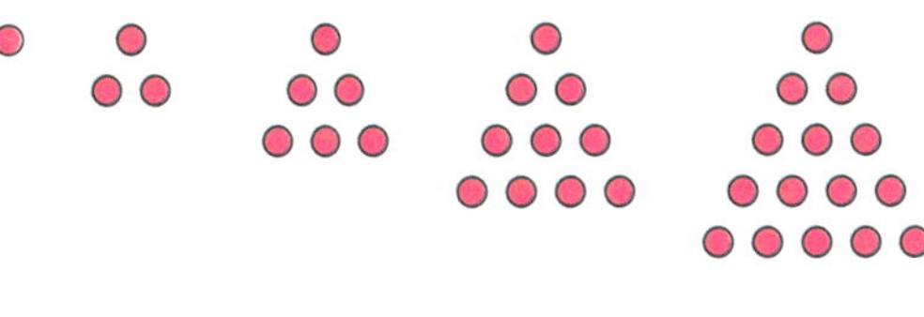

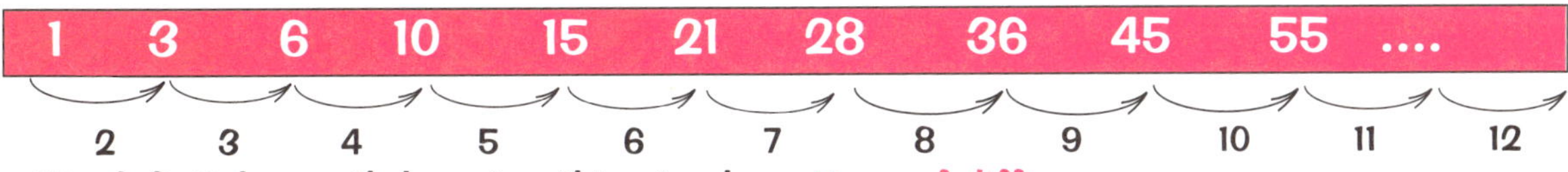

1   3   6   10   15   21   28   36   45   55   ....

2   3   4   5   6   7   8   9   10   11   12

It's definitely worth learning this simple pattern of differences, as well as the formula for the nth term (see P.21) which is:

n^{th} term = ½ n (n + 1)

The Acid Test:

LEARN the first 10 NUMBERS in all six sequences:
EVEN, ODD, SQUARE, CUBE and TRIANGLE NUMBERS.

1) Cover up the page and then write down the first 15 numbers in all six sequences.
2) From this list of numbers: 23, 45, 56, 81, 25, 97, 134, 156, 125, 36, 1, 64
   write down: a) all the even numbers b) all the odd numbers c) all the square numbers
d) all the cube numbers   e) all the powers of 2 and 10.   f) all the triangle numbers.

Multiples, Factors and Prime Factors

Multiples

The **MULTIPLES** of a number are simply its **TIMES TABLE**:

E.g. the multiples of 13 are   13   26   39   52   65   78   91   104 ...

Factors

The **FACTORS** of a number are all the numbers that **DIVIDE INTO IT**.   There's a special way to find them:

Example 1:   *"Find ALL the factors of 24".*

Start off with 1 × the number itself, then try 2×, then 3× and so on, listing the pairs in rows like this. Try each one in turn and put a dash if it doesn't divide exactly. Eventually, when you get a number *repeated*, you *stop*.

$$\begin{array}{l} 1 \times 24 \\ 2 \times 12 \\ 3 \times 8 \\ 4 \times 6 \\ 5 \times - \\ 6 \times 4 \end{array}$$

Increasing by 1 each time

So the **FACTORS OF 24** are 1,2,3,4,6,8,12,24

This method guarantees you find them **ALL** — but *don't forget 1 and 24!*

Factors   Example 2:   *"Find the factors of 64".*

Check each one in turn, to see if it divides or not. Use your calculator when you can, if you're not totally confident.

$$\begin{array}{l} 1 \times 64 \\ 2 \times 32 \\ 3 \times - \\ 4 \times 16 \\ 5 \times - \\ 6 \times - \\ 7 \times - \\ 8 \times 8 \end{array}$$

The 8 has *repeated* so *stop here.*

So the **FACTORS of 64** are 1,2,4,8,16,32,64

Finding Prime Factors — The Factor Tree

Any number can be broken down into a string of **PRIME NUMBERS** (see P.4) all multiplied together — this is called "Expressing it as a product of prime factors", and to be honest it's pretty tedious – but it's in the Exam, and it's not difficult so long as you know what it is.

The mildly entertaining "Factor Tree" method is best, where you start at the top and split your number off into factors as shown.   Each time you get a prime, you ring it and you finally end up with all the prime factors, which you can then arrange in order.

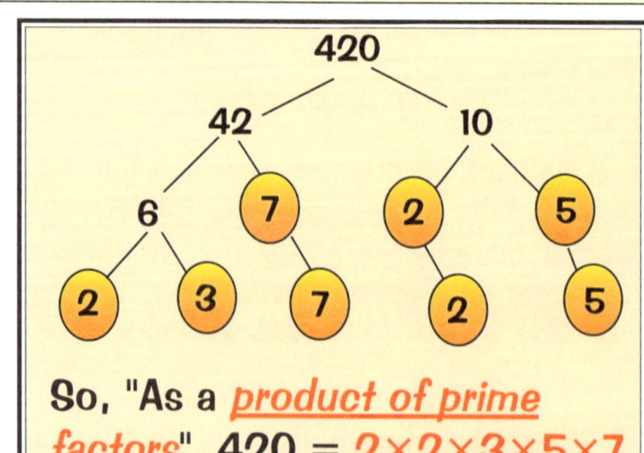

So, "As a *product of prime factors*", 420 = 2×2×3×5×7

The Acid Test:

LEARN what Multiples, Factors and Prime Factors are, **AND HOW TO FIND THEM.** Turn over and write it down.

Then try these without the notes:

1) List the first 10 multiples of 7, and the first 10 multiples of 9.
2) List all the factors of 36 and all the factors of 84.
3) Express as a product of prime factors: a) 990   b) 160.

LCM and HCF

Two big fancy names but don't be put off — they're both *real easy*.

LCM — "Lowest Common Multiple"

"Lowest Common Multiple" — sure, it sounds kind of complicated but *all it means is this*:

> The **SMALLEST** number that will **DIVIDE BY** **ALL** the numbers in question.

Method
1) **LIST** the **MULTIPLES** of **ALL** the numbers.
2) Find the **SMALLEST** one that's in **ALL the lists**.
3) Easy peasy innit.

Example   *Find the lowest common multiple (LCM) of 6 and 7*

Answer   Multiples of 6 are: 6, 12, 18, 24, 30, 36, (42,) 48, 54, 60, 66, …
Multiples of 7 are: 7, 14, 21, 28, 35, (42,) 49, 56, 63, 70, 77, …

> So the *lowest common multiple* (LCM) of 6 and 7 is   **42**.
> Told you it was easy.

HCF — "Highest Common Factor"

"Highest Common Factor" — all it means is *this*:

> The **BIGGEST** number that will **DIVIDE INTO** **ALL** the numbers in question.

Method
1) **LIST** the **FACTORS** of *all* the numbers.
2) Find the **BIGGEST** one that's in **ALL the lists**.
3) Easy peasy innit.

Example   *Find the highest common factor (HCF) of 36, 54, and 72*

Answer   Factors of 36 are: 1, 2, 3, 4, 6, 9, 12, (18,) 36
Factors of 54 are: 1, 2, 3, 6, 9, (18,) 27, 54
Factors of 72 are: 1, 2, 3, 4, 6, 8, 9, 12, (18,) 24, 36, 72

> So the *highest common factor* (HCF) of 36, 54 and 72 is   **18**.
> Told you it was easy.

Just *take care* listing the factors — make sure you use the *proper method* (as shown on the previous page) or you'll miss one and blow the whole thing out of the water.

The Acid Test: LEARN what LCM and HCF are, AND HOW TO FIND THEM.   Turn over and write it all down.

1) List the first 10 multiples of 8, and the first 10 multiples of 9.   What's their LCM?
2) List **all** the factors of 56 and **all** the factors of 104.   What's their HCF?
3) What's the Lowest Common Multiple of 7 and 9?
4) What's the Highest Common Factor of 36 and 84?

Prime Numbers

1) Basically, PRIME Numbers don't divide by anything

And that's the best way to think of them.
So Prime Numbers are all the numbers that DON'T come up in Times Tables:

| 2 | 3 | 5 | 7 | 11 | 13 | 17 | 19 | 23 | 29 | 31 | 37 | ... |

As you can see, they're an awkward-looking bunch (that's because they don't divide by anything!).   For example:

| The only numbers that multiply to give 7 are | 1×7 |
| The only numbers that multiply to give 31 are | 1×31 |

In fact the only way to get ANY PRIME NUMBER is $1 \times$ ITSELF

2) They All End in 1, 3, 7 or 9

1) 1 is NOT a prime number

2) The first four prime numbers are 2, 3, 5 and 7

3) 2 and 5 are the EXCEPTIONS because
all the rest end in 1, 3, 7 or 9

4) But NOT ALL numbers ending in 1, 3, 7 or 9
are primes, as shown here:
(Only the circled ones are primes)

3) HOW TO FIND PRIME NUMBERS — a very simple method

1) Since all primes (above 5) end in 1, 3, 7, or 9, then to find a prime number between say, 70 and 80, the only possibilities are: 71, 73, 77 and 79

2) Now, to find which of them ACTUALLY ARE primes you only need to divide each one by 3 and 7. If it doesn't divide exactly by either 3 or 7 then it's a prime.
(This simple rule using just 3 and 7 is true for checking primes up to 120)

So, to find the primes between 70 and 80, just try dividing 71, 73, 77 and 79 by 3 and 7:

$71 \div 3 = 23.667$, $71 \div 7 = 10.143$ so 71 IS a prime number
(because it ends in 1, 3, 7 or 9 and it doesn't divide by 3 or 7)

$73 \div 3 = 24.333$, $73 \div 7 = 10.429$ so 73 IS a prime number

$79 \div 3 = 26.333$ $79 \div 7 = 11.286$ so 79 IS a prime number

$77 \div 3 = 25.667$ BUT: $77 \div 7 = 11$ — 11 is a whole number (or 'integer'),
so 77 is NOT a prime, because it will divide by 7 $(7 \times 11 = 77)$

The Acid Test: LEARN the main points in ALL 3 SECTIONS above.

Now cover the page and write down everything you've just learned.
1) Write down the first 15 prime numbers (without looking them up).
2) Using the above method, find all the prime numbers between 90 and 110.

Fractions, Decimals And Percentages

The one word that could describe all these three is _PROPORTION_. Fractions, decimals and percentages are simply _three different ways_ of expressing a _proportion_ of something — and it's pretty important you should see them as _closely related and completely interchangeable_ with each other. This table shows the really common conversions which you should know straight off without having to work them out:

Fraction	Decimal	Percentage
1/2	0.5	50%
1/4	0.25	25%
3/4	0.75	75%
1/3	0.333333	33%
2/3	0.666667	67%
1/10	0.1	10%
2/10	0.2	20%
X/10	0.X	X0%
1/5	0.2	20%
2/5	0.4	40%

⅓ and ⅔ have what're known as '_recurring_' decimals — the same pattern of numbers carries on _repeating_ itself forever. (Except here, the pattern's just a single 3 or a single 6. You could have, for instance: 0.143143143...) The ⅔ decimal ends in a 7 because it's been rounded up.

The more of those conversions you learn, the better — but for those that you _don't know_, you must _also learn_ how to _convert_ between the three types. These are the methods:

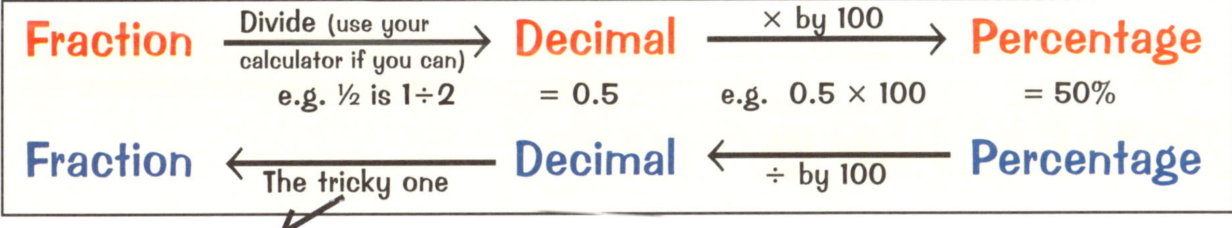

Converting decimals to fractions is only possible for _exact decimals_ that haven't been rounded off.

It's simple enough, but it's best illustrated by examples so look now at P.12 and work out what the simple rule is. You should then be able to fill in the rest of this table:

Fraction	Decimal	Percentage
1/5		
	0.35	
		45%
	0.12	
1/8		
	0.77	

The Acid Test:
LEARN the _whole of the top table_ and the 4 conversion processes for FDP.

Now cover the page and write out the top FDP table from memory, and then the four conversion rules. Then fill in all the spaces in the 2nd table shown above.

Rounding Off

There are _two different ways_ of specifying _where_ a number should be _rounded off_.
They are: "Decimal Places" and "Significant Figures". Doing "Decimal Places" is easier.

The question might say "... to 5 DECIMAL PLACES", or "... to 4 SIGNIFICANT FIGURES".
Don't worry, these are just different ways of _setting the position_ of the _LAST DIGIT_.
Whichever way is used, the _basic method_ is _always the same_ and is _shown below_:

The Basic Method Has Three Steps

1) _Identify_ the position of the LAST DIGIT.

2) Then look at the _next digit to the RIGHT_ – called the DECIDER.

3) If the DECIDER is _5 or more_, then ROUND-UP the LAST DIGIT.
If the DECIDER is _4 or less_, then leave the LAST DIGIT as it is.

EXAMPLE: _"What is 7.45839 to 2 Decimal Places?"_

$$7.45839 \qquad = 7.46$$

LAST DIGIT to be written
(2nd decimal place because
we're rounding to 2 D P)

DECIDER

The _LAST DIGIT_ rounds _UP_
because the _DECIDER_ is _5
or more_

Decimal Places (D.P)

This is pretty easy:
1) To round off to, say, _4 decimal places_, the _LAST DIGIT_ will be
the _4th one after the decimal point_.
2) There must be _no more digits_ after the LAST DIGIT (not even zeros).

DECIMAL PLACES EXAMPLES

Original number: 45.319461

Rounded to 5 decimal places (5 d p)   45.31946   (DECIDER was 1, so don't round up)
Rounded to 4 decimal places (4 d p)   45.3195   (DECIDER was 6, so do round up)
Rounded to 3 decimal places (3 d p)   45.319   (DECIDER was 4, so don't round up)
Rounded to 2 decimal places (2 d p)   45.32   (DECIDER was 9, so do round up)

The Acid Test:

LEARN the _3 Steps of the Basic Method_ and
the _2 Extra Points_ for Decimal Places.

Now turn over and write down what you've learned. Then try again till you know it.
1) Round 3.5743 to 2 decimal places
2) Give 0.0481 to 2 decimal places
3) Express 12.9096 to 3 DP
4) Express 3546.054 to 1 d.p.

Rounding Off

Significant Figures (Sig. Fig.)

The method for sig. fig. is _identical_ to that for DP except that finding the _position_ of the _LAST DIGIT_ is more difficult — it wouldn't be so bad, but for the ZEROS ...

1) The 1st significant figure of any number is simply THE FIRST DIGIT WHICH ISN'T A ZERO.

2) The 2nd, 3rd, 4th, etc. significant figures follow on immediately after the 1st, REGARDLESS OF BEING ZEROS OR NOT ZEROS.

e.g.   0.002309   2.03070

SIG FIGS: 1st 2nd 3rd 4th   1st 2nd 3rd 4th

(If we're rounding to say, 3 sig. fig. then the LAST DIGIT is simply the 3rd sig. fig.)

3) After _Rounding Off_ the LAST DIGIT, _end ZEROS_ must be filled in up to, BUT NOT BEYOND, the decimal point.

No _extra zeros_ must ever be put in _after_ the decimal point.

Examples	_to 4 SF_	_to 3 SF_	_to 2 SF_	_to 1 SF_
1) 54.7651	54.77	54.8	55	50
2) 17.0067	17.01	17.0	17	20
3) 0.0045902	0.004590	0.00459	0.0046	0.005
4) 30895.4	30900	30900	31000	30000

POSSIBLE ERROR OF HALF A UNIT WHEN ROUNDING

Whenever a measurement is _rounded off_ to a _given UNIT_ the actual measurement can be anything up to HALF A UNIT bigger or smaller.

Examples:

1) A room is given as being _"9m long to the nearest METRE"_ — its actual length could be anything from _8.5m to 9.5m_ — i.e. HALF A METRE either side of 9m.

2) If it was given as _"9.4m, to the nearest 0.2m"_, then it could be anything from _9.3m to 9.5m_ — i.e. _0.1m either side_ of 9.4m.

3) _"A school has 460 pupils to 2 Sig Fig"_ (i.e. to the nearest 10) — the actual figure could be anything _from 455 to 464_. — (Why isn't it 465?)

The Acid Test:

LEARN the whole of this page, then turn over and write down everything you've learned. It's all good clean fun.

1) Round these to 2 D.P: a) 3.408 b) 1.051 c) 0.068 d) 3.596
2) Round these to 3 S.F, and for each one say which of the 3 rules about ZEROS applies: a) 567.78 b) 23445 c) 0.04563 d) 0.90876
3) A car is described as 17 feet long to the nearest foot. What is the longest and shortest it could be, in feet and inches? (e.g. 14 feet 4 inches)

Accuracy and Estimating

Appropriate Accuracy

In the Exam you may well get a question asking for *"an appropriate degree of accuracy"* for a certain measurement.

So how do you decide what is *appropriate accuracy?* The key to this is *the number of significant figures* (See P.7) that you give it to, and these are the simple rules:

1) For fairly casual measurements, 2 SIGNIFICANT FIGURES is most appropriate.

> EXAMPLES:
> COOKING — 250 g (2 sig. fig.) of sugar,
> (*not* 253 g (3 S.F.), or 300 g (1 S.F.))
> DISTANCE OF A JOURNEY — 450 miles or 25 miles or 3500 miles (All 2 S F)
> AREA OF A GARDEN OR FLOOR — 330 m² or 15 m²

2) For MORE IMPORTANT OR TECHNICAL THINGS, 3 SIGNIFICANT FIGURES is essential.

> EXAMPLES:
> A LENGTH that will be CUT TO FIT, e.g. You'd measure a shelf as 25.6cm long
> (*not* 26cm or 25.63cm)
> A TECHNICAL FIGURE, e.g. 34.2 miles per gallon,
> (*rather than* 34 mpg)
> Any ACCURATE measurement with a ruler: e.g. 67.5cm, (*not* 70cm or 67.54cm)

3) Only for REALLY SCIENTIFIC WORK would you have more than 3 SIG FIG.

> For example, only someone *really keen* would want to know the length of a piece of string *to the nearest tenth of a mm* — like 34.46cm, for example. (*Get a life!*)

Estimating Calculations

As long as you realise what's expected, this is *VERY EASY*. People get confused because they *over-complicate it*. To *estimate* something this is all you do:

> **1) ROUND EVERYTHING OFF to nice easy CONVENIENT NUMBERS.**
> **2) Then WORK OUT THE ANSWER using those nice easy numbers**
> **— and that's it!**

You don't worry about the answer being "wrong", because we're only trying to get a rough idea of the size of the proper answer, e.g. is it about 20 or about 200?

Don't forget though, in the Exam you'll need to *show all the steps you've done*, to prove you didn't just use a calculator.

Example: Q: ESTIMATE the value of $\dfrac{127.8 + 41.9}{56.5 \times 3.2}$ *showing all your working.*

ANSWER:

$$\frac{127.8 + 41.9}{56.5 \times 3.2} \approx \frac{130 + 40}{60 \times 3} \approx \frac{170}{180} \approx 1 \quad (\text{"}\approx\text{" means "}roughly\ equal\ to\text{"})$$

Accuracy and Estimating

Estimating Areas and Volumes

This isn't bad either — so long as you _LEARN_ the _TWO STEPS_ of the method:

1) Draw or imagine a <u>RECTANGLE OR CUBOID</u> of similar size to the object in question.

2) <u>Round off all lengths to the NEAREST WHOLE</u>, and work it out — easy.

EXAMPLES:

a) <u>Estimate</u> the <u>area of this splodge</u>:

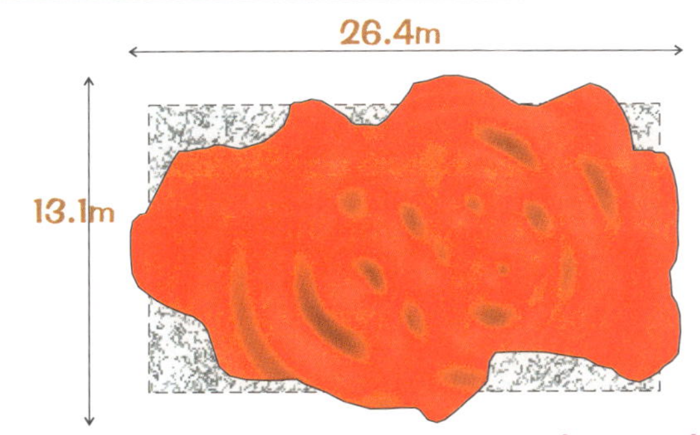

<u>Area of splodge</u> is _approximately equal to_ area of dashed rectangle:
i.e. 26m x 13m = <u>338m²</u>
(or, without a calculator:
30 x 10 = 300m²)

b) <u>Estimate</u> the <u>volume of the bottle</u>:

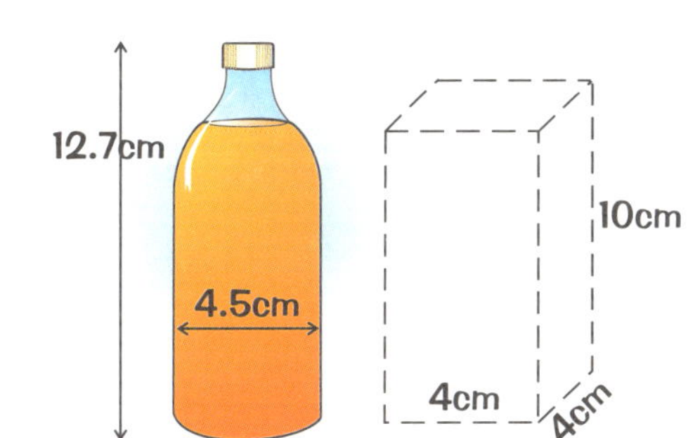

<u>Volume of bottle</u> is _approximately equal to_ volume of dashed cuboid
= 4 x 4 x 10
= <u>160cm³</u>

Estimating Square Roots

Looks horrible — but it's OK if you know your square numbers (page 1).

1) Find the TWO SQUARE NUMBERS EITHER SIDE of the number in question.
2) Find the SQUARE ROOTS and pick a SENSIBLE NUMBER IN BETWEEN.

EXAMPLE: "Estimate $\sqrt{85}$ without using a calculator."

For square roots, see P.82

① The square numbers either side of 85 are _81_ and _100_.

② The square roots are 9 and 10, so $\sqrt{85}$ must be _between 9 and 10_. But 85 is much nearer 81 than 100, so $\sqrt{85}$ must be much _nearer 9 than 10_. So pick _9.1, 9.2 or 9.3_.
(The answer's actually 9.2195... if you're interested.)

The Acid Test:

LEARN the <u>3 RULES</u> about <u>Appropriate Accuracy</u> and the <u>4 RULES</u> for <u>Estimating</u>.

Then cover the page and <u>write them all down</u> from memory.

THEN TRY THESE:

1) Decide which category of accuracy these <u>should</u> belong in and round them off accordingly: a) <u>A jar of jam</u> weighs 34.56g   b) <u>A car</u> has a max speed of 134.25mph   c) <u>A cake</u> needs 852.3g of flour   d) <u>A table</u> is 76.24cm high.

2) Estimate: a) the area of the UK in square miles, b) the volume of a milk bottle in cm³.

3) Estimate: a) $\sqrt{34}$ b) $\sqrt{5}$ c) $\sqrt{61}$ d) $\sqrt{22}$

Conversion Factors

Conversion Factors are a very powerful tool for dealing with a wide variety of questions and the method is very easy.

Method

1) Find the <u>Conversion Factor</u> (always easy)

2) <u>Multiply by it AND divide by it</u>

3) Choose the <u>common sense answer</u>

Three Important *Examples*

1) *"Convert 2.55 hours into minutes."*   (This is NOT 2hrs 55mins)

1) Conversion factor = <u>60</u>   — (simply because 1 hour = <u>60</u> mins)
2) 2.55 hrs × 60 = 153 mins (makes sense)
   2.55 hrs ÷ 60 = 0.0425 mins (ridiculous answer!)
3) So plainly the answer is that 2.55hrs = <u>153 mins</u>   (=2hrs 33mins)

2) *"If £1 = 7.75 French Francs, how much is 47.36 Francs in £ and p?"*

1) Obviously, Conversion Factor = <u>7.75</u>   (The "exchange rate")
2) 47.36 × 7.75 = £367.04
   47.36 ÷ 7.75 = £6.11
3) Not quite so obvious this time, but if roughly 8 Francs = £1, then 47
   Francs can't be much — certainly not £367, so the answer must be
   <u>£6.11p</u>

3) *"A map has a scale of 1:20,000. How big in real life is a distance of 3cm on the map?"*

1) Conversion Factor = 20 000	<u>To Convert 60,000cm to m</u>:
2) 3cm × 20 000 = 60 000cm (looks OK)	1) C.F. = 100 (cm ⟷ m)
3cm ÷ 20 000 = 0.00015cm (not good)	2) 60,000 × 100 = 6,000,000m (hmm)
3) So 60,000cm is the answer.	60,000 ÷ 100 = <u>600m</u> (more like it)
How do we convert to metres?	3) So answer = <u>600m</u>

The Acid Test:

LEARN the <u>3 steps</u> of the <u>Conversion Factor method</u>.
Then turn over and <u>write them down</u>.

1) Convert 2.3 km into metres.
2) Which is more, £34 or 260 French Francs? (Use 7.75)
3) A map is drawn to a scale of 2cm = 5km. A road is 8 km long. How many cm
   will this be on the map? (Hint, C.F. = 5÷2, i.e. 1 cm = 2.5 km)

Metric and Imperial Units

This topic is *Easy Marks!* — make sure you get them.

Metric Units

1) Length — mm, cm, m, km
2) Area — mm², cm², m², km²,
3) Volume — mm³, cm³, m³, litres, ml
4) Weight — g, kg, tonnes
5) Speed — km/h, m/s

MEMORISE THESE KEY FACTS:

1cm = 10mm	1 tonne = 1000kg
1m = 100cm	1 litre = 1000ml
1km = 1000m	1 litre = 1000cm³
1kg = 1000g	1 cm³ = 1 ml

Imperial Units

1) Length — Inches, feet, yards, miles
2) Area — Square inches, square feet, square yards, square miles
3) Volume — Cubic inches, cubic feet, gallons, pints
4) Weight — Ounces, pounds, stones, tons
5) Speed — mph

LEARN THESE TOO!

1 Foot = 12 Inches
1 Yard = 3 Feet
1 Gallon = 8 Pints
1 Stone = 14 Pounds (lbs)
1 Pound = 16 Ounces (Oz)

Metric-Imperial Conversions

YOU NEED TO LEARN THESE — they DON'T promise to give you these in the Exam and if they're feeling mean (as they often are), they won't.

APPROXIMATE CONVERSIONS

1 kg = 2¼ lbs	1 gallon = 4.5 litres
1m = 1 yard (+ 10%)	1 foot = 30cm
1 litre = 1¾ pints	1 metric tonne = 1 imperial ton
1 inch = 2.5 cm	1 mile = 1.6km or 5 miles = 8 km

Using Metric-Imperial Conversion Factors   (See P.10)

1) Convert 45 mm into cm.
   ANS: C.F. = 10, so × or ÷ by 10, which gives 450cm or 4.5cm. (Sensible)

2) Convert 37 inches into cm.
   ANS: C.F. = 2.5, so × or ÷ by 2.5, which gives 14.8cm or 92.5cm.

3) Convert 5.45 litres into pints
   ANS: C.F. = 1¾, so × or ÷ by 1.75, which gives 3.11 or 9.54 pints.

The Acid Test:

LEARN THE 21 Conversion Factors in the boxes above then cover up the page and write them all down.

1) How many litres is 3½ gallons?   2) Roughly how many yards is 200m?
3) A rod is 46 inches long. What is this in cm?
4) Petrol costs £2.83 per gallon. What should it cost per litre?
5) A car travels at 65 mph. What is its speed in km/h?

Fractions Without the Calculator!

Doing fractions _by hand_ is always a pest... so you'd better learn this little lot <u>before your exam!</u>

1) Converting **Fractions to Decimals** — Just **DIVIDE**

Just remember that " / " means " $\div$ ",   so ¼ means $1 \div 4 = 0.25$

The _denominator_ (bottom number) of a fraction, tells you if it'll be a _recurring_ or _terminating decimal_ when you convert it.

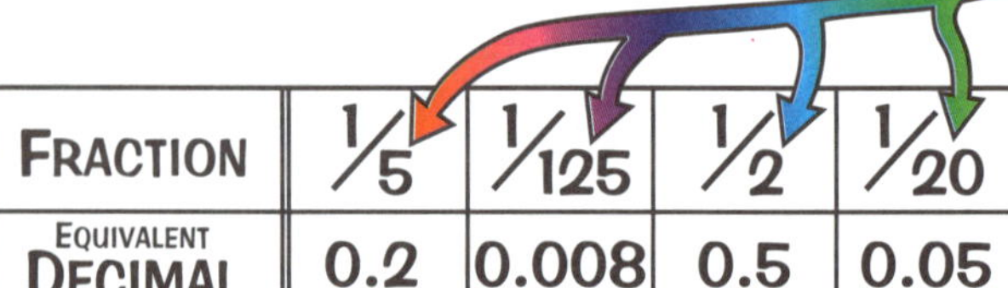

only _prime_ factors: **2 & 5**

also _other_ prime factors

For prime factors, see p.2

FRACTION	$\frac{1}{5}$	$\frac{1}{125}$	$\frac{1}{2}$	$\frac{1}{20}$
EQUIVALENT DECIMAL	0.2	0.008	0.5	0.05

$\frac{1}{7}$	$\frac{1}{35}$	$\frac{1}{3}$	$\frac{1}{6}$
$0.\overline{142857}$	$0.0\overline{285714}$	$0.\overline{3333}$	$0.1\overline{6666}$

Fractions where the denominator has _prime factors_ of _only 2 or 5_ will give _terminating decimals_. All _other fractions_ will give _recurring decimals_.

2) Converting **Decimals to Fractions**

— it's a simple rule, so work it out yourself!:

$0.6 = \frac{6}{10}$, $0.3 = \frac{3}{10}$, $0.7 = 7/10$, $0.X = X/10$, etc.

$0.12 = \frac{12}{100}$, $0.78 = \frac{78}{100}$, $0.45 = 45/100$, $0.05 = 5/100$, etc.

These can then be _cancelled down_.

$0.345 = \frac{345}{1000}$, $0.908 = 908/1000$, $0.024 = 24/1000$, $0.XYZ = XYZ/1000$, etc.

And remember — all _recurring_ decimals are just (exact) fractions in disguise.

1) **Multiplying** — _easy_

Multiply top and bottom separately:

$$\frac{3}{5} \times \frac{4}{7} = \frac{3\times4}{5\times7} = \frac{12}{35}$$

2) **Dividing** — _quite easy_

Turn the 2nd fraction _UPSIDE DOWN_ and then _multiply:_

$$\frac{3}{4} \div \frac{1}{3} = \frac{3}{4} \times \frac{3}{1} = \frac{3\times3}{4\times1} = \frac{9}{4}$$

3) **Adding, subtracting** — _fraught_

Add or subtract _TOP LINES ONLY_
but _only if the bottom numbers are the same._
(If they're not the same it gets very tricky – see opposite.)

$$\frac{2}{6} + \frac{1}{6} = \frac{3}{6}$$

$$\frac{5}{7} - \frac{3}{7} = \frac{2}{7}$$

4) **Cancelling down** — _easy_

Divide top and bottom by the same number,
till they won't go any further:

$$\frac{18}{24} \overset{\div3}{=} \frac{6}{8} \overset{\div2}{=} \frac{3}{4}$$

5) **Finding a fraction of something** — _just multiply._

Multiply the 'something' by the _TOP_ of the fraction,

$$\frac{9}{20} \text{ of £360} = \{(9) \times £360\} \div (20) = \frac{£3240}{20} = £162$$

then _divide_ it by the _BOTTOM_:

$$\text{or: } \frac{9}{20} \text{ of £360} = \frac{9}{1} \times £360 \times \frac{1}{20} = £162$$

More Fractions

6) Equalising the Denominator — why oh why...

You need this whether you're using your _calculator or not_. It comes in handy with ordering fractions by size, and you need it for addition and subtraction by hand.

To make the bottom number the same, you need to find a common multiple of all the denominators:

Example: Put these fractions in ascending order of size: $\frac{8}{3}$, $\frac{6}{4}$, $\frac{12}{5}$

$\Longrightarrow$ Lowest Common Multiple = $3 \times 4 \times 5 = 60 \Longrightarrow \frac{8}{3} = \frac{8}{3} \times \frac{20}{20} = \frac{160}{60}$

See P.3 so put all the fractions over 60... $\frac{6}{4} = \frac{6}{4} \times \frac{15}{15} = \frac{90}{60} \Longrightarrow \frac{90}{60}, \frac{144}{60}, \frac{160}{60}$

(remember that anything divided by itself = 1) $\frac{12}{5} = \frac{12}{5} \times \frac{12}{12} = \frac{144}{60}$ _OR:_ $\frac{6}{4}, \frac{12}{5}, \frac{8}{3}$

When you can though, use your calculator to do all fractions in your exams. It makes sense...

The Fraction Button:

Use this as much as possible in the Exam.
It's very easy, so make sure you know how to use it — or you'll lose a lot of marks:

1) **TO ENTER A NORMAL FRACTION** like $\frac{1}{4}$ Just press: `1` `a b/c` `4`

2) **TO ENTER A MIXED FRACTION** like $1\frac{3}{5}$ Just press: `1` `a b/c` `3` `a b/c` `5`

3) **TO DO A REGULAR CALCULATION** such as $\frac{1}{5} \times \frac{3}{4}$

Just press: `1` `a b/c` `5` `X` `3` `a b/c` `4` `=`

4) **TO REDUCE A FRACTION TO ITS LOWEST TERMS**

Just enter it and then press `=`

e.g. $\frac{9}{12}$: `9` `a b/c` `12` `=` 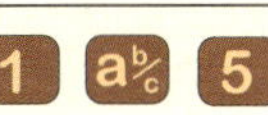 $= \frac{3}{4}$

5) **TO CONVERT BETWEEN MIXED AND TOP HEAVY FRACTIONS**

Just press `SHIFT` `a b/c` e.g. to give $2\frac{3}{8}$ as a top heavy fraction:

Press: `2` `a b/c` `3` `a b/c` `8` `=` to enter the fraction, then `SHIFT` `a b/c` to convert it to $\frac{19}{8}$.

The Acid Test:

LEARN the 2 Rules for converting Fractions ↔ Decimals, the 4 Manual Methods and the 5 features of the Fraction Button.

Then cover up these two pages and write down what you've learned.

1) Do these _WITH YOUR CALCULATOR_:

a) 1/2 x 3/4   b) 3/5 ÷ 2/9   c) 1/3 + 2/5   d) Find x: $2\frac{3}{5} = \frac{x}{5}$ e) Find y: $\frac{14}{98} = \frac{y}{7}$
f) Convert 3/8 into a decimal   g) Convert 0.035 into a fraction, and cancel it down.

2) Do these _BY HAND_:
a) 2/3 x 4/5   b) 4/5 ÷ 3/10   c) 5/6 – 2/6   d) Express 36/84 in its simplest form.
e) Work out 12/19 × 133. f) Work out 12/19 × 134. Express your answer as a fraction.

(Psssssst... what that means is that rather than a decimal of eg. 1·25, you'd give the answer as 1¼. Make sure you can do that — 'coz they could ask you it in the Exam.)

<u>*Percentages*</u>

Contrary to popular belief there are *three distinct types* of percentage question. Obviously then, it's going to be pretty *essential* that you can:

> 1) Distinguish between the three types
> 2) Remember the METHOD for each of them

Type 1 — <u>THESE ARE IDENTIFIED BY THE "%" SYMBOL IN THE QUESTION</u>

This is the easiest type — they're always of the form:

FIND "something" % OF "something-else"

For example: Find 15% *of* £25

Method

> 1) *WRITE:*   15%   OF   £25
> 2) *TRANSLATE:* $\frac{15}{100}$ ×   25   =   £3.75
> 3) *CHECK* THAT IT'S A *SENSIBLE ANSWER*.

Remember:

1) "OF" means "X"

2) "PER CENT" means "OUT OF 100", so 15% *means* "15 out of 100", i.e. $\frac{15}{100}$

Type 2 — <u>THESE ARE IDENTIFIED BY THE WORD "PERCENTAGE"</u> <u>IN THE QUESTION</u>

These are always of the form:

EXPRESS "one thing" AS A PERCENTAGE OF "another"

For example: Express 35p *as a percentage* of £2.80

Method — FDP

F D P : Fraction – Decimal – Percentage

(See P.5) $\frac{35}{280}$ $\xrightarrow{35 \div 280}$ 0.125 $\xrightarrow{\times 100}$ 12.5%

Make a <u>fraction</u> using the two numbers — always with the <u>smallest on top</u>

<u>Divide</u> them to get a <u>decimal</u>

Then <u>multiply by 100</u> to get a <u>percentage</u>

Percentages

Type 3 — THESE ARE IDENTIFIED BY THEM _NOT_ GIVING YOU THE "_ORIGINAL VALUE_"

These are the type most people get wrong — but only because they don't recognise them as a type 3 and don't apply this simple method:

Example:

A house increases in value by 20% to £72,000. Find its value _before_ the rise.

Method

	£72,000	=	120%
÷ 120	£600	=	1%
× 100	£60,000	=	100%

So the original price was £60,000

An _increase_ of 20% means that £72,000 represents _120% of the original_ value.
If it was a _DROP_ of 20%, then we would put "_£72,000 = 80%_" instead, and then divide by _80_ on the LHS, instead of 120.

Always set them out exactly like this example. The trickiest bit is deciding the top % figure on the RHS — the 2nd and 3rd rows are _always_ 1% and 100%

Percentage Change (_An important example of type 2_)

It's quite common to give a _change in value_ as a _percentage_.
This is the formula for doing so — _LEARN IT, AND USE IT_:

$$\text{PERCENTAGE "CHANGE"} = \frac{\text{"CHANGE"}}{\text{ORIGINAL}} \times 100$$

By "change", we could mean all sorts of things such as: "profit", "loss", "appreciation", "depreciation", "increase", "decrease", "error", "discount", etc.

Example: "A shopkeeper buys pens at 8p each and sells them for 10p each. What is his profit _AS A PERCENTAGE_?"

The two numbers we want to _compare_ are the PROFIT (which is 2p) with the ORIGINAL cost (which is 8p).

$$\text{percentage "profit"} = \frac{\text{"profit"}}{\text{original}} \times 100 = \frac{2}{8} \times 100 = 25\%$$

so the shopkeeper makes a _25% profit on the pens_.

The Acid Test:

LEARN The 3 Types, how you _identify_ them, and the Method for each. Also LEARN the Formula for Percentage Change.

Now _turn over and write down all the details_ you've just learned.

Identify the following questions as Type 1, 2, or 3, and apply the method for each.
Practise until you can do them without the notes:

1) A trader buys watches for £5 and sells them for £7. Find his profit in £ and then express it as a percentage.
2) Find the total cost of a plumber's bill given as: "£36 + 17.5% VAT".
3) A car depreciates by 30% to £14,350. What was it worth before?

Calculator Buttons 1

The next few pages are full of lovely calculator tricks to save you a lot of button-bashing. There's basically two types of calculator — the old-style and the new fancy two-line displayers.

The Old-Style Calculators:

These ones only display numbers. They do the calculation each time you press an operation key.

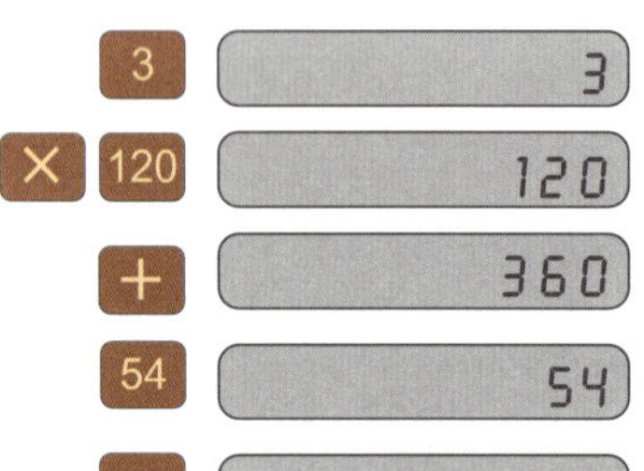

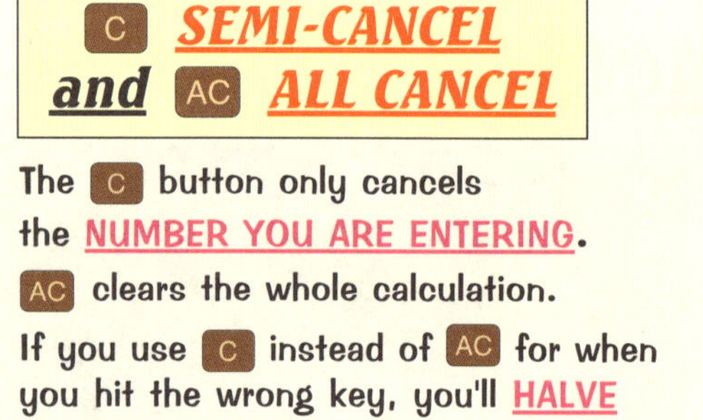

The C button only cancels the NUMBER YOU ARE ENTERING.
AC clears the whole calculation.

If you use C instead of AC for when you hit the wrong key, you'll HALVE the time you spend correcting mistakes!

2-line Display Calculators:

These fancy ones are dead common now. They're pretty easy to use because you just type most calculations exactly as they're written. Like this:

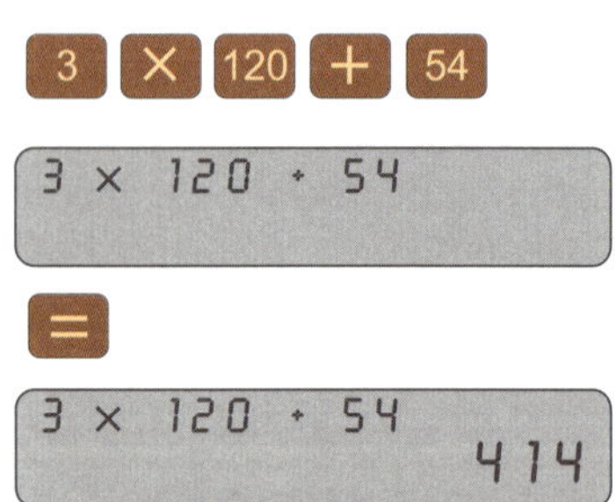

DEL The Delete button

Pressing the DEL button deletes what you've typed, one key at a time (just like on a computer), so it's much quicker than pressing AC and re-typing the whole lot. Use DEL or you'll be in BIG TROUBLE!

Cursor buttons ◄ ►

These cursor buttons ◄ and ► are pretty useful for editing what you've typed in. (You'll probably find you overwrite what was there before, but you can change this with the INS key to insert, rather than overwrite.)

1) Entering negative numbers

On some calculators, there's a +/− button. To enter a minus number, you need to press this after you've entered the number. A lot of calculators just have a minus button (−) which you press before entering the number.

So to work out − 5 × − 6 you'd either press...   (−) 5 × (−) 6 =

or...   5 +/− × 6 +/− =

Why can't they all just be the same...
(The examples in this book will use the (−) button, but if yours is different make sure you know how to use it!)

Calculator Buttons 2

2) *Square*, *Square Root* and *Cube Root*

The SQUARE, SQUARE ROOT, and CUBE ROOT buttons are x^2, $\sqrt{}$ and $\sqrt[3]{}$.

1) The x^2 button squares the number you typed, i.e. IT MULTIPLIES IT BY ITSELF.
   It's ideal for finding the area of a circle, using the well-known (hah!) formula:

   $A = \pi r^2$ e.g. if r = 5 then press 3.14 × 5 x^2 = which gives you 78.5.

   (To get a more accurate answer, use the π button which is usually the second function of the EXP key)

2) $\sqrt{}$ is the REVERSE PROCESS of x^2 — it calculates the SQUARE ROOT of the
   number you enter. Pressing $\sqrt{}$ 25 = gives 5,

   then x^2 = takes you back to 25.

3) $\sqrt[3]{}$ gives the CUBE ROOT (See P.82) which is the reverse of CUBING a number.

   E.g. $\sqrt[3]{}$ 27 = gives 3,

   then pressing x^3 = takes you back to 27.

3) *Older Calculators do stuff Backwards*

On some calculators, especially older ones, you need to enter a lot of
calculations *backwards*. E.g. if you're working out the square root a number, you'd enter
the number first and __then__ press the square root.

   25 $\sqrt{}$ 5

Or if you were typing a trigonometry function like sin 45°, you'd do:

   45 SIN 0.70716718

You don't need to press equals when you do functions on one of these
calculators. It'll work it out automatically. Which is jolly nice of it.

4) *The MEMORY BUTTONS* (STO *Store*, RCL *Recall*)

(On some calculators the memory buttons are called Min (memory in) and MR (memory recall)).
Contrary to popular belief, the memory is not intended for storing your favourite
phone number, but in fact is a mighty useful feature for keeping a number you've just
calculated, so you can use it again shortly afterwards.

For something like $\dfrac{16}{15+12SIN40}$, you could just work out the *bottom line* first
and *stick it in the memory*:

Press 15 + 12 SIN 40 = and then STO (Or STO M or STO 1 or Min)
to keep the result of the bottom line in the memory.
Then you simply press 16 ÷ RCL =, and the answer is 0.7044.

(Instead of RCL, you might need to type RCL M or RCL 1 or MR on yours.)

Once you've practised with the memory buttons a bit, you'll soon find them very
useful. They can speed things up no end.

Calculator Buttons 3

5) Bodmas and the Brackets Buttons

The BRACKETS BUTTONS are [( ] and [ )].

One of the biggest problems people have with their calculators is not realising that the calculator always works things out IN A CERTAIN ORDER, which is summarised by the word BODMAS (see P.83), which stands for:

Brackets, Other, Division, Multiplication, Addition, Subtraction

This becomes really important when you want to work out even a simple thing like $\dfrac{23+45}{64\times3}$ — it's no good just pressing [23] [+] [45] [÷] [64] [×] [3] [=] — it will be

completely wrong. The calculator will think you mean $23+\dfrac{45}{64}\times3$ because the calculator will do the *division and multiplication* BEFORE it does the *addition*.

The secret is to OVERRIDE the automatic BODMAS order of operations using the BRACKETS BUTTONS. Brackets are the ultimate priority in BODMAS, which means anything in brackets is worked out before anything else happens to it.
So all you have to do is

1) Write a couple of pairs of brackets into the expression:	$\dfrac{(23+45)}{(64\times3)}$
2) Then just type it as it's written:	

[( ] [23] [+] [45] [ )] [÷] [( ] [64] [×] [3] [ )] [=]

You might think it's difficult to know where to put the brackets in.
It's not that difficult, you just put them in pairs around each group of numbers.
It's OK to have brackets within other brackets too, e.g. (4 + (5÷2))
As a rule, you can't cause trouble by putting too many brackets in,
SO LONG AS THEY ALWAYS GO IN PAIRS.

6) The Fraction Button:

— It's absolutely essential that you learn how to use this button for doing fractions.
Full details are given on P.13.

7) The Powers Button:

It's used for working out powers of numbers quickly. For example to find 7^5, instead of pressing $7\times7\times7\times7\times7$ you should just press [7] [x^y] [5] [=]

Calculator Buttons 4

8) The Standard Form Button

The STANDARD FORM BUTTON is EXP or EE.

All you ever use this for is entering numbers written in *standard form* into the calculator.

It would be a lot more helpful if the calculator manufacturers labelled it as x10ⁿ because that's what you should call it as you press it: "*Times ten to the power...*"

> For example to enter 6×10^3 YOU MUST ONLY PRESS: 6 EXP 3
> and NOT, as a lot of people do: 6 X 10 EXP 3 .

Pressing X 10 as well as EXP is HORRIBLY WRONG, because the EXP ALREADY CONTAINS the "× 10" in it. That's why you should always say to yourself "TIMES TEN TO THE POWER..." every time you press the EXP button, to prevent this very common mistake.

9) Modes

This is tricky and you wouldn't really need to know about it except that you'll sometimes accidentally get into the wrong mode, and it can make life pretty difficult if you don't know how to get back to normality.

There are 3 SEPARATE MODES that your calculator has to make a choice about:

CALCULATION MODES
You want COMP mode. This is the mode for doing normal calculations.
On CASIOs, this is on the first menu you get from pressing MODE

ANGLES MODES
You want degrees mode (there'll be a small DEG or D on the display when you're in this mode).
On CASIOs, you'd press MODE twice to get the right menu.

DISPLAY MODES
You want NORM mode most of the time. The other display modes are for showing a certain number of decimals places (FIX) or number of significant figures (SCI).
(have a play with these — they're great fun... err, I mean they might be useful... or something.)

The Acid Test:

LEARN YOUR CALCULATOR BUTTONS.
PRACTISE until you can do all of these without having to refer back:

1) What do the x² and √ buttons do?

2) What must you press to find 17^2?   3) How do you enter -5 × -8?

4) Explain what STO and RCL do and give an example of using them.

5) What is the aᵇ/c button used for?

6) How do you enter 6^8?   7) How do you enter 6×10^8?

8) Which should be showing at the top of your display: DEG, RAD or GRAD?

Number Patterns

This is an easy topic, but make sure you know *ALL SIX* types of sequence, not just the first few. The *main secret* is to *write the differences in the gaps* between each pair of numbers. That way you can usually see what's happening whichever type it is.

1) "Common Difference" Type — dead easy

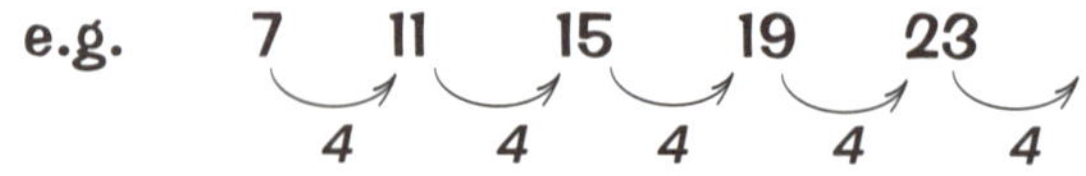
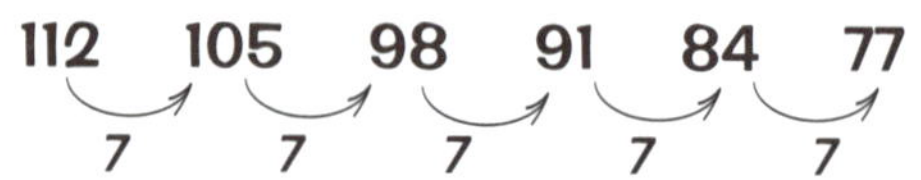

2) "Increasing Difference" Type

Here the differences increase by the same amount each time:

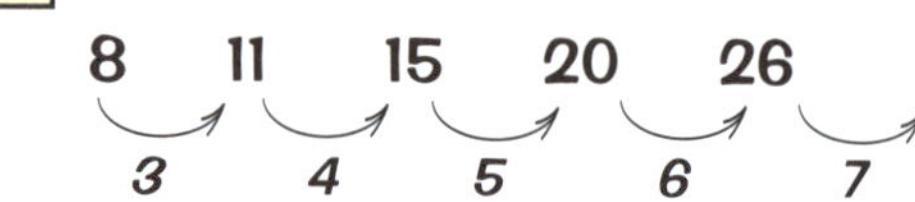

3) "Decreasing Difference" Type

Here the differences decrease by the same amount each time:

e.g.

53 43 34 26 19 13

   10   9   8   7   6

4) "Multiplying Factor" Type

This type has a common **MULTIPLIER** linking each pair of numbers:

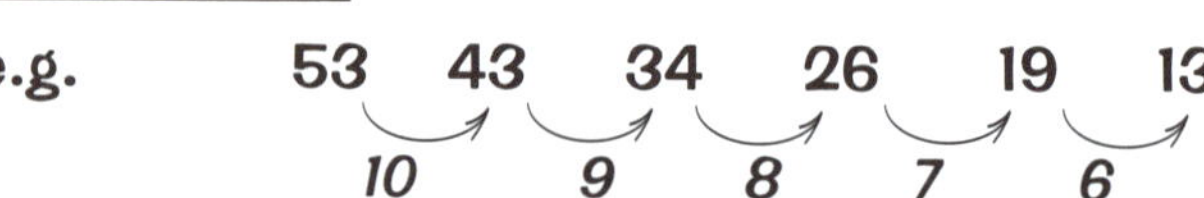

5) "Dividing Factor" Type

This type has a common **DIVIDER** linking each pair of numbers:

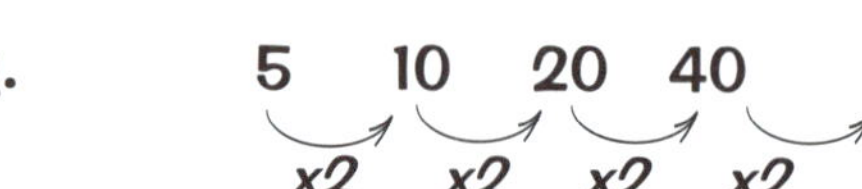

6) "Adding Previous Terms" Type

Add the *first two terms* to get the *3rd*, then add the *2nd and 3rd* to get the *4th*, etc.

e.g.

1 1 2 3 5 8 13 21

1+1 1+2 2+3 3+5 5+8 8+13 13+21

The Acid Test:

LEARN the 6 types of number pattern. Then cover the page and answer these:

1) Write down **FROM MEMORY** the name of each type of number sequence and give an example of each.
2) Find the next two terms in these sequences:
   a) 2,6,18,54...   b) 1,3,4,7,11....   c) 3,5,8,12,17,...   d) 128,64,32,...

Finding the nth Term

"The nth term" is a formula with "n" in it which gives you every term in a sequence when you put different values for n in. There are two different types of sequence (for "nth term" questions) which have to be done in different ways:

Common Difference Type: "dn + (a – d)"

For any sequence such as   3, 7, 11, 15,   where there's a COMMON DIFFERENCE:

you can always find "the nth term" using the FORMULA: n^{th} **Term = dn + (a–d)**

Don't forget:

> 1) "a" is simply the value of **THE FIRST TERM** in the sequence.
> 2) "d" is simply the value of **THE COMMON DIFFERENCE** between the terms.
> 3) To get the nth term, you just find the values of "a" and "d" from the sequence and stick them in the formula.
> *You don't replace n though — that wants to stay as n*
> 4) Of course **YOU HAVE TO LEARN THE FORMULA**, but life is like that.

Example:

"Find the nth term of this sequence: 5,   8,   11,   14, …"

ANSWER: 1) The formula is dn + (a-d)
2) The first term is 5, so a = 5   The common difference is 3 so d = 3
3) Putting these in the formula gives: n^{th} term = 3n + (5–3)
so n^{th} term = 3n + 2

Changing Difference Type:

"a + (n–1)d + ½(n–1)(n–2)C"

If the number sequence is one where the *difference* between the terms is *increasing or decreasing* then it gets a whole lot more complicated (as you'll have spotted from the above formula — which you'll have to *learn!*). This time there are *THREE* letters you have to fill in:

"a" is the **FIRST TERM**,
"d" is the **FIRST DIFFERENCE** (between the first two numbers),
"C" is the **CHANGE BETWEEN ONE DIFFERENCE AND THE NEXT**.

Example:

"Find the nth term of this sequence: 2,   5,   9,   14, …"

ANSWER: 1) The formula is   "a + (n–1)d + ½(n–1)(n–2)C"
2) The first term is 2, so a = 2   The first difference is 3 so d = 3
3) The differences increase by 1 each time so C = +1
Putting these in the formula gives: *"2 + (n–1)3 + ½(n–1)(n–2)×1"*
Which becomes: $2 + 3n - 3 + \tfrac{1}{2}n^2 - 1\tfrac{1}{2}n + 1$
Which simplifies to: $\tfrac{1}{2}n^2 + 1\tfrac{1}{2}n = \tfrac{1}{2}n(n+3)$
so the nth term = ½n(n+3)   (Easy peasy, huh!)

The Acid Test:

LEARN the definition of the nth term and the **4 steps** for finding it, and **LEARN THE FORMULA**.

1) Find the nth term of the following sequences:
a) 4, 7, 10, 13…. b) 3, 8, 13, 18,….   c) 1, 3, 6, 10, 15,….   d) 3, 4, 7, 12,…

Revision Summary for Section One

I know these questions seem difficult, _but they're the very best revision you can do_.
The whole point of revision, remember, is <u>to find out what you _don't_ know</u> and then
learn it <u>until you do</u>. These searching questions test how much you know <u>better
than anything else ever can</u>. They follow the sequence of pages in Section One,
so you can easily look up anything you don't know.

Keep learning these basic facts until you know them

1) List the first ten terms in each of these sequences:
    a) Even numbers   b) Odd numbers   c) Square numbers   d) Cube Numbers
    e) Powers of 2   f) Powers of 10   g) Triangle numbers   h) Prime numbers

2) What are the multiples of a number?   What are the factors of a number?

3) What is the best method for finding all the factors of a number?

4) What are the prime factors of a number? How do you find them?

5) Explain exactly what HCF and LCM mean.

6) State the two rules for finding Prime numbers (below 120).

7) What does FDP stand for? Give full details of the four conversion methods.

8) What are the three steps for rounding off?

9) What are the 3 extra details concerning sig. fig. rounding?

10) What is the possible error when rounding to a specified unit of accuracy?

11) State three rules for deciding on appropriate accuracy.

12) State two rules for estimating the answer to a calculation.

13) State two rules for estimating an area or volume.

14) State the 3 steps of the method for applying conversion factors.

15) Give 7 different conversions from one metric unit to another.

16) Give 5 different conversions from one imperial unit to another.

17) Give 8 conversions between metric and imperial units.

18) Give an example of a fraction that divides to give a terminating decimal.
    And one that doesn't.

19) Describe in words the 5 rules for doing fractions by hand.

20) Order these fractions by their size, smallest first: $^{13}/_{128}$, $^{7}/_{64}$, $^{4}/_{32}$, $^{121}/_{128}$, $^{15}/_{16}$.

21) Which is the fraction button? What must you press to enter $2\frac{3}{4}$?

22) How would you convert it to a top heavy fraction?

23) Describe the 3 types of percentage question and how to identify them.

24) Give details of the method for each of the 3 types.

25) Give the formula for percentage change, and give 3 examples of it.

26) Which are the memory buttons? What are they used for?

27) What does BODMAS mean and what has it got to do with your calculator?

28) When would you use the brackets buttons?

29) Which is the powers button? What must you press to find 8^{15}?

30) Which is the Standard Form button? What must you press to enter 3×10^{-4}?

31) What would the number 5×10^{7} look like on the calculator display?

32) Which 3 modes should your calculator be in?

33) Name the 6 different types of number pattern and give an example of each.

34) Write down the 2 formulas for finding the nth term of a number pattern.

Regular Polygons

A <u>POLYGON</u> is a <u>MANY-SIDED SHAPE</u>. A <u>REGULAR</u> polygon is one where <u>ALL THE SIDES AND ANGLES ARE THE SAME</u>. The <u>REGULAR POLYGONS</u> are a <u>never-ending</u> series of shapes with some fancy features. <u>They're very easy to learn</u>. Here are the first few but they don't stop – you can have one with 12 sides or 25, etc.

EQUILATERAL TRIANGLE

 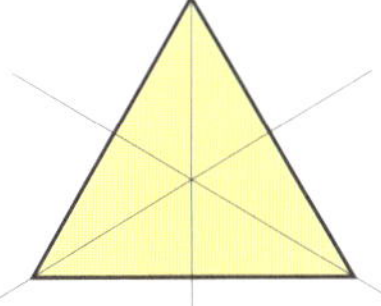

<u>3 sides</u>
<u>3 lines</u> of symmetry
Rot^{nl} symm. <u>order 3</u>

SQUARE

 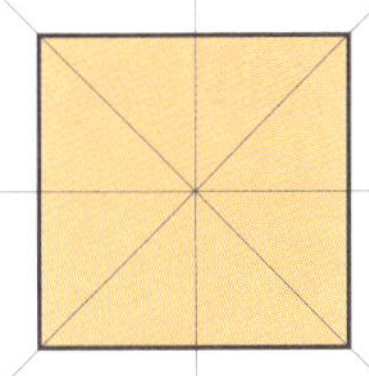

<u>4 sides</u>
<u>4 lines</u> of symmetry
Rot^{nl} symm. <u>order 4</u>

REGULAR PENTAGON

 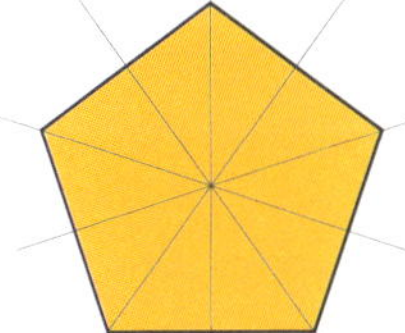

<u>5 sides</u>
<u>5 lines</u> of symmetry
Rot^{nl} symm. <u>order 5</u>

REGULAR HEXAGON

 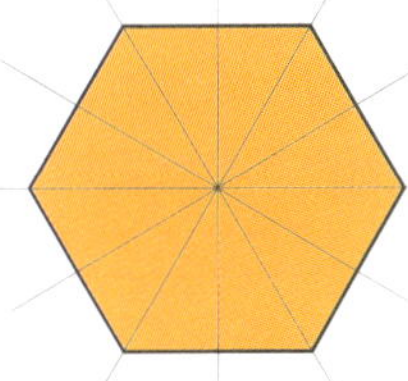

<u>6 sides</u>
<u>6 lines</u> of symmetry
Rot^{nl} symm. <u>order 6</u>

REGULAR HEPTAGON

 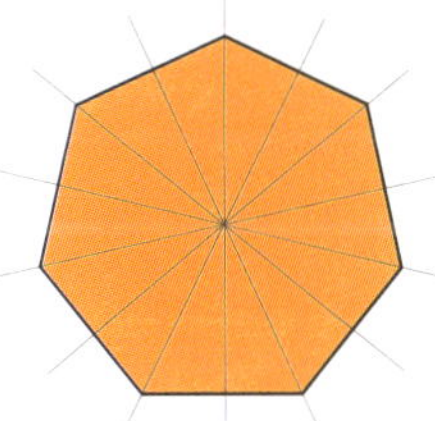

<u>7 sides</u>
<u>7 lines</u> of symmetry
Rot^{nl} symm. <u>order 7</u>

A 50p piece is like a heptagon

REGULAR OCTAGON

 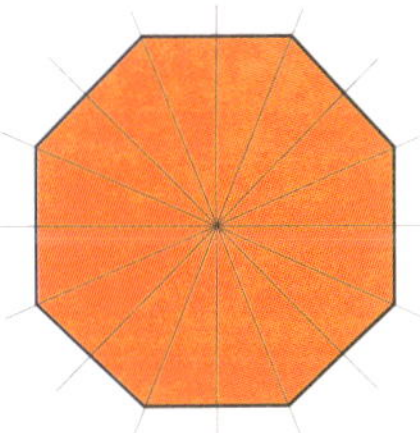

<u>8 sides</u>
<u>8 lines</u> of symmetry
Rot^{nl} symm. <u>order 8</u>

Interior And Exterior Angles

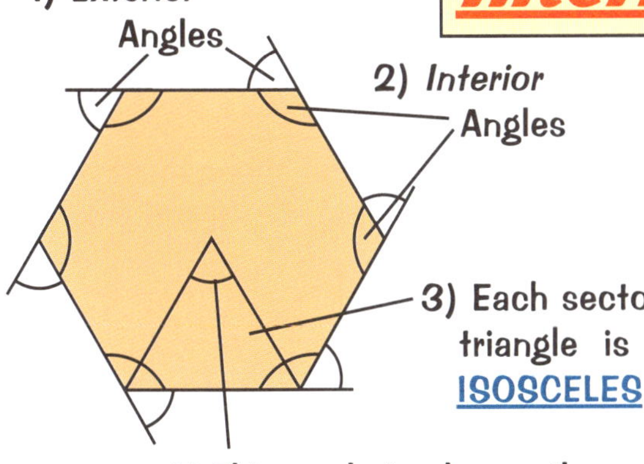

This is the <u>MAIN BUSINESS</u>. Whenever you get a <u>Regular Polygon</u>, it's a <u>cosmic certainty</u> you'll need to work out the <u>Interior and Exterior Angles</u>, because they are the *KEY* to it all.

$$\text{EXTERIOR ANGLE} = \frac{360°}{\text{No. of Sides}}$$

$$\text{INTERIOR ANGLE} = 180° - \text{EXTERIOR ANGLE}$$

The Acid Test:

LEARN THIS PAGE. Then cover it up and answer these little jokers:

1) What is a Regular Polygon?   2) Name the first six of them.
3) Draw a Pentagon and a Hexagon and put in all their lines of symmetry.
4) What are the two important formulae?
5) Work out the two key angles for a Pentagon   6) And for a 12-sided Regular Polygon

Symmetry

<u>SYMMETRY</u> is where a shape or picture can be put in <u>DIFFERENT POSITIONS</u> that <u>LOOK EXACTLY THE SAME</u>. There are <u>THREE TYPES</u> of symmetry:

1) *Line* Symmetry

This is where you can draw a <u>MIRROR LINE</u> (or more than one) across a picture and <u>both sides will fold exactly together</u>.

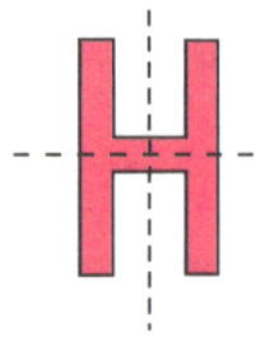
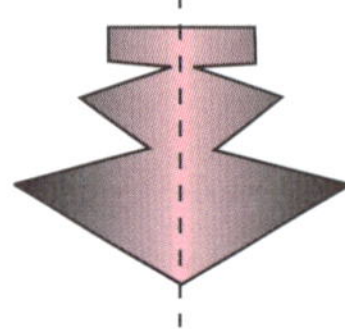

2 LINES OF SYMMETRY	1 LINE OF SYMMETRY	1 LINE OF SYMMETRY	3 LINES OF SYMMETRY	NO LINES OF SYMMETRY	1 LINE OF SYMMETRY

How to draw a *reflection*:

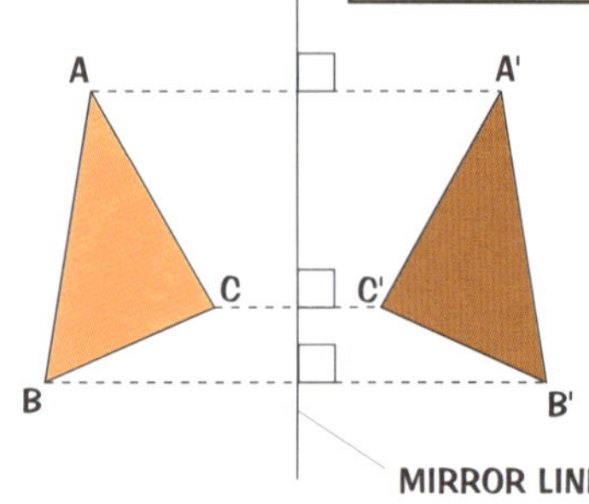

1) Reflect each point one by one

2) Use <u>a line which crosses the mirror line at 90° and goes *EXACTLY* the same distance on the other side of the mirror line</u>, as shown.

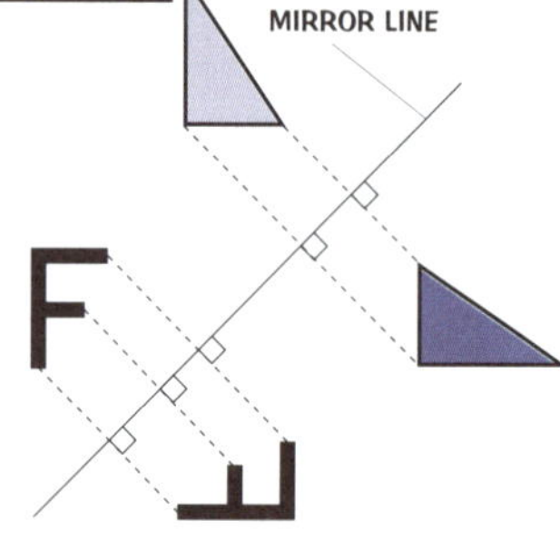

2) *Plane* Symmetry

<u>Plane Symmetry</u> is all to do with <u>3-D SOLIDS</u>. Whereas <u>flat shapes</u> can have a <u>mirror line</u>, <u>solid 3-D objects</u> can have <u>planes of symmetry</u>.

A plane mirror surface can be drawn through many regular solids, but the shape must be <u>EXACTLY THE SAME ON BOTH SIDES OF THE PLANE</u> (i.e. mirror images), like these are:

Planes of Symmetry

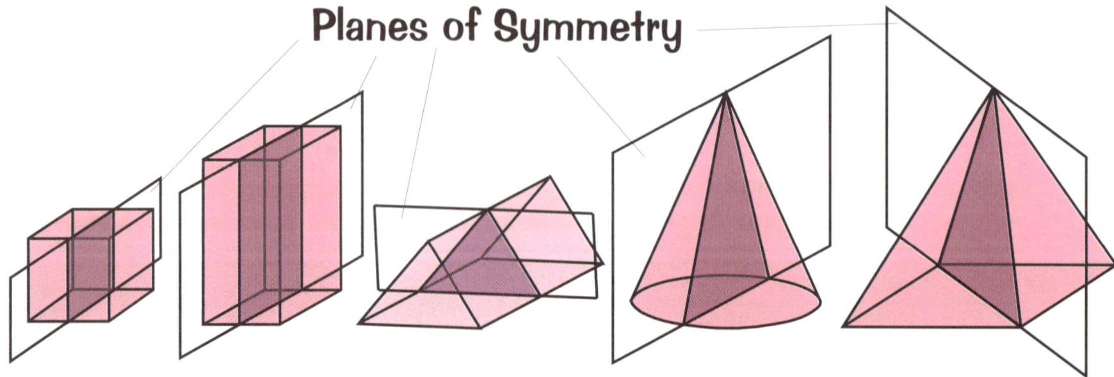

The shapes drawn here all have <u>MANY MORE PLANES OF SYMMETRY</u> but there's only one drawn in for each shape, because otherwise it would all get really messy and you wouldn't be able to see anything.

Symmetry

3) *Rotational* Symmetry

This is where you can <u>ROTATE</u> the shape or drawing into different positions that <u>all look exactly the same</u>.

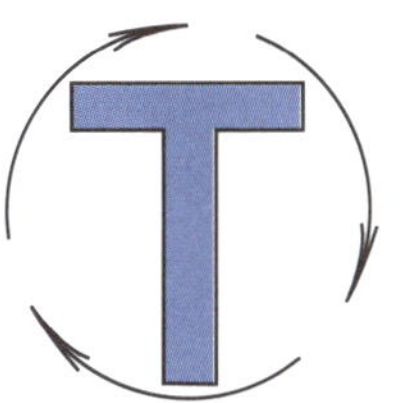

Order 1

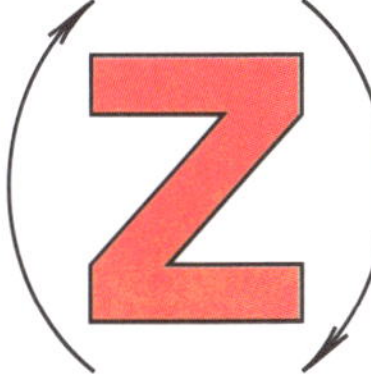

Order 2

Order 2

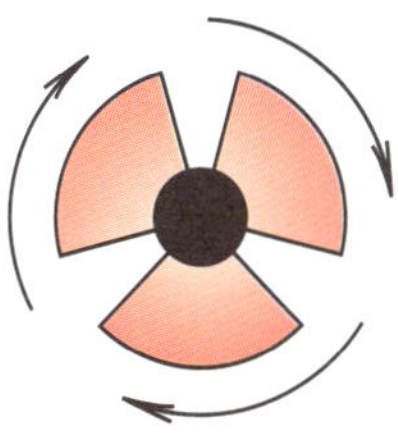

Order 3

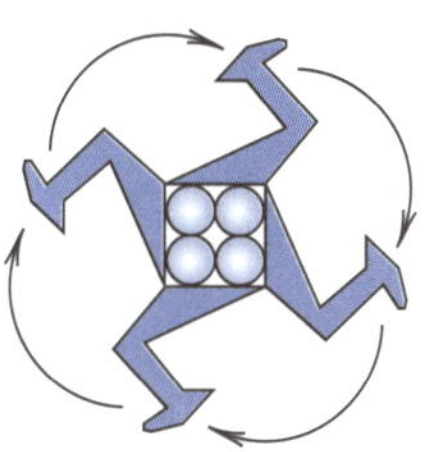

Order 4

Two *Key* Points:

1) The <u>ORDER OF ROTATIONAL SYMMETRY</u> is the fancy way of saying:
"<u>HOW MANY DIFFERENT POSITIONS LOOK THE SAME</u>".
e.g. you should say the Z shape above has "<u>Rotational symmetry order 2</u>"

2) BUT... when a shape has <u>ONLY 1 POSITION</u> you can <u>EITHER</u> say that it has
"<u>Rotational Symmetry order 1</u>"   <u>OR</u>   that it has "<u>NO Rotational Symmetry</u>".

Tracing Paper

SYMMETRY IS ALWAYS A LOT EASIER WITH TRACING PAPER.

1) For <u>REFLECTIONS</u>, trace one side of the drawing and the mirror line too. Then
<u>TURN THE PAPER OVER</u> and line up the mirror line in its original position again.
(If you put a blob on the mirror line it helps you get it back in position again)

2) For <u>ROTATIONS</u>, just swizzle the tracing paper round.
It's really good for <u>finding the CENTRE of rotation</u> (by trial and error)
as well as the <u>order of rotational symmetry</u>.

3) You can use tracing paper in the <u>EXAM</u> — so <u>ASK FOR IT</u>, or else take your
own in with you.

The Acid Test:

<u>LEARN</u> the important details about <u>LINE AND PLANE SYMMETRY</u>, the <u>2 points</u> about <u>ROTATIONAL SYMMETRY</u> and the <u>3 points</u> about <u>TRACING PAPER</u>.

Now <u>TURN OVER</u> and <u>WRITE IT ALL DOWN</u> *with examples,* to see what you've learned.

1) Copy these letters and mark in all the <u>lines of symmetry</u>.
Also say what the <u>rotational symmetry</u> is for each one.

H   N   E   Y   M   O   S   T

2) Copy all the five solids on the last page <u>without their plane of symmetry</u>
(see P.26). Then draw in a <u>different</u> plane of symmetry for each one.
(Drawing 3-D objects ain't easy but it's good laughing at everyone else's dismal efforts.)

The Shapes You Need to Know

These are easy marks in the Exam — make sure you know them all.

1) SQUARE

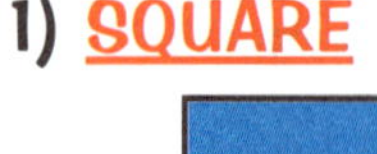

4 lines of symmetry.
Rotational symmetry order 4

2) RECTANGLE

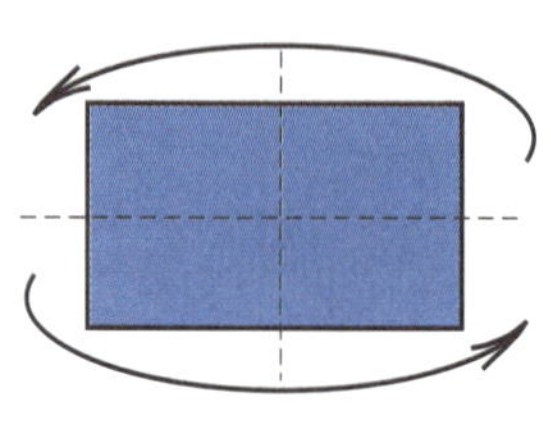

2 lines of symmetry.
Rotational symmetry order 2

3) RHOMBUS (A square pushed over)
(It's also a diamond)

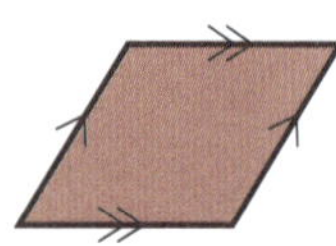
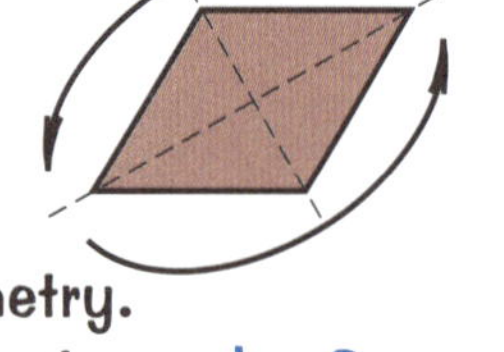

2 lines of symmetry.
Rotational symmetry order 2

4) PARALLELOGRAM
(A rectangle pushed over —
two pairs of parallel sides)

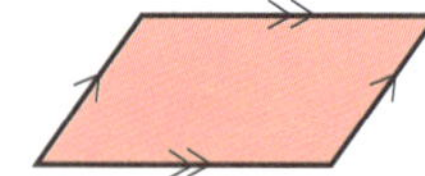
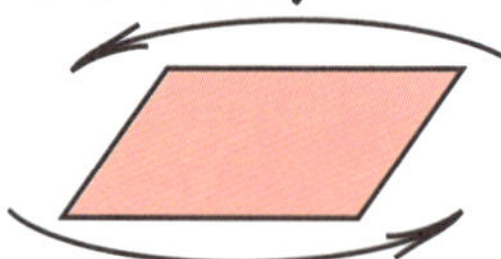

NO lines of symmetry.
Rotational symmetry order 2

5) TRAPEZIUM (One pair of parallel sides)

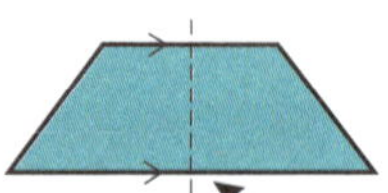
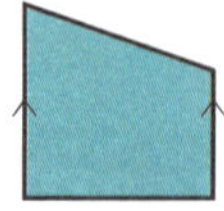
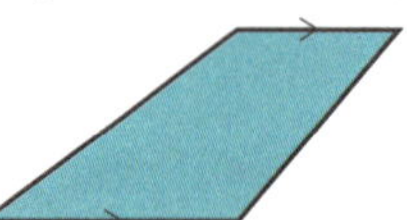

Only the isosceles trapezium has a line of symmetry.
None have rotational symmetry

6) KITE

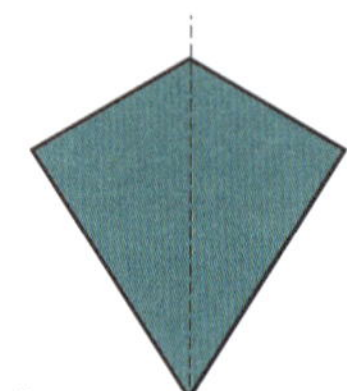

1 line of symmetry.
No rotational symmetry

7) EQUILATERAL Triangle

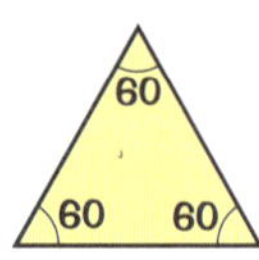

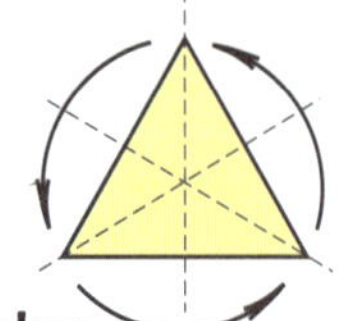

3 lines of symmetry.
Rotational symmetry order 3

8) RIGHT-ANGLED Triangle

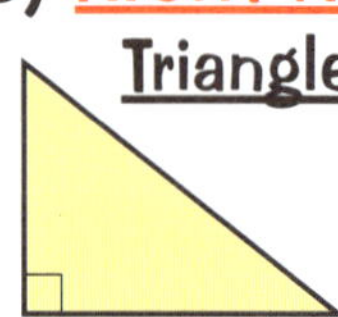

No symmetry unless
the angles are 45°

9) ISOSCELES Triangle

2 sides equal
2 angles equal

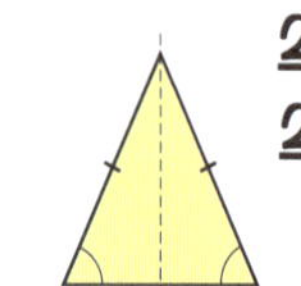

1 line of symmetry.
No rotational symmetry

10) SOLIDS

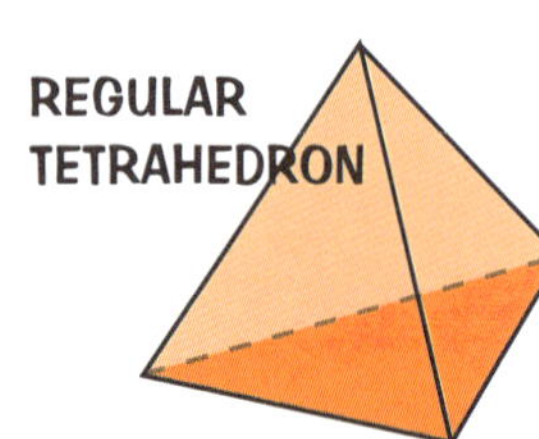

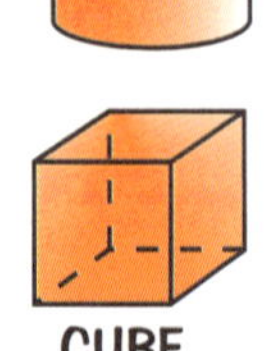

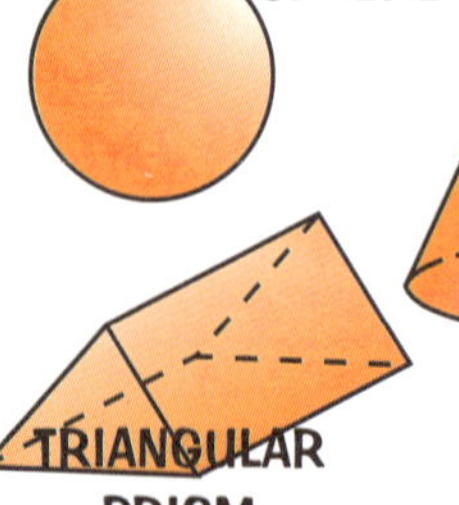

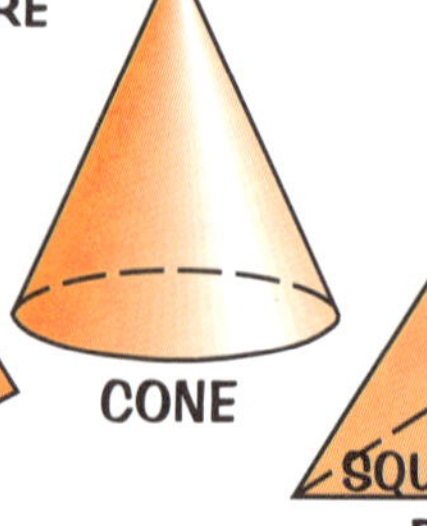

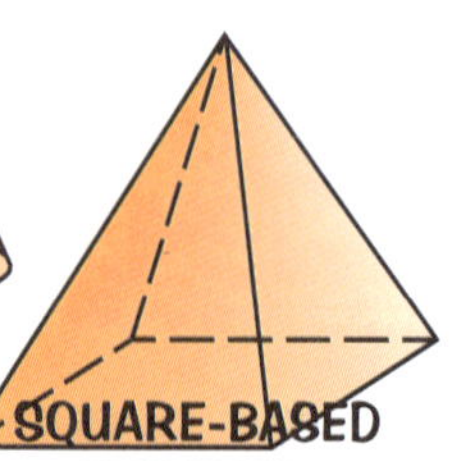

The Acid Test: LEARN everything on this page.

Then turn over and write down all the details that you can remember. Then try again.

Areas

YES IT'S TRUE, these formulae are given inside the front cover of the Exam, but I GUARANTEE that if you don't learn them beforehand, you'll be *totally incapable* of using them in the Exam – *REMEMBER, I ABSOLUTELY GUARANTEE IT* !

YOU MUST LEARN THESE FORMULAE:

1) RECTANGLE

Area of *RECTANGLE* = length × width

$$A = l \times w$$

2) TRIANGLE

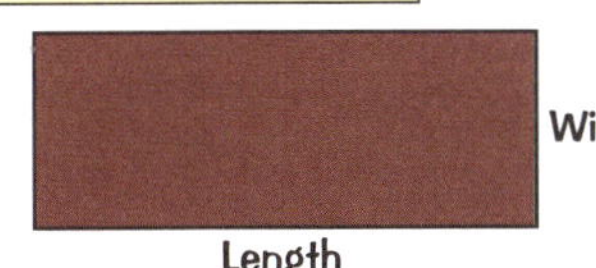

Area of *TRIANGLE* = ½ × base x vertical height

$$A = \tfrac{1}{2} \times b \times h_v$$

Note that the *height* must always be the *vertical height*, not the sloping height.

3) PARALLELOGRAM

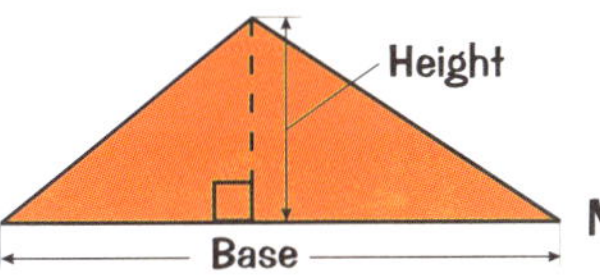

Area of *PARALLELOGRAM* = base × vertical height

$$A = b \times h_v$$

4) TRAPEZIUM

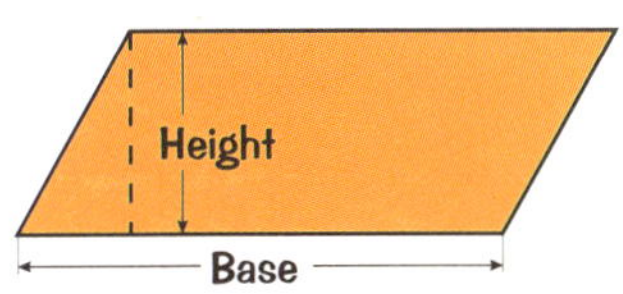

Area of *TRAPEZIUM* = average of parallel sides × distance between them

$$A = \tfrac{1}{2} \times (a + b) \times h$$

5) CIRCLE

DON'T MUDDLE UP THESE TWO CIRCLE FORMULAE!

$\pi = 3.141592....$
$= 3.14$ (approx)

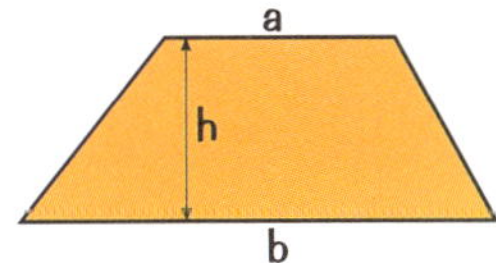

Circumference = distance round the outside of the circle

AREA of *CIRCLE* = $\pi \times$ (radius)^2

$$A = \pi \times r^2$$

e.g. if the radius is 4cm, then
A = 3.14×(4×4)
= 50.24cm^2

CIRCUMFERENCE = π x Diameter

$$C = \pi \times D$$

YOU NEED TO KNOW WHAT THESE ARE TOO:

5a) SECTOR OF CIRCLE

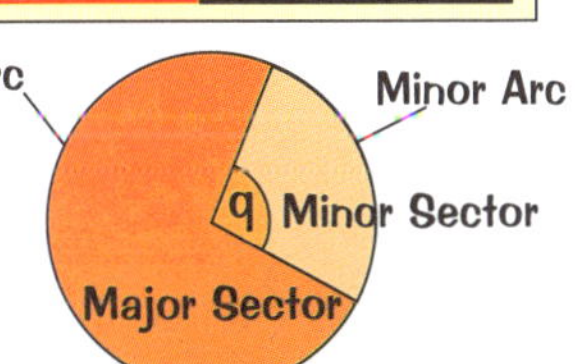

5b) SEGMENT OF CIRCLE

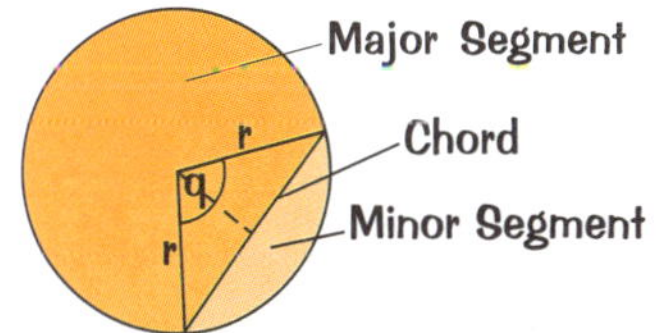

The Acid Test:

LEARN THIS PAGE — then **COVER THE PAGE AND WRITE DOWN** as much of it as you can **FROM MEMORY**.

Check your effort and *try again*!

Circle Questions

1) π "A Number a Bit *Bigger than 3*"

The big thing to remember is that π (called "pi") only seems confusing because it's a scary-looking Greek letter. In the end, it's just an ordinary number (3.14159...) which is rounded off to either 3 or 3.14 or 3.142 (depending on how accurate you want to be). And that's all it is: *A NUMBER A BIT BIGGER THAN 3*.

2) Diameter is TWICE the Radius

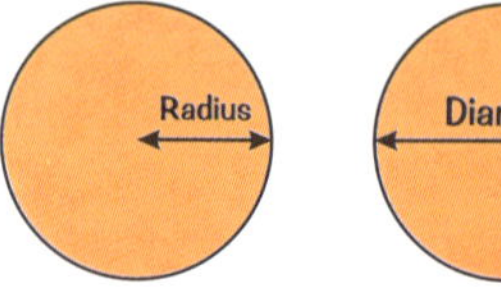

The DIAMETER goes right across the circle.
The RADIUS only goes *halfway* across.

EXAMPLES:

If the radius is 4cm, the diameter is 8cm,   If D = 12cm, then r = 6cm,
If the radius is 12m, the diameter is 24m,   If diameter = 2mm, then radius = 1mm

3) Arc, Chord and Tangent

A TANGENT is a straight line that just touches the outside of the circle.

A CHORD is a line drawn across the inside of a circle.

AN ARC is just part of the circumference of the circle.

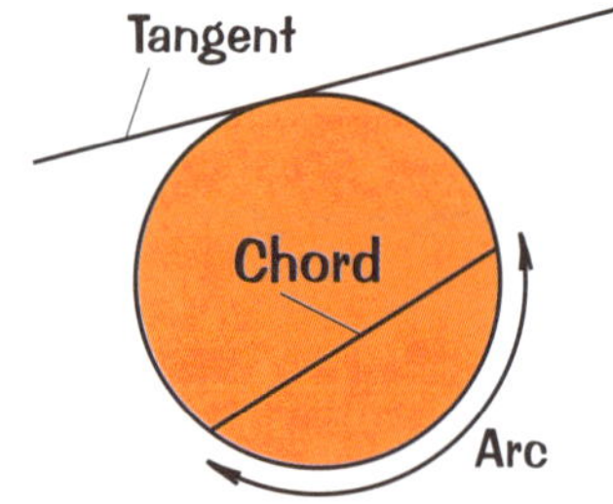

4) The Big Decision: "Which circle formula do I use?"

WORKING OUT AREA OR CIRCUMFERENCE — there is a difference you know!

1) If the question asks for "the area of the circle",

   YOU MUST use the FORMULA FOR AREA:

$$A = \pi \times r^2$$

2) If the question asks for "circumference" (the distance around the circle)

   YOU MUST use the FORMULA FOR CIRCUMFERENCE:

$$C = \pi \times D$$

AND REMEMBER, it makes no difference at all whether the question gives you the radius or the diameter, because it's dead easy to work out one from the other.

EXAMPLE: "Find the circumference and the area of the circle shown below."

ANSWER: Radius = 5 cm, so Diameter = 10 cm (easy)

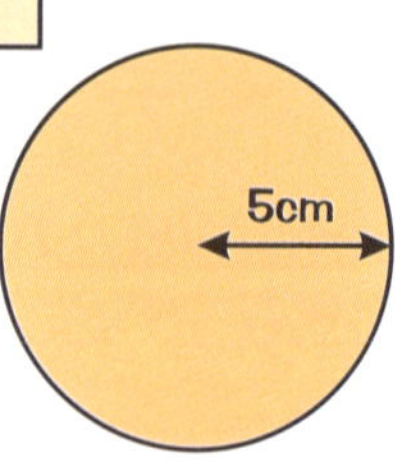

Formula for CIRCUMFERENCE is:
$C = \pi \times D$, so
$C = 3.14 \times 10$
$= \underline{31.4 \text{ cm}}$

Formula for AREA is:
$A = \pi \times r^2$
$= 3.14 \times (5 \times 5)$
$= 3.14 \times 25 = \underline{78.5 \text{ cm}^2}$

The Acid Test: There are 4 SECTIONS on this page. They're all *mighty important* — LEARN THEM.

Now cover the page and *write down* everything you've learnt. Frightening isn't it.
1) A plate has a diameter of 14cm. Find the area and the circumference of it using the methods you've just learnt. Remember to show all your working out.
2) A flower bed has a radius of 6m. Find the area and circumference of it.

Perimeters and Areas

1) *Perimeters* of Complicated Shapes

Make sure you know these *nitty gritty details* about perimeter:

1) Perimeter is the distance *all the way around the outside of a 2-D shape*.

2) To find a PERIMETER, you *ADD UP THE LENGTHS OF ALL THE SIDES* , but....
THE ONLY RELIABLE WAY to make sure you get *all the sides* is this:

> 1) Put a big blob at one corner and then go around the shape.
> 2) Write down the length of every side as you go.
> 3) Even sides that seem to have no length given — you must *work them out*.
> 4) Keep going until you get back to the BIG BLOB.

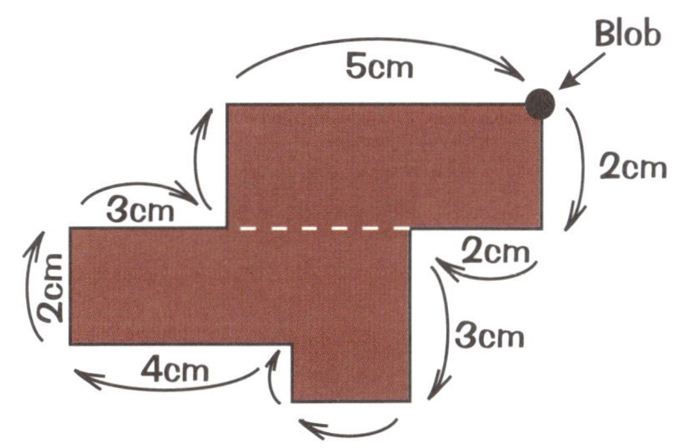

e.g. 2+2+3+2+1+4+2+3+2+5 = 26 cm

Yes, I know you think it's *yet another fussy method*, but believe me, it's so easy to miss a side. You must use GOOD RELIABLE METHODS for EVERYTHING — or you'll lose marks willy nilly.

2) *Areas* of Complicated Shapes

> 1) SPLIT THEM UP into *the 3 basic shapes*: RECTANGLE, TRIANGLE, AND CIRCLE.
> 2) Work out the area of each bit SEPARATELY.
> 3) Then ADD THEM ALL TOGETHER (or sometimes SUBTRACT them).

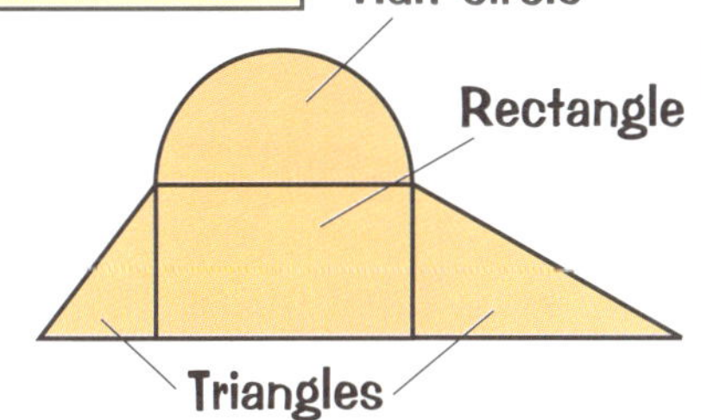

EXAMPLE: *Work out the area of this shape:*

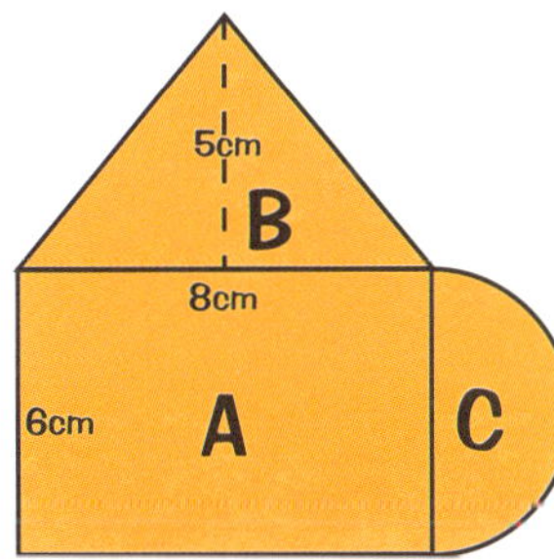

ANSWER:

Rectangle A:

$$\text{Area} = l \times w$$
$$= 8 \times 6$$
$$= \underline{48 \text{ cm}^2}$$

Triangle B:

$$\text{Area} = \tfrac{1}{2} \times b \times h$$
$$= \tfrac{1}{2} \times 8 \times 5$$
$$= \underline{20 \text{ cm}^2}$$

Semicircle C:

$$\text{Area} = (\pi \times r^2) \div 2$$
$$= (3.14 \times 3^2) \div 2$$
$$= \underline{14.13 \text{ cm}^2}$$

TOTAL AREA = 48 + 20 + 14.13 = 82.13 cm²

The Acid Test:

LEARN THE RULES for finding the perimeter and area of complicated shapes.

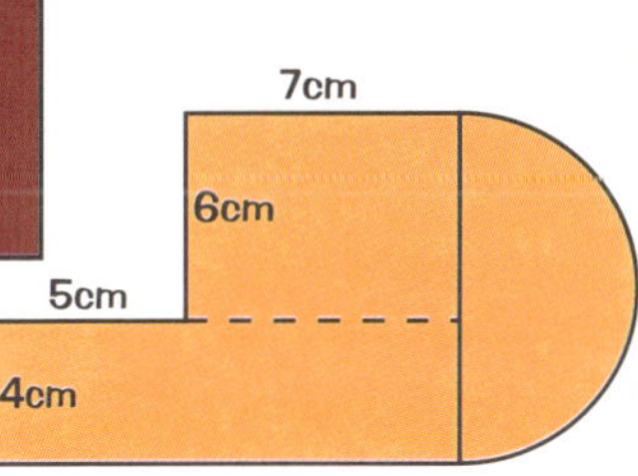

1) *Turn over and write down* what you've learnt.

2) Find the perimeter and area of the shape shown here:

Volume or Capacity

VOLUMES — YOU MUST LEARN THESE TOO!

1) CUBOID (RECTANGULAR BLOCK)

(This is also known as a *'rectangular prism'* — see below to understand why)

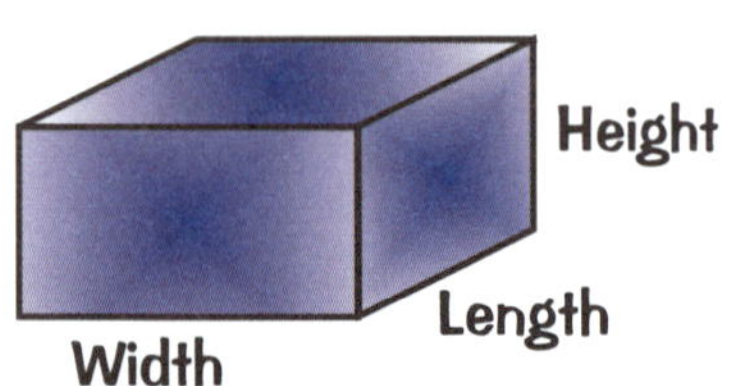

Volume of Cuboid = length × width × height

$$V = l \times w \times h$$

(The other word for volume is *CAPACITY*)

2) PRISM

A PRISM is a solid (3-D) object which has a **CONSTANT AREA OF CROSS-SECTION** — i.e. it's the same shape all the way through.

Now, for some reason, not a lot of people know what a prism is, but they come up all the time in Exams, so make sure **YOU** know.

Circular Prism
(or Cylinder)

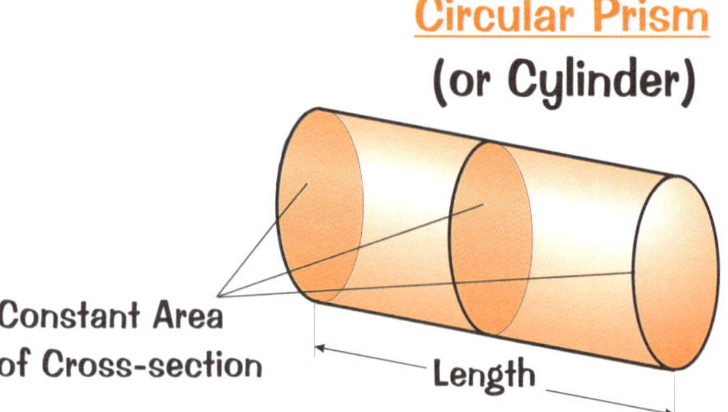

Hexagonal Prism
(a flat one, certainly, but still a prism)

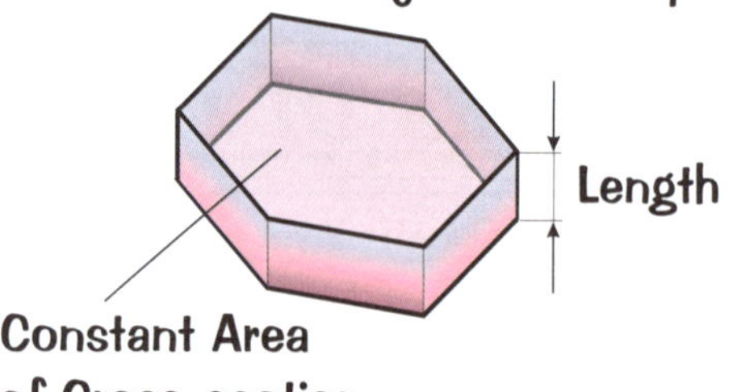

Triangular Prism

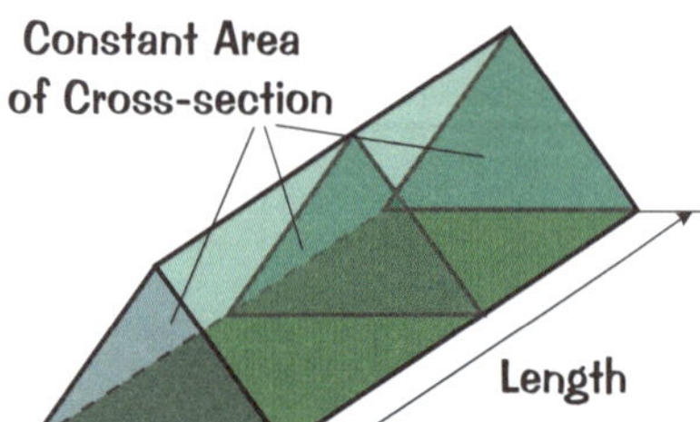

$$\text{Volume of prism} = \text{Cross-sectional Area} \times \text{length}$$

$$V = A \times l$$

As you can see, the formula for the volume of a prism is *very simple*. The *difficult* part, usually, is *finding the area of the cross-section*.

The Acid Test:

LEARN this page. Then turn over and try to write it all down. **Keep trying until you can do it.**

Practise these two questions until you can do them all the way through without any hesitation. Name the shapes and find their volumes:

a)

b)
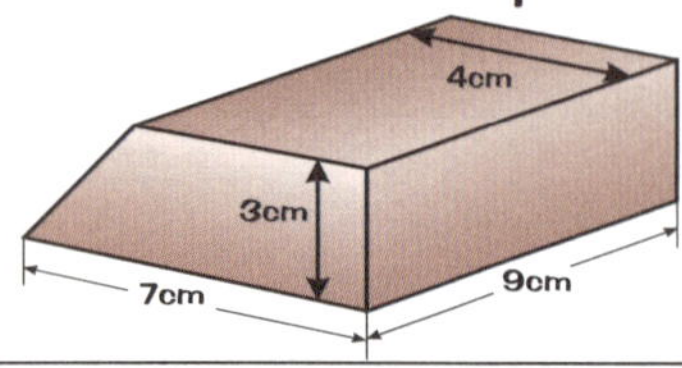

Solids and Nets

You need to know what *Face*, *Edge* and *Vertex* mean:

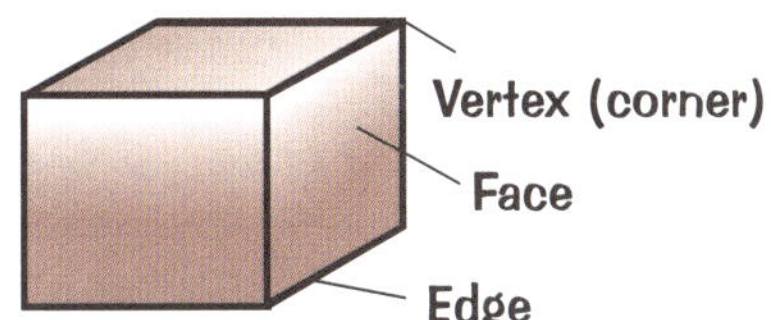

Surface Area and Nets

1) SURFACE AREA only applies to solid 3-D objects, and it's simply *the total area of all the outer surfaces added together*. If you were painting it, it's all the bits you'd paint!

2) There is never a simple formula for surface area — *you have to work out each side in turn and then* ADD THEM ALL TOGETHER.

3) A NET is just A SOLID SHAPE FOLDED OUT FLAT.

4) So obviously: SURFACE AREA OF SOLID = AREA OF NET.

There are 4 nets that you need to know really well for the Exam, and they're shown below. They may well ask you to draw one of these nets and then work out its area.

1) Triangular Prism

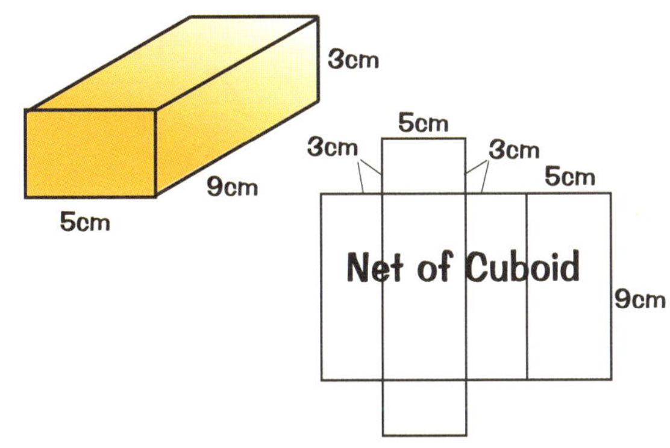

2) Cube

3) Cuboid

4) Pyramid

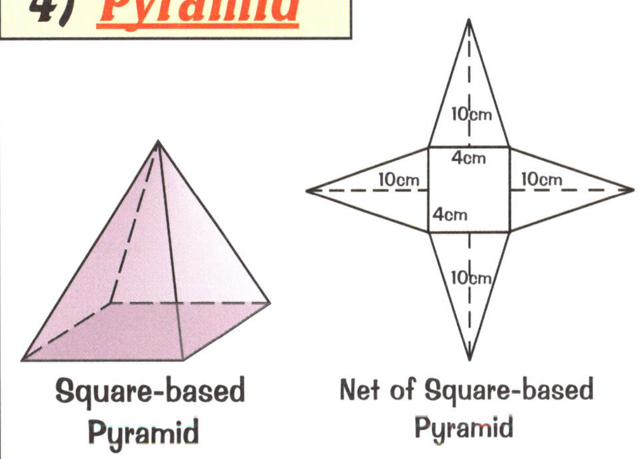

The Acid Test:

LEARN the 4 details on surface area and nets and the FOUR NETS on this page, and also the little diagram at the top of the page.

Now cover the page and write down everything you've learnt.
1) Work out the area of all four nets shown above.

Length, Area And Volume

Identifying Formulas Just by Looking at Them

This isn't as bad as it sounds, since we're only talking about the formulas for 3 things:

LENGTH, AREA and VOLUME

The rules are as simple as this:

> **AREA FORMULAS** always have **LENGTHS MULTIPLIED IN PAIRS**
>
> **VOLUME FORMULAS** always have **LENGTHS MULTIPLIED IN GROUPS OF THREE**
>
> **LENGTH FORMULAS** (such as perimeter) always have **LENGTHS OCCURRING SINGLY**

In formulas of course, **LENGTHS ARE REPRESENTED BY LETTERS**, so when you look at a formula you're looking for:

GROUPS OF LETTERS MULTIPLIED TOGETHER in *ONES*, *TWOS* or *THREES*.
BUT REMEMBER, π is **NOT** a length.

Examples:

$4\pi r^2 + 6d^2$ (area)	$Lwh + 6r^2L$ (volume)	(r^2 means $r \times r$,
$4\pi r + 15L$ (length)	$6hp + \pi r^2 + 7h^2$ (area)	don't forget)
$5p^2L - 4k^3/7$ (volume)	$2\pi d - 14r/3$ (length)	

Watch out for these last two tricky ones: (Why are they tricky?)

$3p(2b + a)$ (area) $3\pi h(L^2 + 4P^2)$ (volume)

Four Extra Facts:

1) A *QUADRILATERAL* is just *a four-sided shape* — *any* four-sided shape. So *squares*, *rectangles*, *parallelograms*, etc. are all *QUADRILATERALS*. And so are the two shown here:

2) *ACUTE ANGLES* are *sharp pointy ones* (between 0° and 90°).
3) *OBTUSE ANGLES* are *flatter* (between 90° and 180°).
4) *REFLEX ANGLES* are *over-extended* (between 180° and 360°).

The Acid Test:
LEARN the Rules for Identifying Formulas, and the Four Extra Facts. Turn over and write it all down.

1) Identify each of these expressions as an area, volume, or perimeter:
πr^2, Lwh, πd, $\frac{1}{2}bh$, $2bh + 4lp$, $4r^2p + 3\pi d^3$, $2\pi r(3L + 5T)$

Enlargements — The 4 Key Features:

1) If the Scale Factor is BIGGER THAN 1 then the shape gets BIGGER.

A to B is an Enlargement, Scale Factor 1½

2) If the Scale Factor is SMALLER than 1 (i.e. a fraction like ½), then the shape gets SMALLER.

(Really this is a *reduction*, but you still call it an Enlargement, Scale Factor ½)

A to B is an Enlargement of Scale Factor ½

3)

Enlargement Scale Factor 3

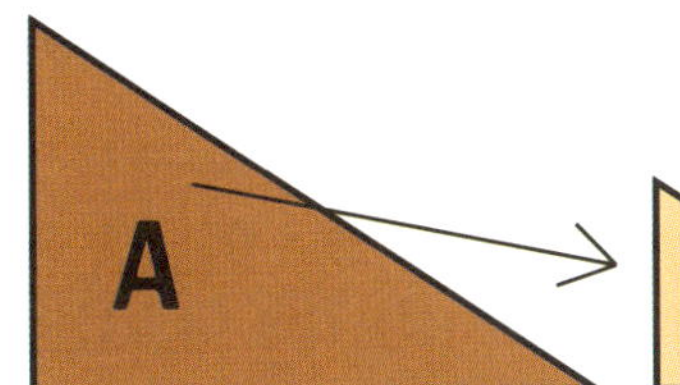

The Scale Factor also tells you the RELATIVE DISTANCE of old points and new points from the Centre of Enlargement.

This is VERY USEFUL FOR DRAWING AN ENLARGEMENT, because you can use it to trace out the positions of the new points from the centre of enlargement, as shown in the diagram.

4) The lengths of the big and small shapes are related to the Scale Factor by this VERY important Formula Triangle WHICH YOU MUST LEARN:

Obviously, if the length of a single side is multiplied by the scale factor, then the perimeter will also change by the same amount — e.g. a square of side-length 1 enlarged by scale factor 2 will have sides of length 2 and a perimeter changed from 4 to 8 (4 × 2).

This now lets you to tackle the classic "Enlarged photo" Exam question with breathtaking triviality:

For formula triangles, see P.52

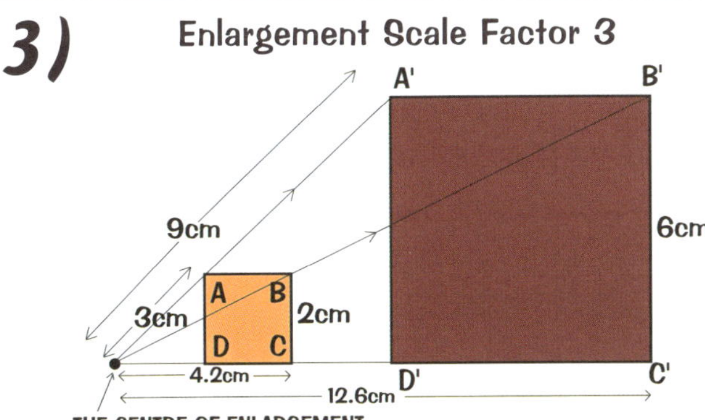

To find the width of the enlarged photo we use the formula triangle TWICE, (firstly to find the Scale Factor, and then to find the missing side):

1) **Scale Factor** = New length ÷ Old length = 13.2 ÷ 8.4 = **1.57**

2) **New width** = Scale Factor × Old width = 1.57 × 5.8 = **9.1 cm**

BUT WITHOUT THE FORMULA TRIANGLE YOU'RE SCUPPERED!

The Acid Test:

LEARN the FOUR KEY FEATURES of enlargements, especially the FORMULA TRIANGLE.

Then, when you think you know it, cover the page and write it all down again, from memory, including the sketches and examples, especially the photo enlargement one. Keep trying till you can.

The Four Transformations

T ranslation — ONE Detail
E nlargement — TWO Details
R otation — THREE Details
R eflection — ONE Detail
Y

1) Use the name <u>TERRY</u> to remember the 4 types.

2) You must always specify <u>all the details</u> for each type.

3) It'll help if you remember which properties remain <u>unchanged</u> in each transformation, too.

1) TRANSLATION

<u>You must Specify this ONE detail:</u>

1) The <u>VECTOR OF TRANSLATION</u> $\begin{pmatrix} x \to \\ \uparrow y \end{pmatrix}$ (See P.44 on vector notation)

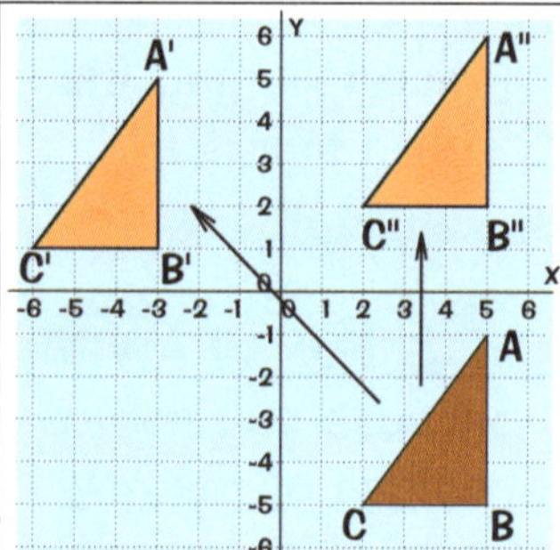

ABC to A'B'C' is a <u>translation of</u> $\begin{pmatrix} -8 \\ 6 \end{pmatrix}$

ABC to A"B"C" is a <u>translation of</u> $\begin{pmatrix} 0 \\ 7 \end{pmatrix}$

All that changes in a translation is the *POSITION* of the object — <u>*everything else*</u> remains <u>unchanged</u>.

2) ENLARGEMENT

<u>You must Specify these 2 details:</u>

1) The <u>SCALE FACTOR</u>
2) The <u>CENTRE</u> of Enlargement

From <u>A to B</u> is an enlargement of <u>scale factor 2</u>, and <u>centre (2,6)</u>

From <u>B to A</u> is an enlargement of <u>scale factor 1/2</u> and <u>centre (2,6)</u>

With enlargement, the *ANGLES* of the object remain <u>unchanged</u>. The *RATIOS* of the lengths of the sides, and the object's *ORIENTATION* remain <u>unchanged</u>. Everything else *can* change.

3) ROTATION

<u>You must Specify these 3 details:</u>

1) <u>ANGLE</u> turned
2) <u>DIRECTION</u> (Clockwise or..)
3) <u>CENTRE</u> of Rotation

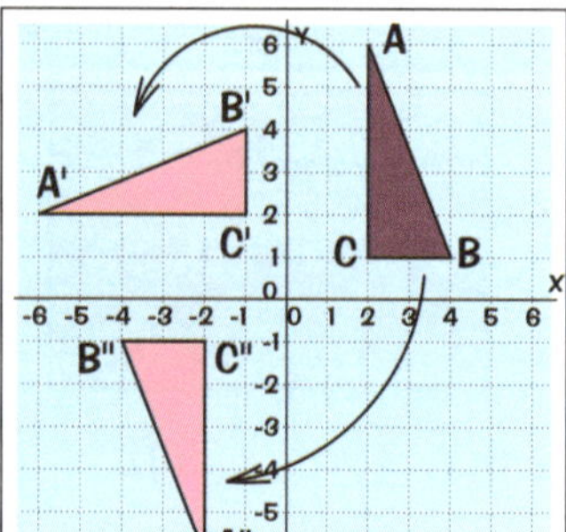

ABC to A'B'C' is a Rotation of <u>90°</u>, <u>anticlockwise</u>, <u>ABOUT the origin</u>.

ABC to A"B"C" is a Rotation of <u>half a turn (180°)</u>, <u>clockwise</u>, <u>ABOUT the origin</u>.

The only things that *change* in a rotation are the *POSITION* and the *ORIENTATION* of the object. <u>*Everything else*</u> remains <u>unchanged</u>.

4) REFLECTION

<u>You must Specify this ONE detail:</u>

1) The <u>MIRROR LINE</u>

A to B is a <u>reflection IN the Y-axis</u>.

A to C is a <u>reflection IN the line Y=X</u>

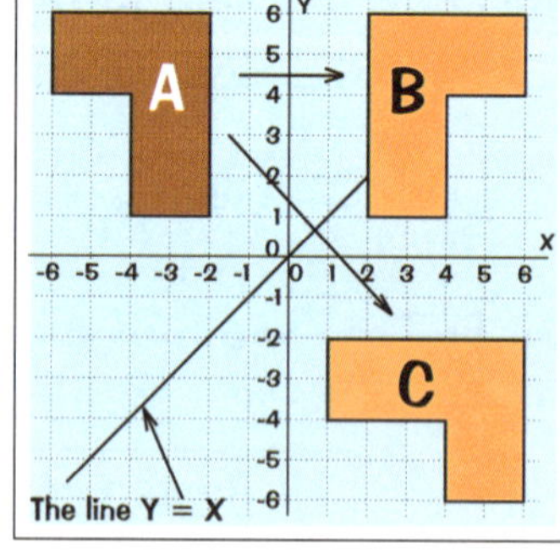

With reflection, the *POSITION* and *ORIENTATION* of the object are the <u>*only things that change*</u>.

The Acid Test:

LEARN the names of the Four Transformations and the details that go with each. When you think you know it, <u>*turn over and write it all down*</u>.

1) Describe <u>*fully*</u> these transformations: A → B, B → C, C → A, A → D.

Combinations of Transformations

In Exam questions they'll often do something _horrid_ like _stick two transformations together_ and then ask you what combination gets you from shape A to shape B.   Be _ready_.

The _Better_ You _Know Them All_ — The _Easier_ it is

These kinds of question aren't so bad — but _ONLY_ if you've _LEARNT_ the _four transformations_ on the last page _really well_ — if you don't know them, then you certainly won't do too well at spotting a _combination_ of one followed by another.
That's because the method is basically _"Try it and see..."_

Example

"What combination of two transformations takes you from triangle A to triangle B?"

(There's usually a few different ways of getting from one shape to the other — but remember you only need to find _ONE_ of them.)

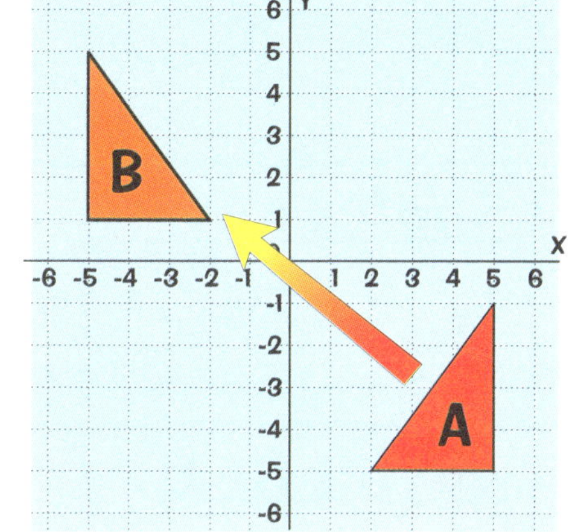

Method: Try an _obvious transformation_ first, and _See..._

If you _think_ about it, the answer can _only_ be a combination of two of the _four types_ shown on the last page, so you can immediately start to _narrow it down_:

1) Since the shapes are the _same size_ we can _rule out enlargements_.
2) Next, _try a reflection_ (in either the X-axis or the Y-axis).
   Here we've tried a reflection in the _Y-axis_, to give shape A':
3) You should now easily be able to see the _final step_

   from A' to B — it's a _translation_ of $\begin{pmatrix} 0 \\ 6 \end{pmatrix}$.

And that's it _DONE_ — from A to B is simply a combination of:

> A _REFLECTION IN THE Y-AXIS_ followed by a _TRANSLATION OF_ $\begin{pmatrix} 0 \\ 6 \end{pmatrix}$

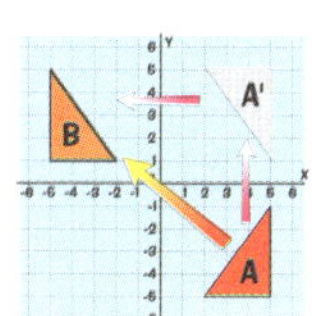

At least that's one answer anyway. If instead we decided to reflect it in the X-axis first (as shown here) then we'd get another answer (see Acid Test below) — but both are right.

"But which transformation do I try first?" I hear you cry.

Well it just depends on _how it looks_.
But the _more transformation questions_ you do, the more obvious that first guess becomes.
In other words: the more you _practise_, the _easier_ you'll be able to do it — surprise surprise...

The Acid Test: LEARN the _main points_ on this page.
Then _cover it up_ and _write them all down_.

1) What pair of transformations will convert shape C into shape D?:
   What pair will convert shape D to shape C?
2) In the example above, find the other transformation needed to
   get to shape B after reflecting shape A in the X-axis.

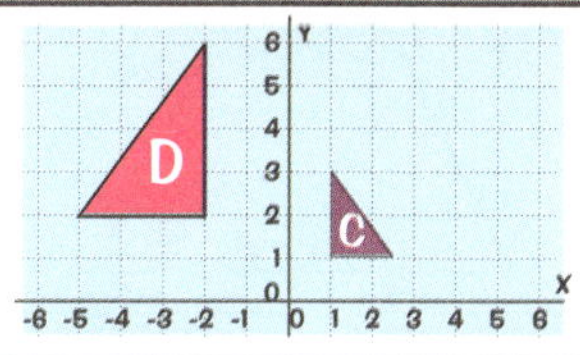

Geometry

8 Simple Rules — that's all:

If you know them ALL — THOROUGHLY, you at least have a fighting chance of working out problems with lines and angles. *If you don't — you've no chance.*

1) Angles in a triangle

Add up to 180°.

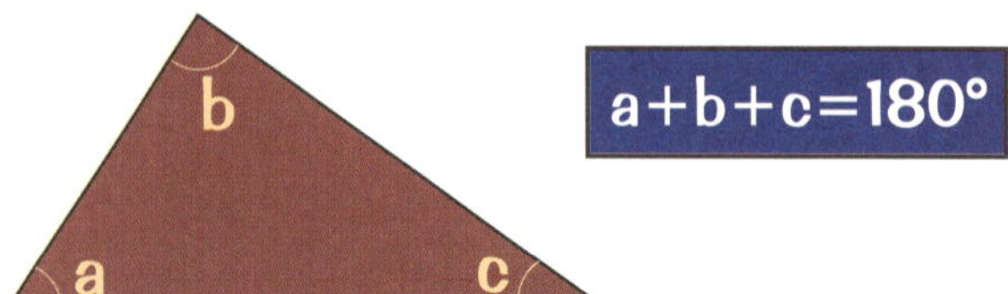

2) Angles on a straight line

Add up to 180°.

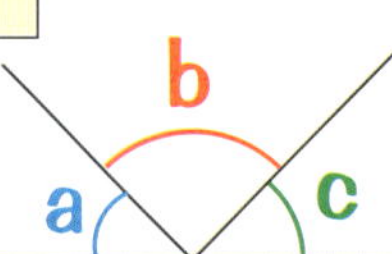

3) Angles in a 4-sided shape

(a "Quadrilateral")

Add up to 360°.

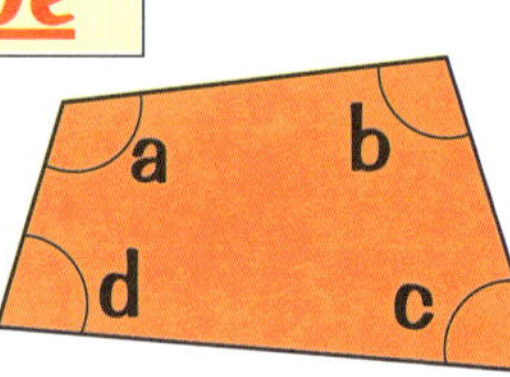

4) Angles round a point

Add up to 360°.

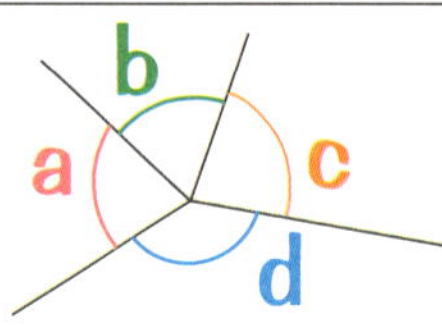

5) Exterior Angle of Triangle

Exterior Angle of triangle
= sum of Opposite Interior angles

i.e. a+b=d

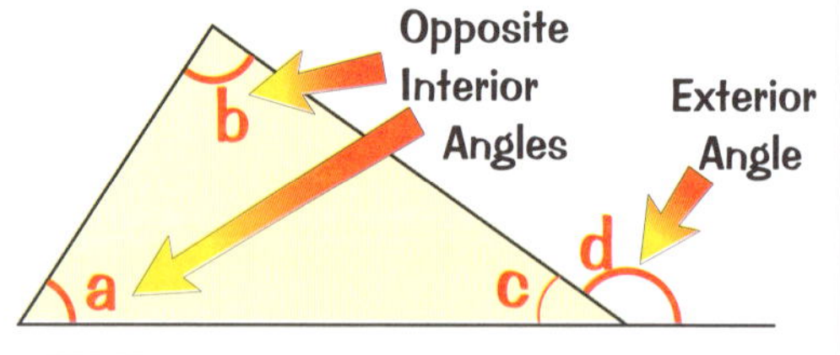

6) Isosceles triangles

2 sides the same
2 angles the same

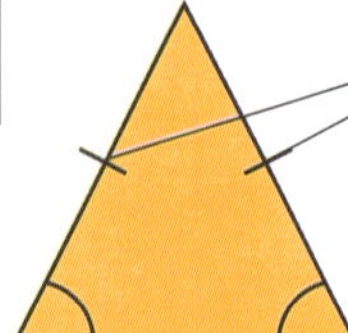

In an isosceles triangle, *YOU ONLY NEED TO KNOW ONE ANGLE* to be able to find the other two, which is *very useful IF YOU REMEMBER IT.*

a)

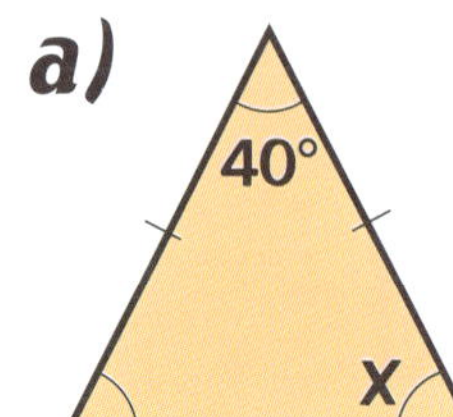

180° – 40° = 140°
The two bottom angles are both the same and they must add up to 140°, so each one must be half of 140° (= 70°). So *X = 70°*.

b)

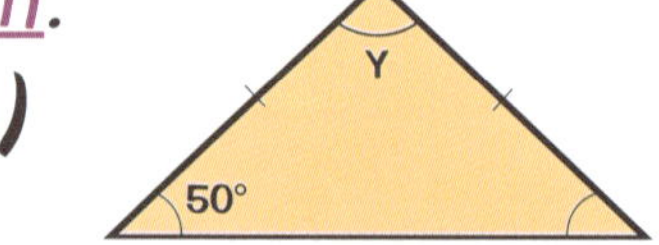

The *two bottom angles must be the same*, so 50° + 50° = 100°.
All the angles add up to 180° so Y = 180° – 100° = *80°*.

Geometry

7) *Parallel* lines

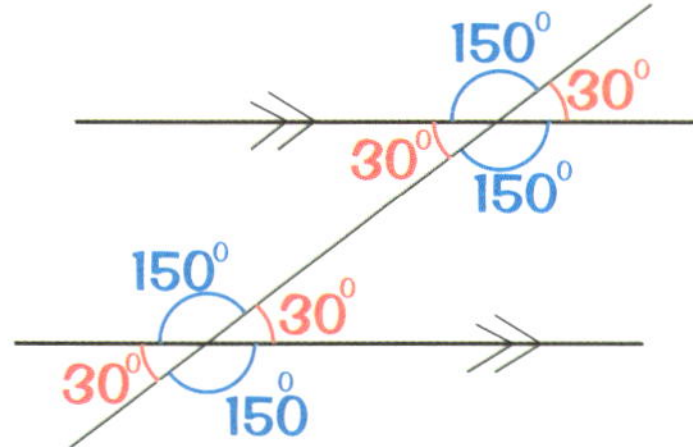

Whenever one line goes across 2 parallel lines, then <u>the two bunches of angles are the same</u>
(The arrows mean those 2 lines are parallel)

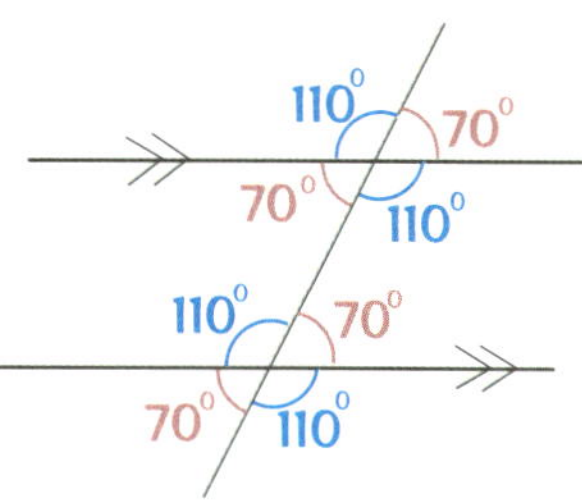

Whenever you have <u>TWO PARALLEL LINES</u> there are *only two different angles*: <u>A SMALL ONE</u> and <u>A BIG ONE</u> and they <u>ALWAYS ADD UP TO 180°</u>.
E.g.   30° and 150°   or   70° and 110°

The trickiest bit about parallel lines is <u>spotting them in the first place</u> — watch out for these "Z", "C", "U" and "F" shapes popping up:

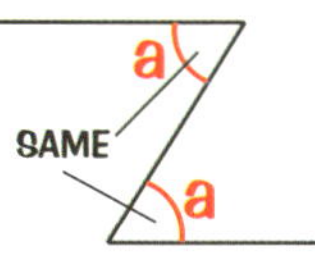
In a <u>Z-shape</u> they're called "ALTERNATE ANGLES"

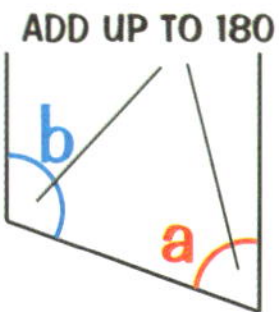
If they add up to 180 they're called "SUPPLEMENTARY ANGLES"

In an F-shape they're called "CORRESPONDING ANGLES"

Alas you're expected to learn these three silly names too!

If necessary, *EXTEND THE LINES* to make the diagram *easier to get to grips with*:

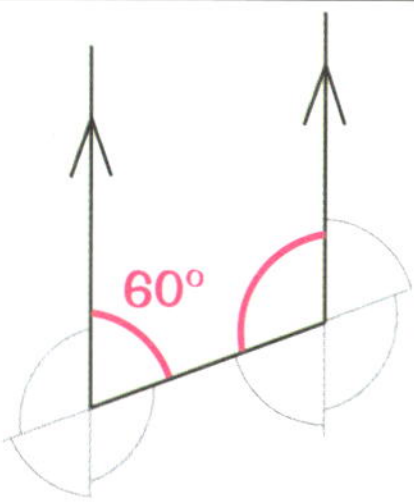

8) *Irregular* Polygons: Interior and Exterior Angles

An irregular polygon is basically any shape with lots of straight sides which aren't all the same. There are two formulas you need to know:

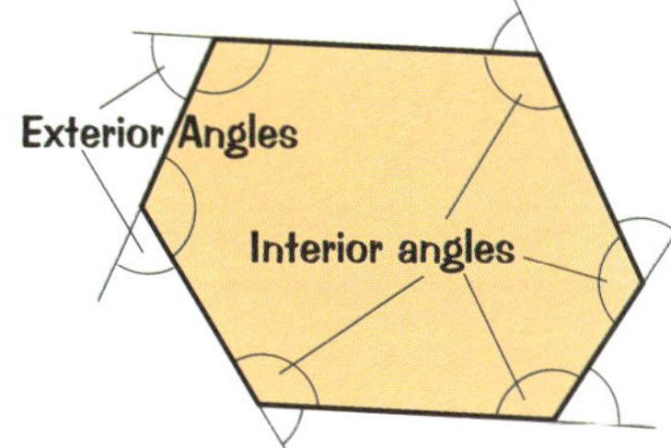

> ### <u>Sum of Exterior angles = 360°</u>

> ### <u>Sum of Interior angles</u> = (n – 2)×180°
> where n is the number of sides

This formula works for any polygon, but I bet you know the angles of a regular polygon anyway.

The (n – 2)×180° formula comes from splitting the inside of the polygon up into triangles using full diagonals. Each triangle has 180° in it so just count up the triangles and times by 180°. There's always **2** less triangles than there are sides, hence the (n – 2).

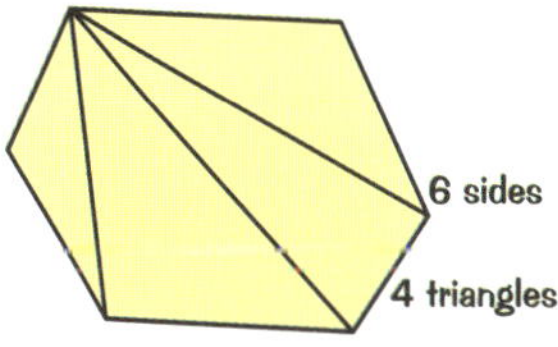

The Acid Test:

<u>LEARN EVERYTHING</u> on these two pages. Then <u>turn over</u> and see how much of it you can <u>write down</u>.

1) Find the size of angle Z in the triangle shown:
2) How much do the exterior angles of a 7-sided polygon add up to?
3) How much do the interior angles of a 5-sided polygon add up to?
4) One of the diagrams above has one angle given as 60°. Find the other 7 angles.

Circle Geometry

Nine Simple Rules — that's all:

You'll have to learn these too if you want to be able to do circle problems.

1) ANGLE IN A SEMICIRCLE = 90°

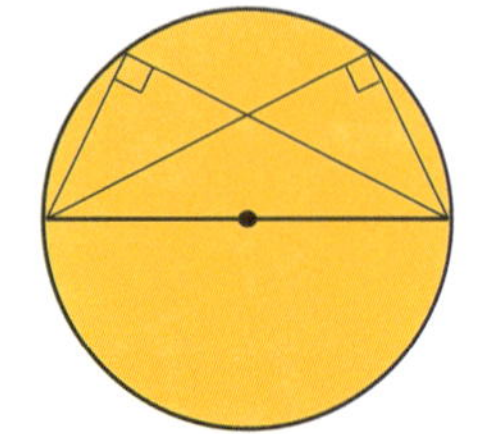

A triangle drawn from the <u>two ends of a diameter</u> will ALWAYS make an <u>angle of 90° where it hits</u> the edge of the circle, no matter where it hits.

2) TANGENT and RADIUS MEET AT 90°

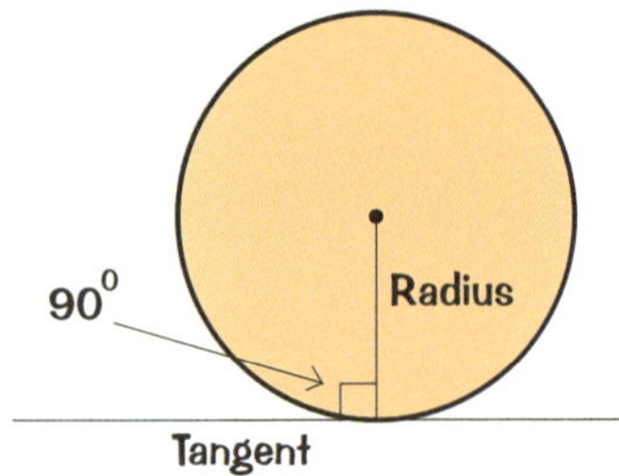

A TANGENT is a line that just touches the edge of a curve. <u>If a tangent and radius meet</u> at the same point, then the angle they make is *EXACTLY 90°*.

3) SNEAKY ISOSCELES TRIANGLES FORMED BY TWO RADII

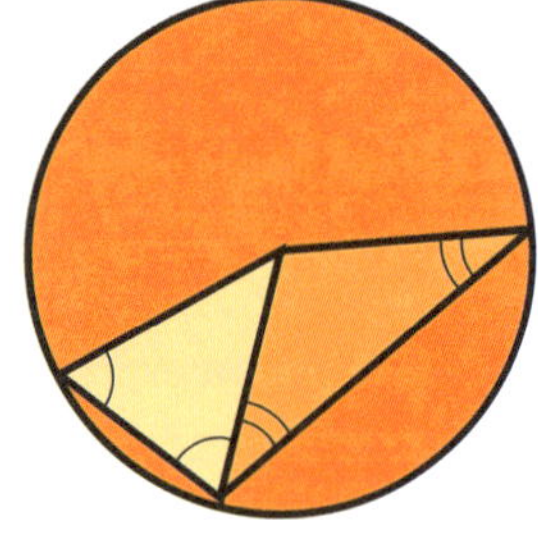

Unlike other isosceles triangles they don't have the little tick marks on the sides to remind you that they're the same — the fact that two sides are radii is enough to make it an isosceles trangle.

4) CHORD BISECTOR IS A DIAMETER

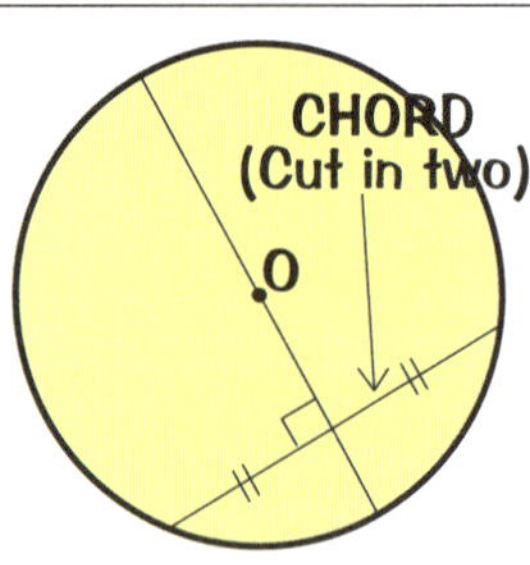

A CHORD is any line <u>drawn across a circle</u>, and no matter where you draw a chord, the line that <u>cuts it exactly in half</u> (at 90°), will go <u>through the centre of the circle</u> and so it'll <u>have to be</u> a *DIAMETER*.

5) ANGLES IN THE SAME SEGMENT ARE EQUAL

All triangles drawn from a chord will have <u>the same angle where they touch the circle</u>.

Also, the two angles on opposite sides of the chord <u>add up to 180°</u>.

When the chord chops the circle in half (to form 2 <u>semicircles</u>), the angle at the edge of the circle is <u>always a right angle</u>.

Circle Geometry

6) ANGLE AT THE CENTRE IS TWICE THE ANGLE AT THE EDGE

The angle subtended at the centre of a circle is EXACTLY DOUBLE the angle subtended at the edge of the circle from the same two points (two ends of the same chord). The phrase "angle subtended at" is nothing complicated, it's just a bit posher than saying "angle made at".

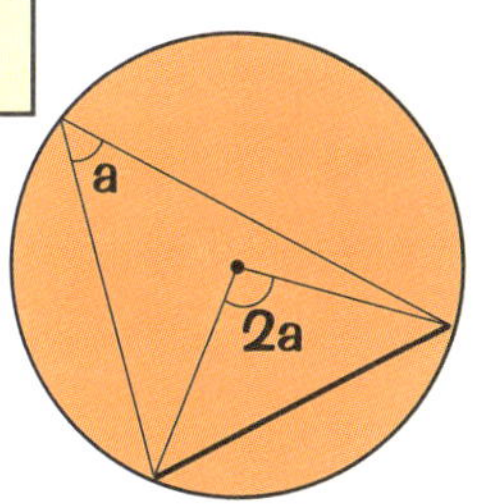

7) OPPOSITE ANGLES OF A CYCLIC QUADRILATERAL ADD UP TO 180°

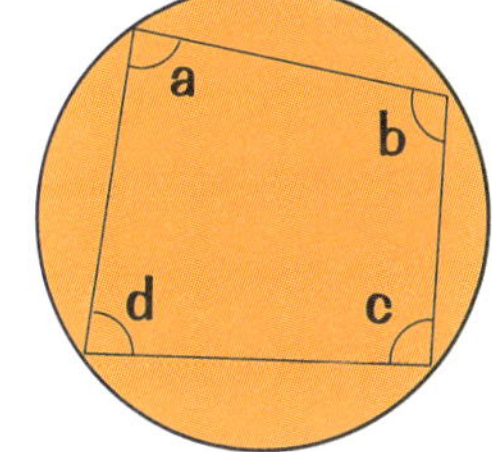

$a+c=180°$

$b+d=180°$

A *cyclic quadrilateral* is a 4-sided shape with every corner touching the circle. Both pairs of opposite angles add up to 180°.

8) EQUALITY OF TANGENTS FROM A POINT

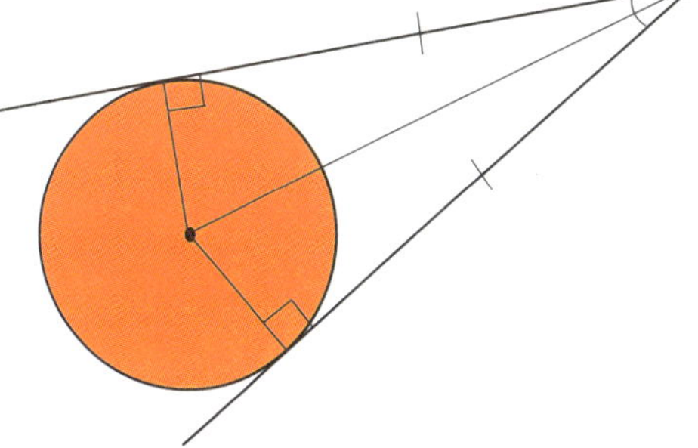

The two tangents drawn from an outside point are always equal in length, so creating an "isosceles" situation, with two congruent right-angled triangles.

9) ANGLE IN OPPOSITE SEGMENT IS EQUAL

This is perhaps the trickiest one to remember. If you draw a tangent and a chord that meet, then the angle between them is always equal to "*the angle in the opposite segment*" (i.e. the angle made at the edge of the circle by two lines drawn from the chord)

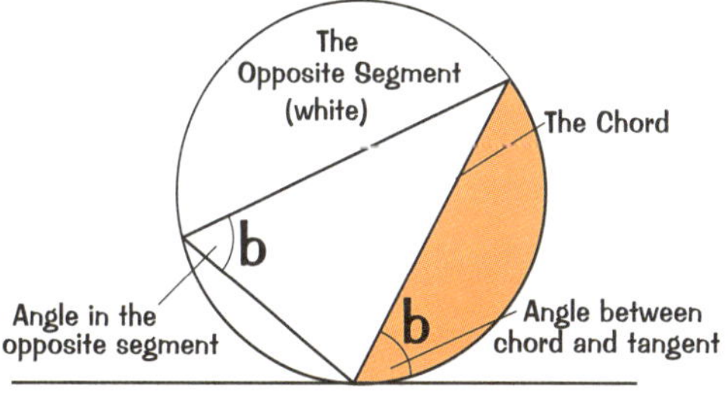

10) WHEN YOU'RE STUCK...

It's all too easy to find yourself staring at a geometry problem and getting nowhere — IF SO, this is what you do:

> **GO THROUGH ALL THE 17 RULES OF GEOMETRY** (on pages 36-39), **ONE BY ONE, and APPLY EACH OF THEM IN TURN in as many ways as possible** — *ONE OF THEM IS BOUND TO WORK.*

In other words, just find ALL the angles in whichever order they become obvious.

The Acid Test: LEARN all Nine Rules on these two pages, and all 8 from the last two pages. Then turn over and write them all down.

Check your effort and try again — and keep trying till you can do it!

Three-letter Angle Notation

Using Three Letters to Specify Angles

The best way to say which angle you're talking about in a diagram is by using THREE letters. For example in the diagram, angle ACB = 25°.

This is the way they'll do it in the Exam so like it or lump it, you'd better get the hang of it. Anyway, it's very simple:

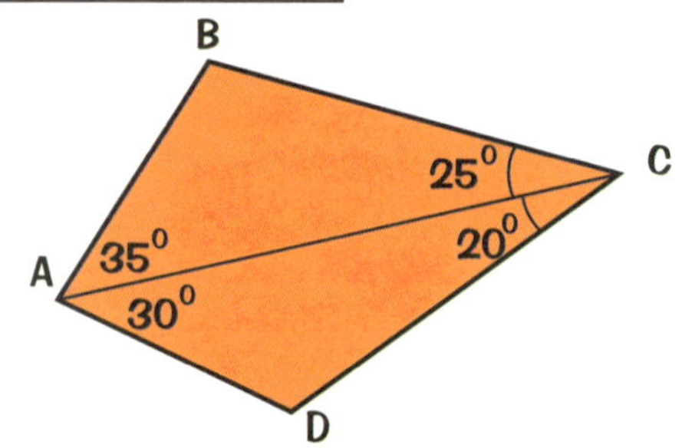

1) The MIDDLE LETTER is where the angle is.

2) The OTHER TWO LETTERS tell you WHICH TWO LINES enclose the angle.

EXAMPLES FROM THE DIAGRAM ABOVE:

1) Angle BCD is AT C and is ENCLOSED BY the lines BC and CD (you just split BCD into BC-CD). So angle BCD = 45°.

2) Angle ACD (AC-CD) is AT C and is ENCLOSED BY the lines AC and CD. ACD = 20°.

A Fairly Tricky Question — Illustrating the 3-letter notation

QUESTION:

"Find all the angles in this diagram."
(Apply Rule 10 from P.39 and see how easy it makes it)

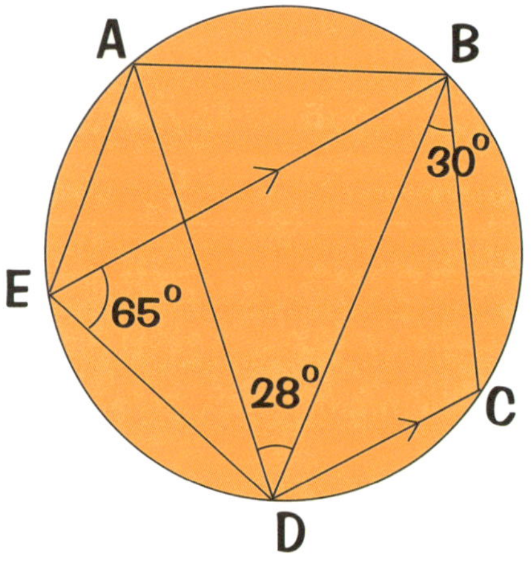

ANSWER:

1) PARALLEL LINES – there are actually 4 different lines crossing the 2 parallel ones, but the most useful one is ED which tells us that EDC is 115°

2) ANGLE IN SAME SEGMENT – there are potentially eight different chords where this rule could apply, but some are more useful than others:
EAD = EBD,   ADB = AEB (so AEB = 28°)
ABE = ADE,   DAB = DEB (so DAB = 65°)

3) ANGLES IN OPPOSITE SEGMENTS – again there are three different chords where this can be applied and two of them bear fruit:
BCD = 180 – 65 = 115°
ABD = 180 – (65+28) = 87°

4) ANGLES IN A TRIANGLE ADD UP TO 180° – this, the simplest of all the rules, will now find all the other angles for you.

The Acid Test:

LEARN what 3-Letter notation is. Then cover the page and give an example of it.

1) Looking at the diagram at the top of the page, write down the size of angle BAC and also give the three-letter notation for the angles which are   a) 30° and   b) 65°.

2) *Practise the above Example* till you *understand every step* and can do it yourself without any help from the notes — keep practising till you can.

Projections, Congruence and Similarity

Projections *show* *the Scale of the Shape*

A '*projection*' shows the relative size and shape of an object from either the *front*, *side* or *back* — they're usually known as '*elevations*'. A '*plan*' shows the view from *above*. They're always *drawn to scale*.

Take this church (naff picture, I know) — you can represent it like this:

FRONT Elevation — the view you'd see if you looked from directly *in front*:

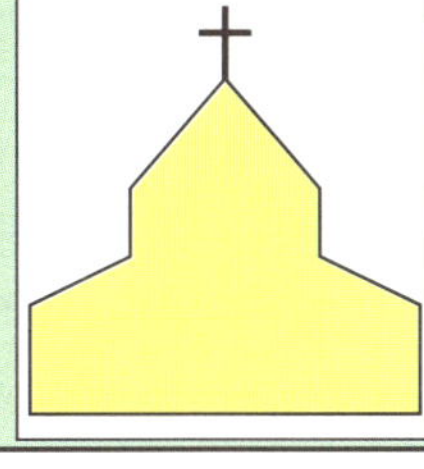

SIDE Elevation — the view you'd see if you looked from directly to *one side*:

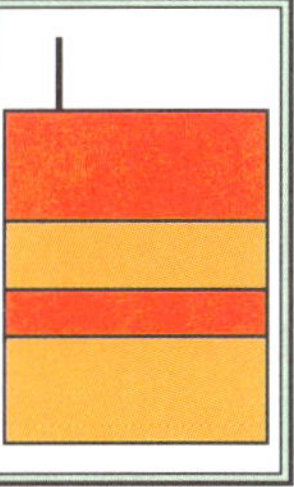

PLAN — the view you'd see if you looked from directly *above*:

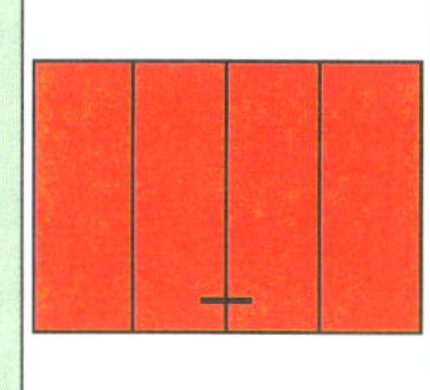

If they're feeling really mean (and they often are), you might get a question on:

This one's a bit trickier, so you might want to spend a little longer practising it — just to get your head round it.

ISOMETRIC Projection — this is where the shape is drawn (again, to scale) from a view at *equal angles to* all three axes (*x, y and z*). Or more simply, it's a drawing like this:

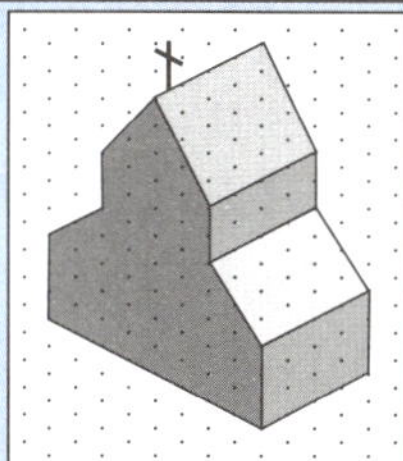

Congruence *and* *Similarity*

Congruence is another ridiculous maths word which sounds really complicated when it's not: If two shapes are *CONGRUENT*, they're simply *the same* — *the same size and the same shape*.

CONGRUENT
— same size, same shape
A, B, and C are <u>CONGRUENT</u>
(with each other)

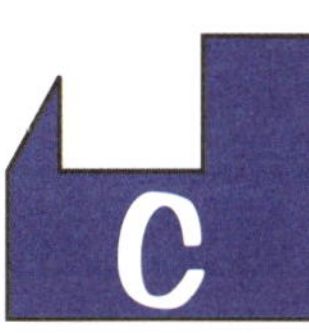

SIMILAR
— same shape, *but can be different size*
D and E are <u>SIMILAR</u>, (but not congruent)

Remember: when you have *similar* shapes *the angles are always the same*.

The Acid Test: Make sure you understand <u>ALL FOUR TYPES OF PROJECTION</u>, and <u>LEARN</u> exactly what "<u>SIMILAR</u>" and "<u>CONGRUENT</u>" mean.

Now cover the page and write down what you've learned. Then REMEMBER it forever!

1) Draw a plan, front and side elevations and an isometric projection of your own house.

2) a) Which of these four shapes are similar?
   b) Which are congruent?

i) 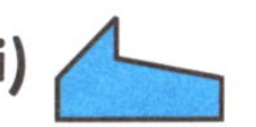 ii)  iii) 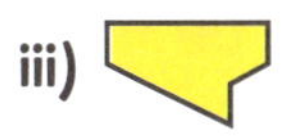 iv) 

Revision Summary for Section Two

More difficult questions, _but just keep reminding yourself that they're the very best revision you can do_. These questions are very plain and very straightforward. They don't ask anything tricky, just whether or not you've actually _learnt_ all the _basic facts_ in Section Two. It's really important to keep practising these as often as you can.

Keep learning these basic facts until you know them

1) What is a regular polygon? Draw the first 6, and describe their symmetry.
2) What are the 2 key angles for regular polygons? How do you find them?
3) What are the 3 types of symmetry called? Draw an example of each.
4) What is the most useful bit of equipment for doing symmetry?
5) Draw and name 6 different quadrilaterals and specify all their symmetry.
6) Name 3 different triangles. Draw them and describe their symmetry in full.
7) Name and draw the 8 different solids with 1 plane of symmetry on each.
8) Write down the formulas for the area of 5 different types of shape.
9) What is π?   What are the two circle formulae?   When do you use them?
10) Draw a circle and show on it: radius, diameter, arc, chord, tangent.
11) State 3 important steps for successfully finding the perimeter of a shape.
12) What are the 3 rules for working out complicated areas?
13) Give the formulas for the volumes of two types of solid.
14) What exactly is a prism? Draw one and show the two important details.
15) Explain what is meant by surface area and what a net is.
16) How are the two related? Is there a formula for working out surface area?
17) Draw the four important nets.
18) What are the 3 rules for identifying formulae as length, area or volume?
19) What is a quadrilateral?
20) Explain what acute and obtuse angles are and give 2 examples of each.
21) In enlargements, what is the effect (on the lengths of the sides) of a scale factor _bigger_ than 1?
22) What is the effect of a scale factor _smaller_ than 1?
23) What is the centre of enlargement?
24) How is it used for drawing an enlargement?
25) What is the Formula Triangle for enlargements?
26) Illustrate its use with the enlarged photo question.
27) In relation to the four enlargements, what does TERRY stand for?
28) Give the details that go with each of the 4 types of transformation.
29) List the first 8 rules of geometry, and give extra details about the last 3.
30) List the 9 rules of circle geometry.
31) What is the 3-letter notation for angles? Give an example.
32) Draw the plan and side and front elevations for this cuboid:

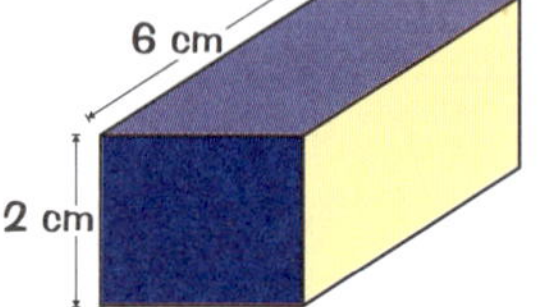

33) Draw an isometric representation of a cube with side lengths of 3 units.*
34) Explain congruence and similarity.

* If you don't have any isometric graph paper, then copy the pattern of the dots from page 41 and answer as best you can.

Bearings

Bearings — 3 Key Points

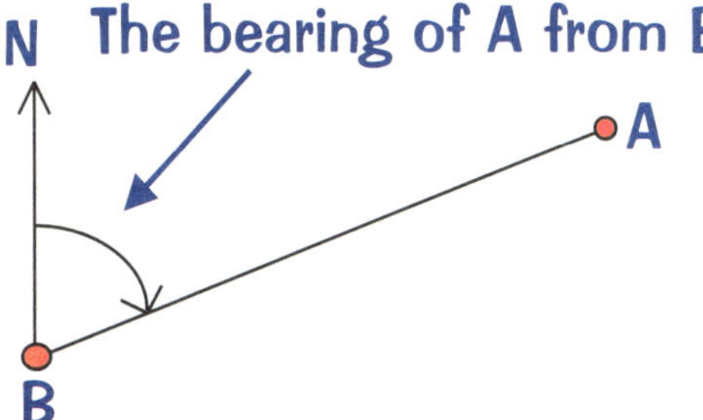

1) A bearing is the **DIRECTION TRAVELLED** between two points, **GIVEN AS AN ANGLE** in degrees.

2) All bearings are measured **CLOCKWISE from the NORTHLINE**.

3) All bearings should be given as _3 figures_, e.g. 243⁰, 060⁰ (not 60⁰), 008⁰ (not 8⁰), 018⁰ etc.

The 3 Key Words

Only learn this if you want to get bearings _RIGHT_

1) "FROM"

Find the word "FROM" in the question, and put your pencil on the diagram at the point you are going "_from_".

2) NORTHLINE

At the point you are going "FROM", _draw in a NORTHLINE_.

3) CLOCKWISE

Now draw in the angle CLOCKWISE _from the northline to the line joining the two points_. This angle is the BEARING.

Example

Find the bearing of Q from P:

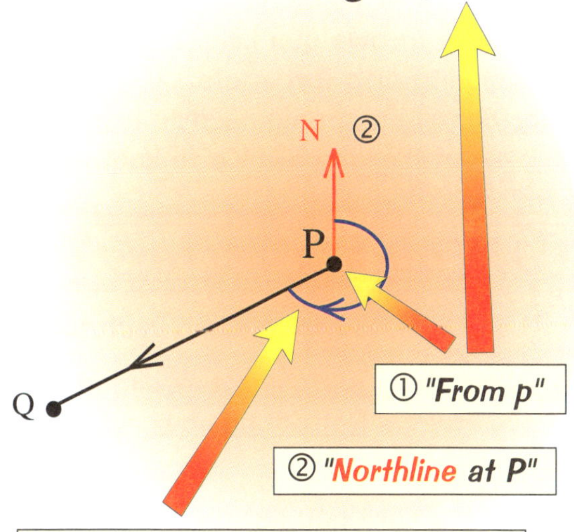

This angle is the _bearing of Q from P_ and is _245°_.

The Acid Test:

LEARN the _3 Features of Bearings_ and the _3 Key Steps of the method_ for finding them.

Now _turn over_ and write down what you've just learnt.
Keep trying _till you can write down all six points from memory_.

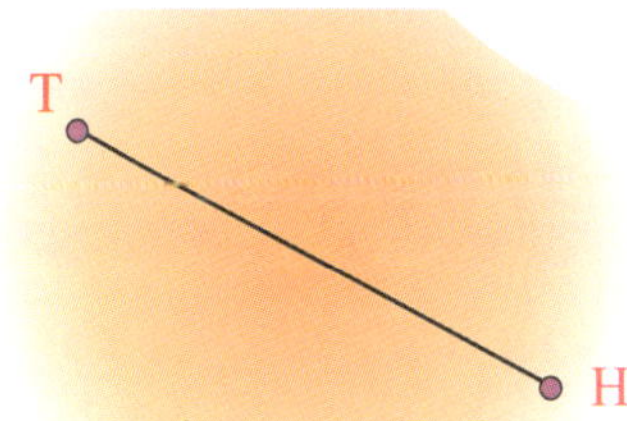

1) Find the bearing of H from T.   (Use a protractor)
2) Find the bearing of T from H.

Vectors

<u>SOME MONSTROUSLY IMPORTANT THINGS</u> you need to know about Vectors:

1) *A VECTOR is just a certain length in a certain direction*

1) Vectors are *always* shown as <u>lines with arrows on them</u>.

2) The length and direction of the line represent the size and direction of the thing in question.

3) There are *four notations* you need to know.
The vector shown above can be referred to as either:

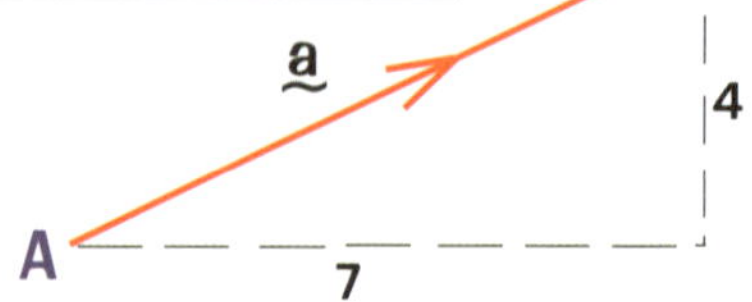

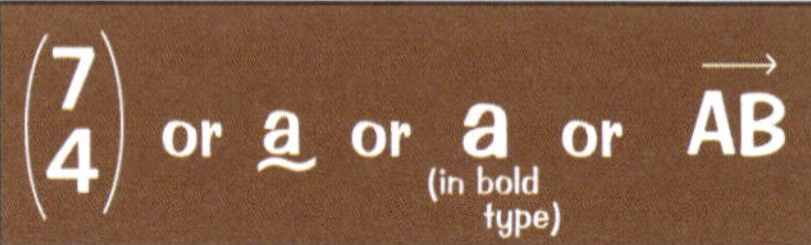
$$\begin{pmatrix}7\\4\end{pmatrix} \text{ or } \underline{a} \text{ or } \mathbf{a} \text{ (in bold type) or } \overrightarrow{AB}$$

2) What *Exactly* are Vectors?

<u>VECTORS HAVE BOTH SIZE AND DIRECTION</u> — and you're supposed to remember that.

"But what <u>is</u> a vector?" I hear you cry.

Well vectors represent *real-life things* which have <u>SIZE</u> and <u>DIRECTION</u>: you know, things like *position*, *velocity*, *acceleration*, *force* — things that are not only *big or small*, but also *act in a certain direction*.

(Temperature on the other hand, is *NOT a vector*, because it only has a value, e.g. 80°C, — it never points in a certain direction as well.)

So these arrows you keep dealing with are supposed to represent something <u>real</u> like a velocity or a force, etc.

Fortunately you only need to learn these simple rules to be able to do vector questions — but it's kind of nice to know they're not *completely* irrelevant really, isn't it!

3) *Column Vectors*

1) The notation for column vectors is: $\begin{pmatrix} x \to \\ y \uparrow \end{pmatrix}$, i.e. two numbers in brackets,

where: <u>Top number</u> = distance moved in the <u>+ X-direction</u> ($\to$)
<u>Bottom number</u> = distance moved in the <u>+ Y-direction</u> ($\uparrow$).

2) Make sure you get the x and y <u>the right way round</u>.

The two vectors shown are $\begin{pmatrix}7\\3\end{pmatrix}$ and $\begin{pmatrix}6\\-4\end{pmatrix}$

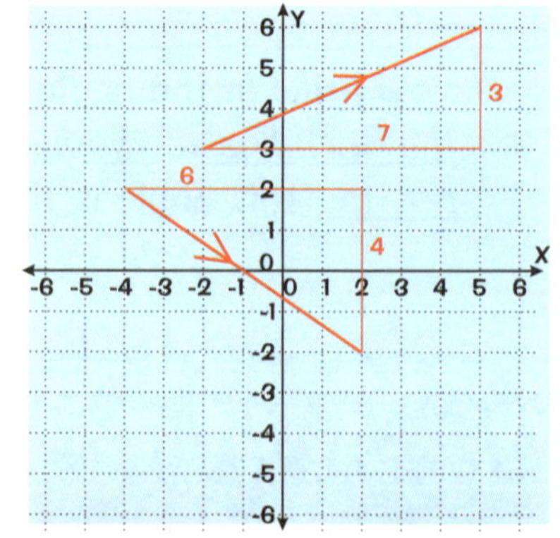

3) Also note that moving ← way or ↓ way will mean a <u>negative</u> number in the column vector, like the −4 in the one above.

The Acid Test:

<u>LEARN this page</u>. There are several important points in each of the 3 sections — <u>LEARN THEM ALL</u>.

1) Now cover up the page and write down all you know about vectors, including the 4 notations, the 3 rules for column vectors and 4 examples of real-life vectors.

Pythagoras' Theorem

1) PYTHAGORAS' THEOREM goes hand in hand with SIN, COS and TAN because they're both involved with RIGHT ANGLED TRIANGLES.

2) The big difference is that PYTHAGORAS DOES NOT INVOLVE ANY ANGLES — it just uses *two sides* to find the *third side*. (SIN, COS and TAN always involve ANGLES)

Method

The basic formula for Pythagoras' theorem is : $a^2 + b^2 = h^2$

Remember that Pythagoras can only be used on RIGHT-ANGLED TRIANGLES.

The trouble is, the formula can be quite difficult to use. *Instead*, it's a lot better to *just remember* these THREE SIMPLE STEPS, which work every time:

1) Square Them

SQUARE THE TWO NUMBERS that you are given,

(use the x^2 button if you've got your calculator — if you haven't, make sure you know the squares on P.1)

2) Add or Subtract

To find the *longest side*, ADD the two squared numbers.

To find *a shorter side*, SUBTRACT the smaller one from the larger.

3) Square Root

Once you've got your answer, take the SQUARE ROOT.

(By pressing $\sqrt{\ }$, then checking that your answer is SENSIBLE, or by *remembering everything on P.1*.)

Example 1: *"Find the missing side in the triangle shown."*

ANSWER: ❶ Square them: $5^2 = 25$, $3^2 = 9$

❷ You want to find a shorter side,

so SUBTRACT: $25 - 9 = 16$

❸ Square root: $\sqrt{16} = 4$ So the missing side = 4m

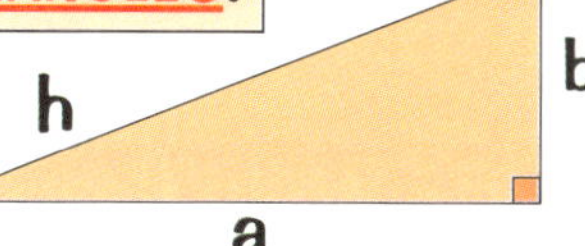

(You should always ask yourself: "Is it a *sensible answer*?" — in this case you can say "YES, because it's shorter than 5m, as it should be since 5m is the longest side, but not too much shorter")

Example 2: *"Find the length of the line segment shown."* For coordinates, see P.68

ANSWER: ❶ Work out how far across and up it is from A to B

❷ Treat this exactly like a normal triangle...

❸ Square them: $3^2 = 9$, $4^2 = 16$

❹ You want to find the longer side (the hypotenuse), so ADD: $9 + 16 = 25$

❺ Square root: $\sqrt{25} = 5$

So the length of the line segment = 5 units

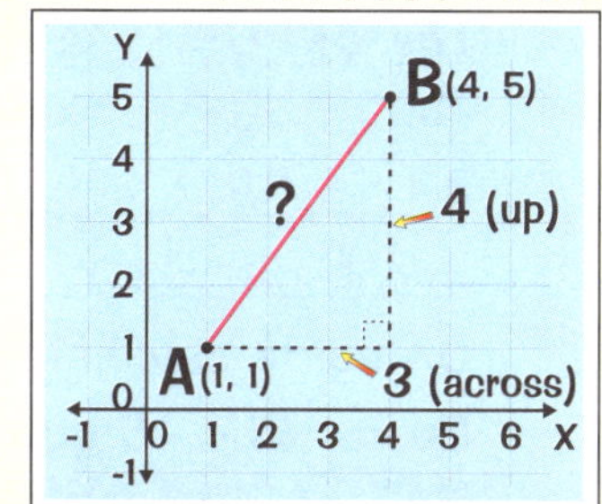

The Acid Test:

LEARN the 2 facts relating Pythag. with SIN, COS, TAN, and the 3 steps of the Pythag. method.

Now *turn over and write down what you've learned*.

1) Then apply the above method to find the missing side BC:

2) Another triangle has sides of 5 m, 12 m and 13 m.
   Is it a right-angled triangle? How do you know?

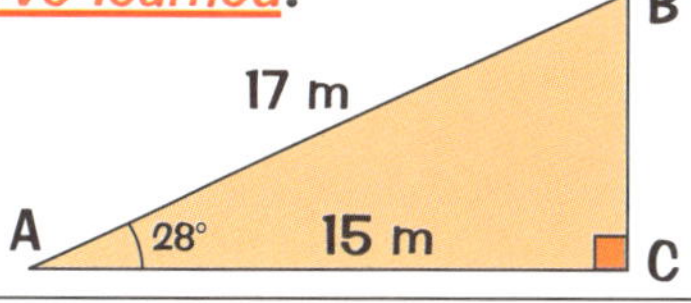

Trigonometry — SIN, COS, TAN

Using formula triangles to do Trigonometry makes the whole thing *a whole lot easier*, but ALWAYS follow all these steps in this order. If you miss any out *you're asking for trouble*.

Method

Using SIN, COS and TAN to solve right-angled triangles

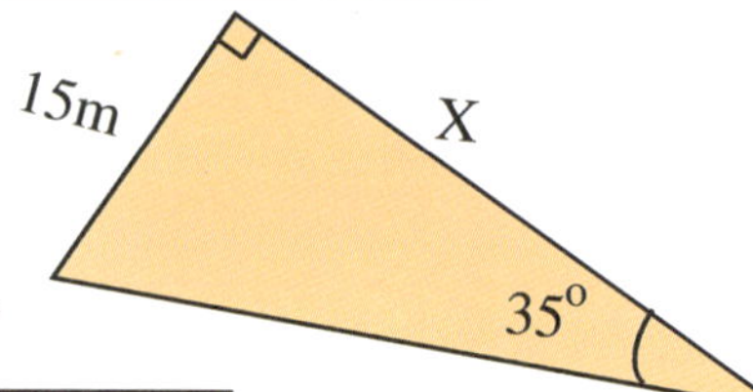

1) Label the three sides O, A and H

(Opposite, Adjacent and Hypotenuse).

2) Write down FROM MEMORY "SOH CAH TOA"

(Sounds like a Chinese word, "Sockatoa!")

3) Decide WHICH TWO SIDES are involved O,H A,H or O,A

and select SOH, CAH or TOA accordingly

4) Turn the one you choose into a FORMULA TRIANGLE, thus:

(See P.52)

S O H  **C A H** 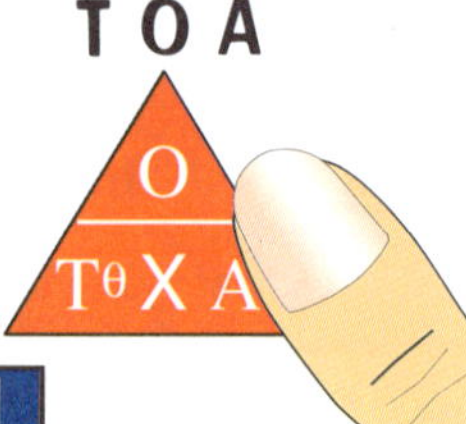 **T O A**

5) Cover up the thing you want to find

with your finger, and write down whatever is left showing.

6) Translate into numbers and work it out

7) Finally, check that your answer is sensible.

Seven Nitty Gritty Details

☺ The HYPOTENUSE is the LONGEST SIDE.
The OPPOSITE is the side OPPOSITE the angle being used (θ).
The ADJACENT is the side NEXT TO the angle being used (θ).

☺ θ IS A GREEK LETTER called "theta", *and is used to represent ANGLES*

☺ In the formula triangles, S^θ represents SIN θ, C^θ is COS θ, and T^θ is TAN θ.

☺ On some calculators, you have to enter trig functions BACKWARDS.
So for SIN 45 you might have to press `45` `SIN` (but most calculators do it the right way now).

☺ Remember, TO FIND THE ANGLE — USE INVERSE (see opposite page →).

☺ ALWAYS USE A DIAGRAM — *draw your own if necessary*.

☺ You can only use SIN, COS and TAN on RIGHT-ANGLED TRIANGLES — you may
have to *add lines to the diagram to create one* — especially on ISOSCELES triangles.

The Acid Test:

LEARN the 7 Steps of the Method and....
...the 7 Nitty Gritty Details.

Then turn over and write them all down from memory.

Trigonometry — SIN, COS , TAN

Example 1) *"Find x in the triangle shown."*

1) Label O,A,H
2) Write down "SOH CAH TOA"
3) Two sides *involved*: O,H

4) So use 

5) We want to find H so cover it up to leave: $H = \dfrac{O}{S\,q}$

6) Translate: $X = \dfrac{15}{SIN\ 35}$

Press  26.151702   So ans = <u>26.2</u>m

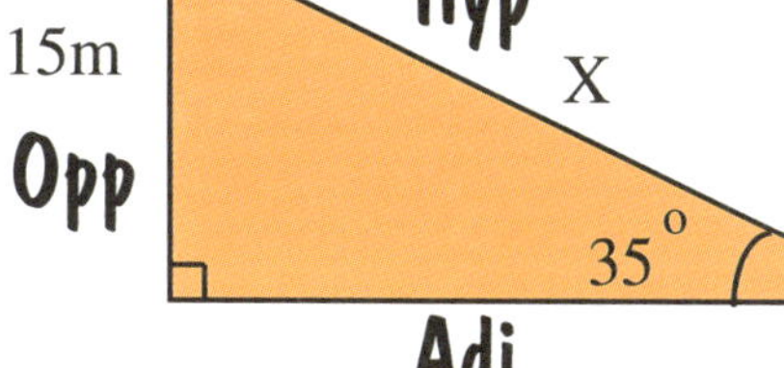

7) Check it's sensible: yes it's about twice as big as 15, as the diagram suggests.

Example 2) *"Find the angle θ in this triangle."*

1) Label O, A, H
2) Write down "SOH CAH TOA"'
3) Two sides *involved*: A,H

4) So use 

5) We want to find θ so cover up Cθ to leave: $C\theta = \dfrac{A}{H}$

6) Translate: $COS\ \theta = \dfrac{15}{25} = 0.6$

Note the usual way of dealing with an *ISOSCELES TRIANGLE*: split it <u>down the middle</u> to get a *RIGHT ANGLE*:

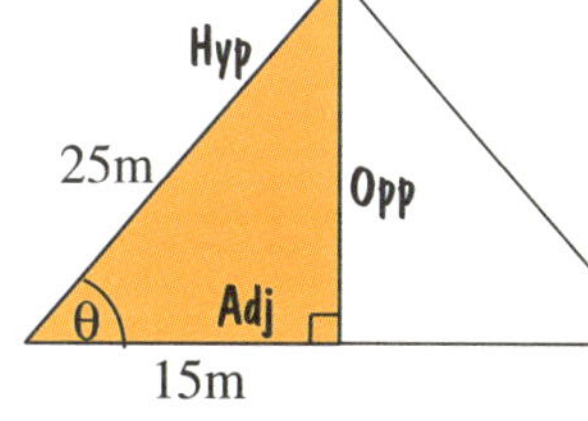

NOW USE INVERSE :   θ = INV COS (0.6)

Press INV COS 0.6 =   53.130102   So ans. = <u>53.1</u>°

7) Finally, is it sensible? — Yes, the angle looks like about 50°.

Angles of *Elevation* And *Depression*

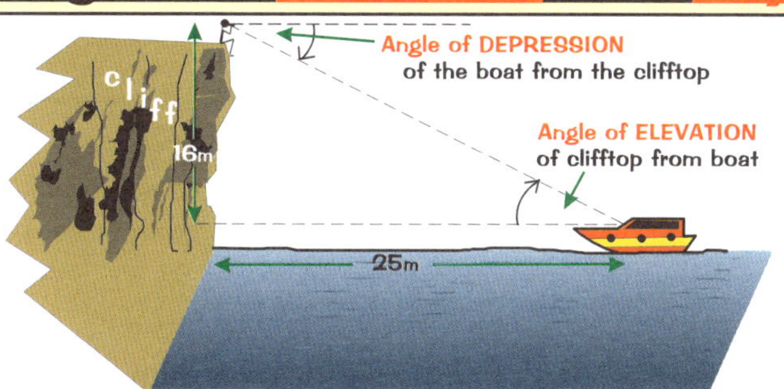

1) The *Angle of Depression* is the angle <u>downwards</u> from the horizontal.

2) The *Angle of Elevation* is the angle <u>upwards</u> from the horizontal.

3) The *Angle of Elevation* and *Angle of Depression* are <u>*ALWAYS EQUAL*</u>.

The Acid Test:
Practise these questions until you can apply the method <u>fluently</u> and without having to refer to it <u>at all</u>.

1) Find X 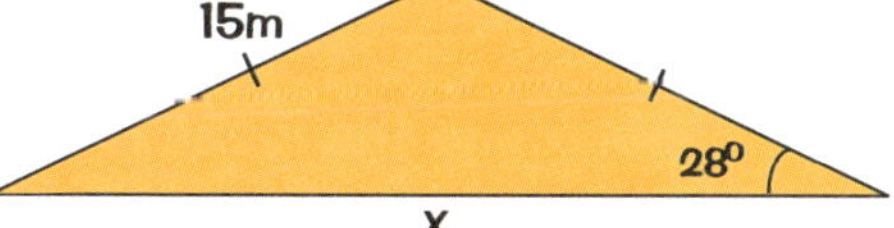

2) Find θ 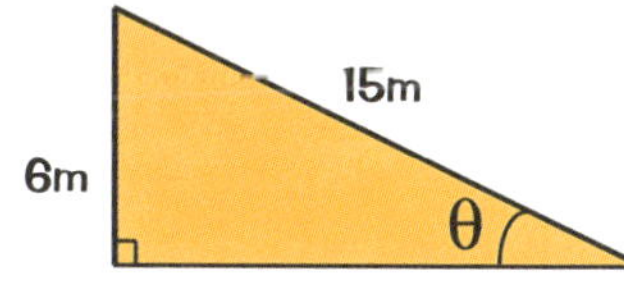

3) Calculate the angles of elevation and depression in the boat drawing above.

Loci and Constructions

A **LOCUS** (another ridiculous maths word) is simply:

> **A LINE that shows <u>all the points which fit in with a given rule</u>**

Make sure you <u>learn</u> how to do these **PROPERLY** using a **RULER AND COMPASSES** as shown on these two pages

1) The locus of points which are "*A FIXED DISTANCE from a given POINT*"

This locus is simply a *CIRCLE*.

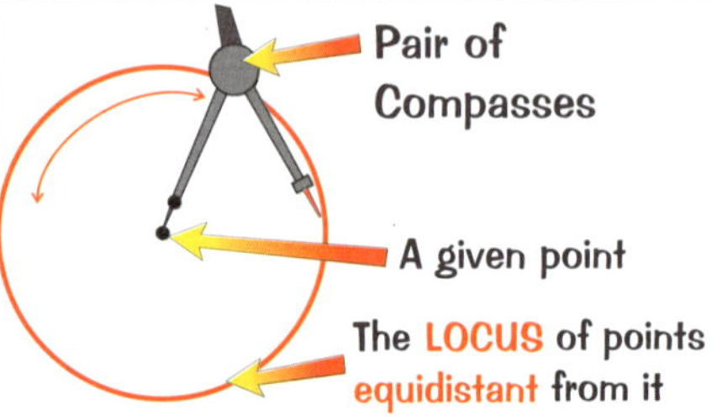

2) The locus of points which are "*A FIXED DISTANCE from a given LINE*"

This locus is an *OVAL SHAPE*

It has *straight sides* (drawn with a *ruler*) and *ends* which are *perfect semicircles* (drawn with *compasses*).

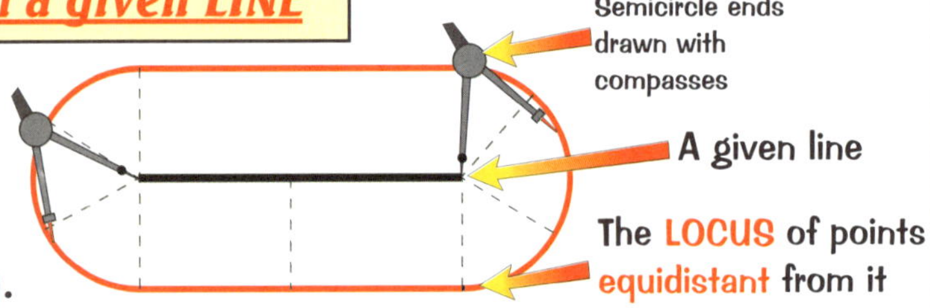

3) The locus of points which are "*EQUIDISTANT from TWO GIVEN LINES*"

1) Keep the compass setting *THE SAME* while you make *all four marks*.

2) Make sure you *leave* your compass marks *showing*.

3) You get *two equal angles* — i.e. this *LOCUS* is actually an *ANGLE BISECTOR*.

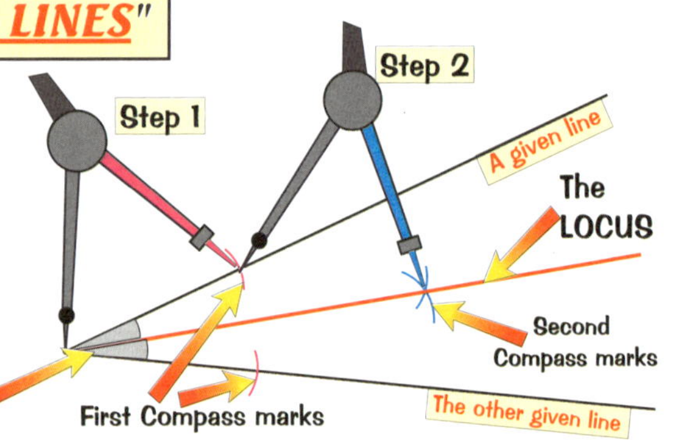

4) The locus of points which are "*EQUIDISTANT from TWO GIVEN POINTS*"

(In the diagram below, A and B are the two given points)

This LOCUS is all the points which are the *same distance* from A and B.

This time the locus is actually the *PERPENDICULAR BISECTOR* of the line joining the two points.

Loci and Constructions

Constructing accurate 60° angles

1) They may well ask you to draw an _accurate 60° angle_.

2) One place they're needed is for drawing an _equilateral triangle_.

3) Make sure you _follow the method_ shown in this diagram, and that you can do it _entirely from memory_.

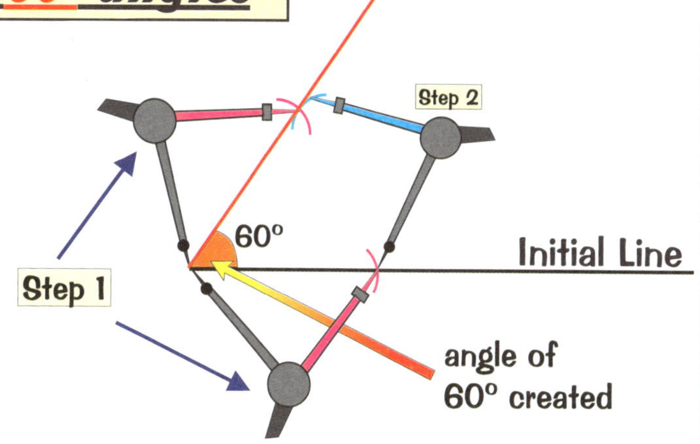

Constructing accurate 90° angles

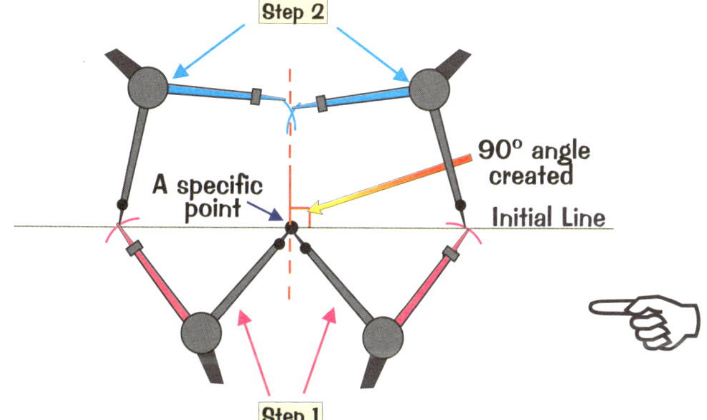

1) They might want you to draw an _accurate 90° angle_.
2) They won't accept it just done "_by eye_" or with a ruler — if you want to get the marks, you've got to do it _the proper way_ with _compasses_ like I've shown you here.
3) Make sure you can _follow the method_ shown in this diagram.

Drawing the Perpendicular from a Point to a Line

1) This is similar to the one above but _not quite the same_ — make sure you can do _both_.

2) Again, they won't accept it just done "_by eye_" or with a ruler — you've got to do it _the proper way_ with _compasses_.

3) _Learn_ the diagram.

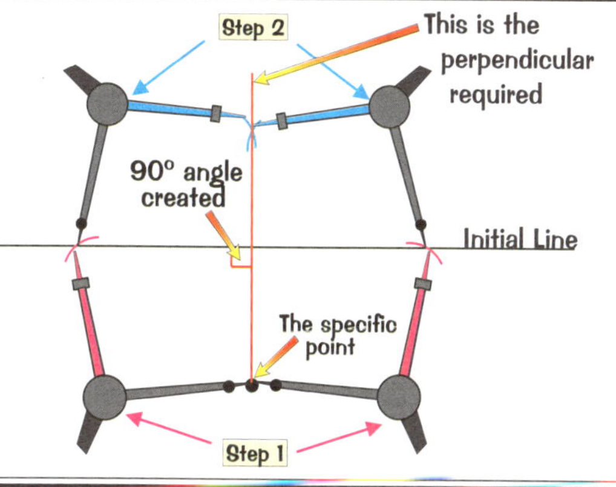

The Acid Test: LEARN EVERYTHING ON THESE TWO PAGES

Now cover up these two pages and draw an example of each of the four loci. Also draw an equilateral triangle and a square, both with fabulously accurate 60° and 90° angles. Also, draw a line and a point and construct the perpendicular from the point to the line.

Ratios

The whole grisly subject of <u>RATIOS</u> gets a whole lot easier when you do this:

Treat RATIOS *like* FRACTIONS

So for the <u>RATIO</u> 3:4, you'd treat it as the <u>FRACTION</u> 3/4, which is 0.75 as a <u>DECIMAL</u>.

What the fraction form of the ratio actually means

Suppose in a class there's <u>girls and boys</u> in the ratio 3 : 4.
This means there's 3/4 as many girls as boys.
So if there were 20 boys, there would be 3/4 × 20 = 15 girls.
You've got to be careful — it <u>doesn't mean</u> 3/4 of the <u>people</u> in the class are girls.

Reducing *Ratios* to their *simplest form*

You reduce ratios just like you'd reduce fractions to their simplest form.

For the ratio 15 : 18, both numbers have a <u>factor</u> of 3, so <u>divide them by 3</u> —
That gives 5 : 6. We can't reduce this any further. So the simplest form of 15 : 18 is <u>5 : 6</u>.

Treat them just like fractions — use your calculator if you can

Now this is really sneaky. If you stick in a fraction using the $a\frac{b}{c}$ button, your calculator automatically cancels it down when you press $=$.
So for the ratio 8 : 12, just press 8 $a\frac{b}{c}$ 12 $=$, and you'll get the reduced fraction 2/3.
Now you just change it back to ratio form ie. <u>2 : 3</u>. Ace.

The More Awkward Cases:

1) The $a\frac{b}{c}$ button will only accept whole numbers

So <u>IF THE RATIO IS AWKWARD</u> (like "2.4 : 3.6" or "1¼ : 3½") then you must:
<u>MULTIPLY BOTH SIDES</u> by the <u>SAME NUMBER</u> until they are both <u>WHOLE NUMBERS</u>
and then you can use the $a\frac{b}{c}$ button as before to simplify them down.
e.g. with "<u>1¼ : 3½</u>", × both sides by 4 gives "<u>5 : 14</u>" (Try $a\frac{b}{c}$, but it won't cancel further)

2) If the ratio is MIXED UNITS

then you must <u>CONVERT BOTH SIDES</u> into the <u>SMALLER UNITS</u> using the
relevant <u>CONVERSION FACTOR</u> (see P.10), and then carry on as normal.
e.g. "24mm : 7.2cm" (× 7.2cm by 10) $\Rightarrow$ 24mm : 72mm = <u>1 : 3</u> (using $a\frac{b}{c}$)

3) To reduce a ratio to the form 1 : n (n can be *any number at all*)

Simply <u>DIVIDE BOTH SIDES BY THE SMALLEST SIDE</u>.
e.g. take "<u>3 : 56</u>" — dividing both sides by 3 gives: <u>1 : 18.7</u> (56÷3) (i.e. 1 : n)
The 1 : n form is often the <u>most useful</u>, since it shows the ratio very clearly.

Ratios

Using The Formula Triangle in Ratio Questions

"Mortar is made from sand and cement in the ratio 7:2.
If 9 buckets of sand are used, how much cement is needed?"

This is a fairly common type of Exam question and it's pretty tricky for most people
— but once you start using the formula triangle method, it's all a bit of a breeze really.

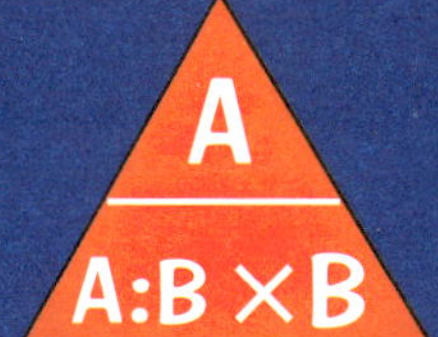

This is the basic **FORMULA TRIANGLE** for **RATIOS**, but **NOTE**:

1) **THE RATIO MUST BE THE RIGHT WAY ROUND,** with the **FIRST NUMBER IN THE RATIO** relating to the item **ON TOP** in the triangle.

2) **You'll always need to CONVERT THE RATIO** into its **EQUIVALENT FRACTION** or Decimal to work out the answer.

The formula triangle for the mortar question is shown below and the trick is to replace the RATIO 7:2 by its EQUIVALENT FRACTION: 7/2, or 3.5 as a decimal ($7 \div 2$)

So, *covering up cement in the triangle*, gives us "cement = sand / (7:2)"
i.e. "9 / 3.5" = $9 \div 3.5 = 2.57$ or about *2½ buckets of cement*.

Proportional Division

In a *proportional division question* a *TOTAL AMOUNT* is to be *split in a certain ratio*.

For example: *"£9100 is to be split in the ratio 2:4:7. Find the 3 amounts"*.

The key word here is **PARTS**. — concentrate on "parts" and it all becomes quite painless:

Method

1) **ADD UP THE PARTS**:

The ratio 2:4:7 means there will be a total of 13 *parts*   i.e. 2+4+7 = **13 PARTS**

2) **FIND THE AMOUNT FOR ONE *"PART"***

Just *divide* the *total amount* by the number of *parts*: £9100 ÷ 13 = **£700**   (= 1 PART)

3) **HENCE FIND THE THREE AMOUNTS**:

2 parts = 2×700 = **£1400**,   4 parts = 4×700 = **£2800**,   7 parts = 7×700 = **£4900**

The Acid Test:

LEARN the **6 RULES for SIMPLIFYING**, the **FORMULA TRIANGLE for Ratios** (plus **2 points**), and the **3 Steps for PROPORTIONAL DIVISION**.

Now *turn over* and *write down what you've learned*. Try again *until you can do it*.

1) Simplify: a) 25:35   b) 3.4 : 5.1   c) 2¼ : 3¾
2) Porridge and ice-cream are mixed in the ratio 7:4 . How much porridge should go with 10 bowls of ice-cream?   3) Divide £8400 in the ratio 5:3:4

Formula Triangles

You may have already come across these in physics, but whether you have or you haven't, the fact remains that they're *extremely potent tools* for quite a number of tricky maths problems — so make sure you know how to use them.
They're *very easy to use* and *very easy to remember*. Watch:

If **3** things are related by a formula that looks either

like this: $A = B \times C$ or like this: $B = \dfrac{A}{C}$

then you can put them into a FORMULA TRIANGLE like this:

1) First *decide* where the letters go:

1) If there are are <u>TWO LETTERS MULTIPLIED TOGETHER</u> in the formula
then they must go <u>ON THE BOTTOM</u> of the Formula Triangle
(and so *the other one* must go *on the top*).

For example the formula "$F = m \times a$" fits into
a formula triangle like this →

2) If there's <u>ONE THING DIVIDED BY ANOTHER</u> in the formula
then the one <u>ON TOP OF THE DIVISION</u> goes <u>ON TOP IN THE
FORMULA TRIANGLE</u> (and so the other two must go *on the bottom*
— it doesn't matter which way round).

For example the formula " $\text{SIN}\theta = \text{Opp/Hyp}$" fits into a formula triangle like this ↑.

2) Using the Formula Triangle:

Once you've got the formula triangle sorted out, the rest is easy:

1) <u>COVER UP</u> *the thing you want to find* and just <u>WRITE DOWN</u> *what's left showing*.
2) <u>PUT IN THE VALUES</u> for the other two things and just <u>WORK IT OUT</u>.

Example:

"Using " $F = m \times a$" , find the value of "a" when F = 20 and m = 50"

<u>ANSWER</u>: Using the formula triangle, we want to find "a" so we
cover "a" up, and that leaves "F/m" showing (i.e. F÷m).
So "a = F/m", and putting the numbers in we get: a = 20/50 = <u>0.4</u>

The Acid Test: <u>LEARN THIS WHOLE PAGE</u> then turn over and <u>write
down</u> all the important details including the examples.

Density and Speed

You might think this is physics, but density is specifically mentioned in the maths syllabus, and it's very likely to come up in your Exam. The standard formula for density is:

Density = Mass ÷ Volume

so we can put it in a FORMULA TRIANGLE like this:

One way or another you MUST remember this formula for density, because they won't give it to you and without it you'll be pretty stuck. The best method by far is to remember the order of the letters in the FORMULA TRIANGLE as $D^{M}V$ or DiMoV (The Russian Agent!).

EXAMPLE: *"Find the volume of an object which has a mass of 40 g and a density of 6.4 g/cm³"*

ANSWER: To find volume, cover up V in the formula triangle. This leaves M/D showing, so V = M ÷ D
= 40 ÷ 6.4
= 6.25 cm³

Speed = Distance ÷ Time

This is very common. In fact it probably comes up every single year — *and they never give you the formula!* Either *learn it beforehand* or wave goodbye to *lots of easy marks.* Life isn't all bad though — there's an easy FORMULA TRIANGLE:

Of course you still have to remember the order of the letters in the triangle ($S^{D}T$) — but this time we have the word SoDiT to help you.

So if it's a question on speed, distance and time just say: SOD IT.

EXAMPLE: *"A car travels 90 miles at 36 miles per hour. How long does it take?"*

ANSWER: We want to find the TIME, so cover up T in the triangle which leaves D/S,

so   T = D/S   = Distance ÷ speed = 90 ÷ 36 = 2.5 hours

> **LEARN THE FORMULA TRIANGLE, AND YOU'LL FIND QUESTIONS ON *SPEED, DISTANCE* AND *TIME* VERY EASY.**

The Acid Test:

LEARN the formulas for DENSITY and SPEED — and also the two Formula triangles.

1) What's the formula triangle for Density?
2) A metal object has a volume of 45 cm³ and a mass of 743 g. What is its density?
3) Another piece of the same metal has a volume of 36.5 cm³. What is its mass?
4) What's the formula for speed, distance and time?
5) Find the time taken, for a person walking at 3.2 km/h to cover 24 km.
   Also, find how far she'll walk in 3 hrs 30 mins.

Two Hints When Using Formulas

These are just the kind of little details that you really do need to know but somehow never quite get to learn — *WELL LEARN THEM NOW!*

1) Units — Getting them Right

By *units* we mean things like *cm, m, m/s, km^2* etc. and as a rule you don't have to worry too much about them. However, when you're using a FORMULA TRIANGLE, there's one special thing you need to know. It's simple enough *but you must know it*:

> The UNITS you get OUT of a Formula
> DEPEND ENTIRELY upon the UNITS you put INTO IT

So for example if you put a *distance in CM* and a *time in SECONDS* into the formula triangle to work out speed, the answer must come out in *CM per SECOND* (cm/s).

Alternatively, if the time is in HOURS and the speed in MILES PER HOUR (mph) then the *distance* you'd calculate would obviously come out as MILES.

It's pretty simple when you think about it. Where you really have to watch out is when you get this sort of question:

Example

"A boy walks 800 m in 10 minutes. Find his speed in km/h"

ANSWER: If you just do *"800 m ÷ 10 minutes"* your answer will be a speed, sure, but in metres per minute (m/min) which is no good at all.
Instead you must CONVERT INTO KM AND HOURS first:
800m = 0.8 km   10 mins = 0.1667 hours (mins÷60).
Then you can divide 0.8 *km* by 0.1667 *hours* to get 4.8 km/h which is much more like it.

2) Converting Time to Hrs, Mins and Secs with °'''

Here's a tricky detail that comes up when you're doing speed distance and time: converting an answer like 2.35 hours into hours and minutes. What it definitely ISN'T is 2 hours and 35 mins — remember your calculator does not work in hours and minutes unless you tell it to, as shown below. You'll need to practise with this button, but you'll be glad you did.

1) To ENTER a time in hours, mins and secs:
E.g. 5hrs 34mins and 23 secs, press 5 °''' 34 °''' 23 °''' = to get `5°34°23`.

2) Converting hours, min and secs to a decimal time:
Enter the number in hours, mins and secs as above.
Then just press °''' and it should convert it to a decimal like this `5.573055556`.
(Though some older calculators will automatically convert it to decimal when you enter a time in hours, minutes and secs.)

3) To convert a decimal time (as you always get from a formula) into hrs, mins and secs:
E.g. To convert 2.35 hours into hrs, mins and secs.
Simply press 2.35 = to enter the decimal, then press SHIFT °'''.
The display should become `2°21°0`, which means 2 hours, 21 mins (and 0 secs).

The Acid Test:

LEARN the two important topics on this page, then turn over and write down everything you've learned.

1) Find the time taken, in *hours, mins and secs*, to travel 9,785 m at a speed of 6 km/h.

Revision Summary for Section Three

Here we are again — more lovely questions for you to test yourself with. Remember you have to keep practising these questions _over and over again_ until you can answer them _all_. Seriously, you do. That's the best kind of revision there is because the whole idea is to find out what you _don't know_ and then learn it _until you do_.   Enjoy.

Keep learning these basic facts until you know them

1) Give three important facts about bearings.
2) What are the three Key Words you use to find or plot a bearing?
3) What is a vector? Give the 4 main examples.
4) What are the 4 types of vector notation? Illustrate with an example.
5) What is the formula for Pythagoras' Theorem?
6) What are the three steps of the easy method for doing Pythagoras?
7) What is trigonometry? What is a typical question involving it?
8) List the seven steps of the method for trigonometry.
9) How do you decide which sides are the adjacent, opposite and hypotenuse?
10) What is the special word to remember for trigonometry?
11) What are the 3 formula triangles that come from it?
12) How do you enter SIN 45° into the calculator?
13) What button will you have to press to find angles?
14) What is θ? What sort of shape is needed for trigonometry?
15) Draw a diagram to illustrate the angles of elevation and depression.
16) What is a locus? Describe in detail the four types you should know.
      Also draw a 60° angle and a 90° angle using the proper methods.
17) Which two things can a ratio be converted into?
18) Which calculator button can you then use to simplify ratios?
19) What is the formula triangle for ratios?
20) What are the 2 rules for using this Ratio formula triangle?
21) What are the three steps of the method for proportional division?
22) What are the two types of formula that can be put into a formula triangle?
23) What are the 2 rules for doing so?
24) What are the 2 steps for using a formula triangle?
25) What is the formula triangle for density?
26) What is the easiest way to tackle speed, distance and time?
27) What can you say about the units that come out of a formula?
28) Which calculator button converts time between _"decimal time"_ and "hours, minutes and seconds"?
29) What exactly do you press to enter a time in hrs, mins and secs?
30) How do you convert this to a decimal time?
31) How do you convert the other way?
32) What is the point of converting them anyway?

Probability

This is nobody's favourite subject — for sure, I've never really spoken to anyone who's said they do like it (not for long anyway).

Although it does seem a bit mysterious to most people, it's not as bad as you might think, but <u>YOU MUST LEARN THE BASIC FACTS</u>, which is what we have on these 2 pages.

All *Probabilities* are between *0 and 1*

A probability of <u>ZERO</u> means it will <u>NEVER HAPPEN</u>,
A probability of <u>ONE</u> means it <u>DEFINITELY WILL</u>.

You can't have a probability bigger than 1.

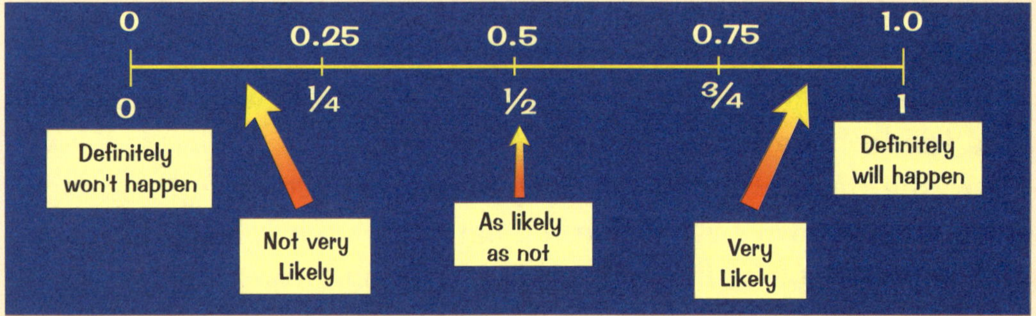

You should be able to put the probability of any event happening on this scale of 0 to 1.

Three *Important Details*

1) <u>PROBABILITIES SHOULD BE GIVEN</u> as either
   <u>A FRACTION (¼)</u>, or <u>A DECIMAL (0.25)</u>

2) <u>THE NOTATION</u> :   "P(x) = ½" <u>SHOULD BE READ AS</u>:
   <u>"The probability of event X happening is ½"</u>

3) <u>PROBABILITIES ALWAYS ADD UP TO 1.</u> This is essential for finding the probability of *the other outcome*. e.g If P(pass) = ¼, then P(fail) = ¾

THREE *IMPORTANT* EXTRAS   *for combined events ready for the next page!)*:

1) <u>USE YOUR CALCULATOR FRACTION BUTTON</u>   *whenever you can* for multiplying or adding fractions.

2) Watch out for "<u>WITH REPLACEMENT</u>" and "<u>WITHOUT REPLACEMENT</u>" and make sure you know what difference it makes.
   (Either you put the thing back after the first go, before having your second go, or you don't — the 2nd tree diagram opposite illustrates what can happen)

3) The <u>COMBINED PROBABILITY</u> of <u>two events</u> <u>BOTH</u> happening is ALWAYS <u>LESS</u> than the probability of either of them occurring alone.

The Acid Test: LEARN the <u>diagram</u> and the <u>6 IMPORTANT POINTS</u> on this page. Then <u>turn over</u> and <u>write it all down</u>.

1) If P(picking a blue ball) is ¼, what is the value of P(not picking a blue ball)?

Probability — Tree Diagrams

General Tree Diagram

Tree Diagrams are all pretty much the same, so it's a pretty darned good idea to learn these basic details (which apply to **ALL** tree diagrams) — ready for the one in the Exam.

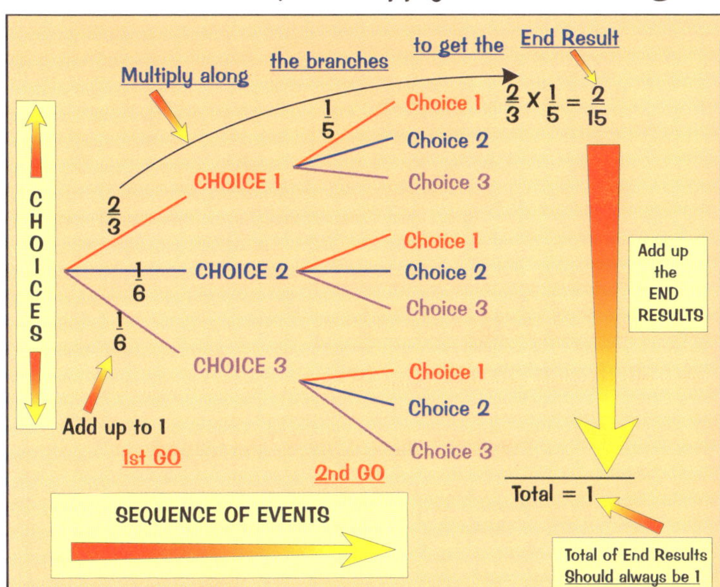

1) Always **MULTIPLY ALONG THE BRANCHES** (as shown) to get the END RESULTS.

2) *On any set of branches which all meet at a point*, the numbers must always ADD UP TO 1.

3) *Check that your diagram is correct* by making sure the End Results ADD UP TO ONE.

4) *To answer any question*, simply ADD UP THE RELEVANT END RESULTS (see below).

A likely Tree Diagram Question

EXAMPLE: *"A box contains 5 red disks and 3 green disks. Two disks are taken* <u>without replacement</u>. *Draw a tree diagram and hence find the probability that both disks are the same colour."*

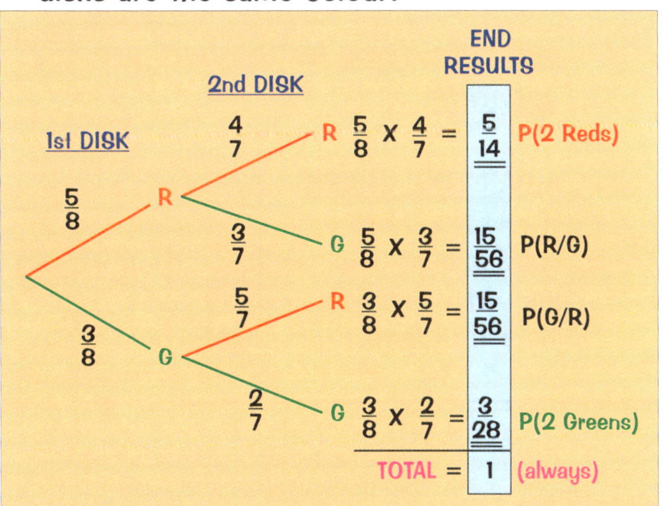

Once the tree diagram is drawn all you then need to do to answer the question is simply <u>select the RELEVANT END RESULTS</u> and then <u>ADD THEM TOGETHER</u>:

| 2 REDS | (5/14) |
| 2 GREENS | (3/28) |

$$\frac{5}{14} + \frac{3}{28} = \frac{13}{28}$$

If you can, use a calculator for this. Otherwise, use the fraction rules on P.12.

The Acid Test:

LEARN the <u>GENERAL DIAGRAM</u> for Tree Diagrams and the <u>4 points</u> that go with them.

1) O.K. let's see what you've learnt shall we:
   TURN OVER AND WRITE DOWN EVERYTHING YOU KNOW ABOUT TREE DIAGRAMS.

2) A bag contains 6 red tarantulas and 4 black tarantulas. If two girls each pluck out a tarantula at random, draw a tree diagram to find the probability that they get different coloured ones.

Graphs And Charts

Make sure you know all these easy details:

1) *Line Graphs* or *"Frequency Polygons"*

A line graph or "frequency polygon" is just a set of points joined up with straight lines.

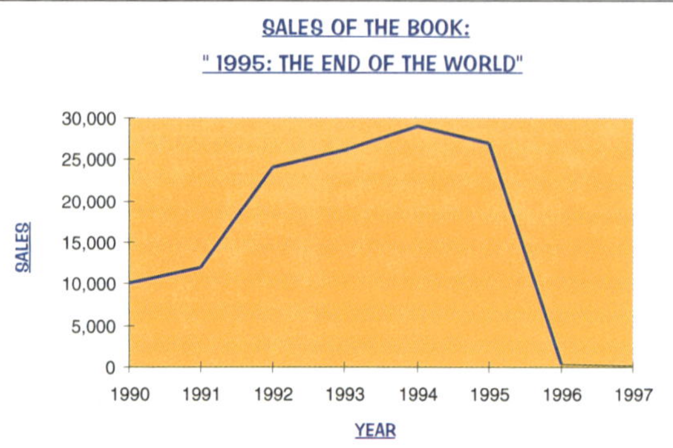

2) *Bar Charts* and *Frequency Diagrams*

Just watch out for when the bars should *touch* or *not touch*:

Number of dried slugs found (various lengths)

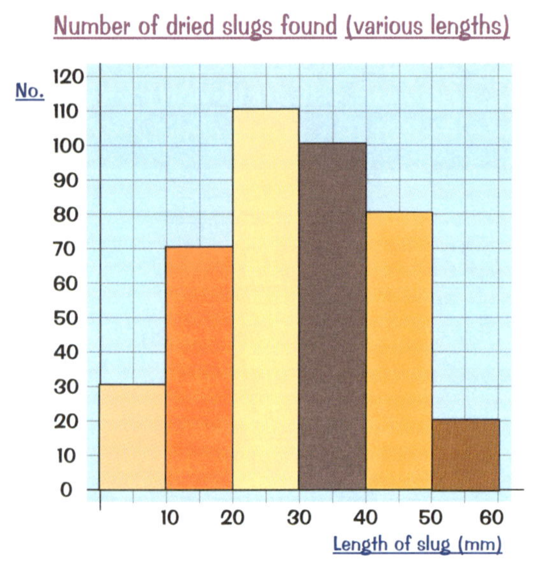

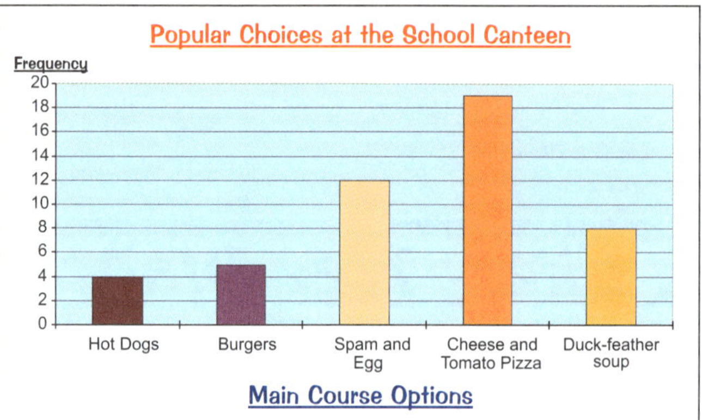

This bar chart compares *totally separate items* so the bars are *separate*.

ALL the bars in this frequency diagram are for **LENGTHS** and you must *put every possible length into one bar or the next* so there mustn't be any spaces.

A **BAR-LINE GRAPH** is just like a bar chart except you just draw thin lines instead of bars.

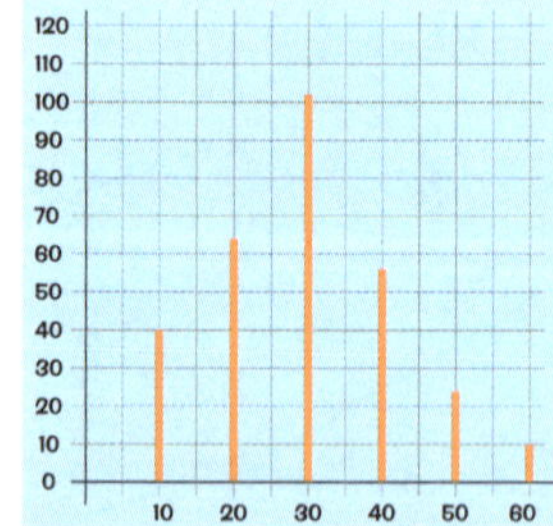

3) *Scatter Graphs*

1) **A SCATTER GRAPH** is just a load of points on a graph that *end up in a bit of a mess* rather than in a nice line or curve.
2) There's a fancy word to say *how much of a mess* they're in — it's **CORRELATION**.
3) *Good Correlation* (or *Strong* Correlation) means the points *form quite a nice line*, and it means *the two things are closely related to each other*.

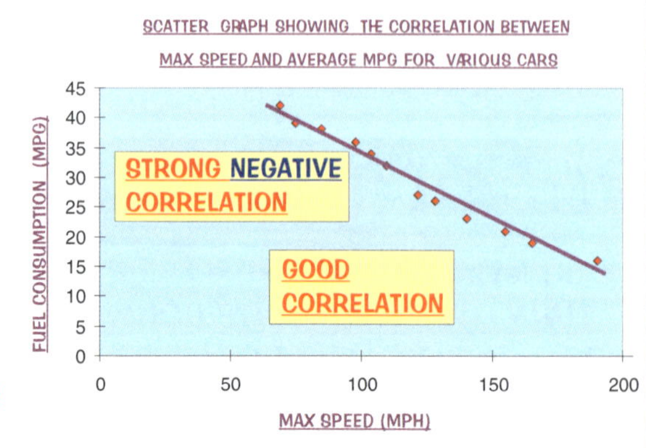

Graphs And Charts

Scatter Graphs (continued)

4) *Poor Correlation* (or *Weak* Correlation) means the points are *all over the place* and so there's *very little relation between the two things*.

5) If the points form a line sloping **UPHILL** from left to right, then there is **POSITIVE CORRELATION**, which just means that *both things increase or decrease together*.

6) If the points form a line sloping **DOWNHILL** from left to right, then there is **NEGATIVE CORRELATION**, which just means that *as one thing increases the other decreases*.

7) So when you're describing a scatter graph you have to mention both things, i.e. whether it's *strong/weak/moderate* correlation *and* whether it's *positive*/*negative*.

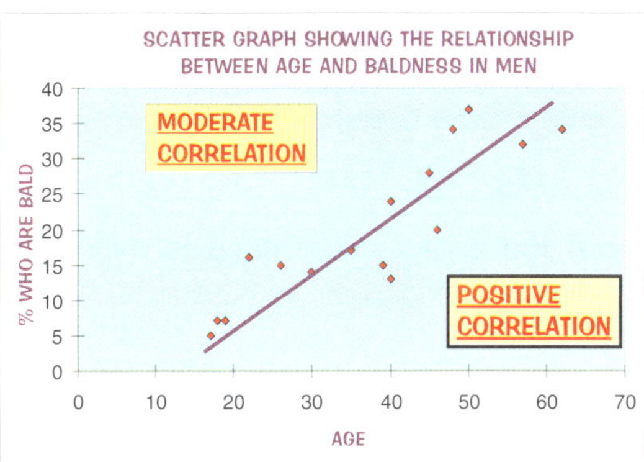

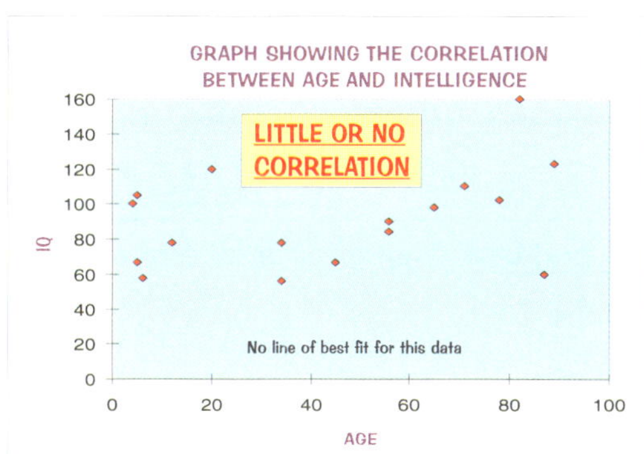

4) Pie Charts

Learn the Golden Rule for Pie Charts:

The TOTAL of Everything = 360°

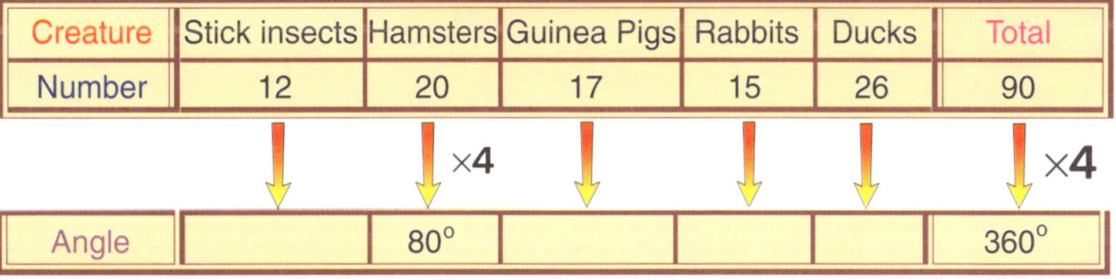

Creature	Stick insects	Hamsters	Guinea Pigs	Rabbits	Ducks	Total
Number	12	20	17	15	26	90

×4   ×4

Angle		80°				360°

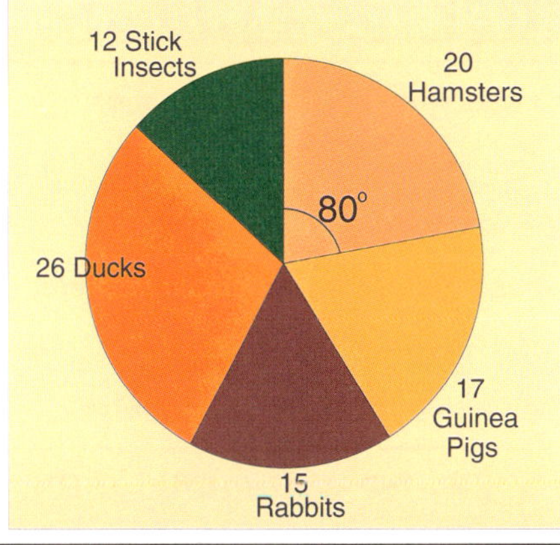

1) Add up all the numbers in each sector to get the **TOTAL** ($\leftarrow$ 90 for this one).

2) Then find the **MULTIPLIER** (or divider) that you need to turn your total into 360°:
For 90 $\rightarrow$ 360 as above, the **MULTIPLIER** is 4.

3) Now **MULTIPLY EVERY NUMBER BY 4** to get the angle for each sector.
E.g. the angle for hamsters will be
20 × 4 = **80°** .

The Acid Test: *LEARN THE NAMES* of the *four types* of *CHART*.

1) Turn over the page and draw an example of each of the 4 charts.

2) Work out the angles for all the other animals in the pie chart shown above.

3) If the points on a scatter graph are all over the place, what does it tell you about the two things that the scatter graph is comparing?

Stem & Leaf Diagrams and Distribution

Shapes of Distributions are Measures of "Spread"

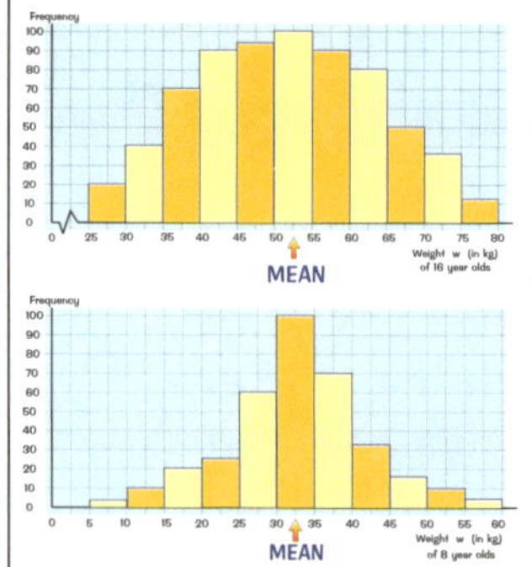

You must *LEARN the significance of the shapes* of these two frequency diagrams:

1) This one shows *high dispersion* i.e. a *large spread* of results away from the mean. (E.g. the weights of a sample of 16 year olds will cover a very wide range.)

2) This second one shows a "*tighter*" distribution of results where most values are within a *narrow range* either side of the mean. (E.g. the weights of a sample of 8 year olds will show very little variation.)

Remember that the *mean* value of a frequency diagram is more or less *IN THE MIDDLE*.

Stem and Leaf diagrams use the actual data

A <u>stem and leaf</u> diagram is a bit like a histogram, but the data itself is used to make the diagram.

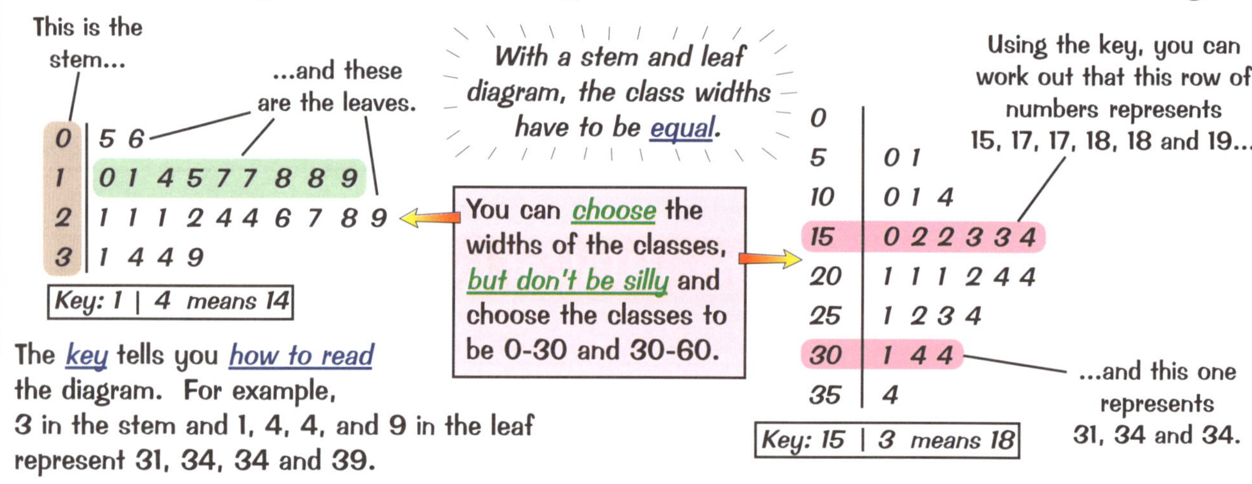

This is the stem...

...and these are the leaves.

0	5 6
1	0 1 4 5 7 7 8 8 9
2	1 1 1 2 4 4 6 7 8 9
3	1 4 4 9

Key: 1 | 4 means 14

The *key* tells you *how to read* the diagram. For example, 3 in the stem and 1, 4, 4, and 9 in the leaf represent 31, 34, 34 and 39.

With a stem and leaf diagram, the class widths have to be equal.

You can *choose* the widths of the classes, *but don't be silly* and choose the classes to be 0-30 and 30-60.

Using the key, you can work out that this row of numbers represents 15, 17, 17, 18, 18 and 19...

0	
5	0 1
10	0 1 4
15	0 2 2 3 3 4
20	1 1 1 2 4 4
25	1 2 3 4
30	1 4 4
35	4

Key: 15 | 3 means 18

...and this one represents 31, 34 and 34.

The Bigger the Sample Size, the Better the Estimate

There are <u>FOUR DIFFERENT TYPES OF SAMPLING</u>: (you don't need to know them in any detail)

RANDOM — this is where you just select individuals "at random".

SYSTEMATIC — start with a random selection and select every 10th or 100th one after that.

STRATIFIED — where there's different 'layers' to choose from — classes/pupils; departments/employees etc.

QUOTA — where the sample reflects the whole population — same ratio of males:females, adults:children etc.

If you *repeated* any of these experiments, you'd get *different* overall results each time. Likewise...

FOR ***ANY*** SAMPLING METHOD, THE *LARGER* THE *SAMPLE SIZE* (I.E. THE MORE PEOPLE ASKED), THE *BETTER* AN *ESTIMATE* YOU'LL GET OF [THE PARAMETERS FOR] THE *WHOLE POPULATION.*

The Acid Test:

LEARN what a <u>stem and leaf diagram</u> is, and <u>how to create your own</u> from some data, and <u>remember this</u>.

1) A survey was done to investigate the average age of cars on Britain's roads by standing on a motorway bridge and noting the registration of the first 200 cars. Give a reason why this is a poor sampling technique and suggest a better approach.

Mean, Median, Mode and Range

If you don't manage to learn the 4 basic definitions then you'll be passing up on some of the easiest marks in the whole Exam. It can't be *that* difficult can it?

1) MODE = **MOST** common

Mode = most (emphasise the 'o' in each when you say them)

2) MEDIAN = **MIDDLE** value

Median = mid (emphasise the m*d in each when you say them)

3) MEAN = **TOTAL of items ÷ NUMBER of items**

Mean is just the average, "but it's mean 'cos you have to work it out"

4) RANGE = **How far from the smallest to the biggest**

THE GOLDEN RULE:

Mean, median, mode and range should be easy marks but even people who've gone to the incredible extent of learning them, still manage to lose marks in the Exam because they don't do this one vital step:

Always REARRANGE the data in ASCENDING ORDER

(and check you have the same number of entries!)

Example: *"Find the mean, median, mode and range of these numbers:"*

2, 5, 3, 2, 6, -4, 0, 9, -3, 1, 6, 3, -2, 3   (14)

1) FIRST... rearrange them: -4, -3, -2, 0, 1, 2, 2, 3, 3, 3, 5, 6, 6, 9   (✓14)

2) MEAN = $\dfrac{\text{total}}{\text{number}}$ = $\dfrac{-4-3-2+0+1+2+2+3+3+3+5+6+6+9}{14}$

$= 31 \div 14 = \underline{2.21}$

3) MEDIAN = the middle value (only when they're arranged in order of size, that is!).

When there are TWO MIDDLE NUMBERS, as in this case, then the median is HALFWAY BETWEEN THE TWO MIDDLE NUMBERS

-4, -3, -2, 0, 1, 2, 2, 3, 3, 3, 5, 6, 6, 9
← seven numbers this side   ↑   seven numbers this side →
Median = 2.5

4) MODE = most common value, which is simply 3. (Or you can say "The modal value is 3")

5) RANGE = distance from lowest to highest value, i.e. from -4 up to 9, = 13

The Acid Test: LEARN The Four Definitions and THE GOLDEN RULE...

..then cover this page and write them down from memory.

1) Apply all that you have learnt to find the mean, median, mode and range for this set of data: 1, 3, 14, -5, 6, -12, 18, 7, 23, 10, -5, -14, 0, 25, 8

Frequency Tables

Frequency Tables can either be done in _rows_ or in _columns_ of numbers,
and they can be quite confusing, _but not if you learn this easy example_:

Example

Here's a typical frequency table shown in
both ROW FORM and COLUMN FORM:

No. of Sisters	0	1	2	3	4	5	6
Frequency	7	15	12	8	3	1	0

Row Form

Column Form

No. of Sisters	Freq.
0	7
1	15
2	12
3	8
4	3
5	1
6	0

There's no real difference between these two forms,
and you could get either one in your Exam.
Whichever you get, make sure you remember
these THREE IMPORTANT FACTS:

1) THE 1ST ROW (or column) gives us the GROUP LABELS
   for the different categories: i.e. "no sisters", "one sister", "two sisters", etc.

2) THE 2ND ROW (or column) is the ACTUAL DATA and tells us HOW MANY (people)
   THERE ARE in each category i.e. 7 people had "no sisters", 15 people had "one sister", etc.

3) BUT YOU SHOULD SEE THE TABLE AS _UNFINISHED_, because it still needs a
   THIRD ROW (or column) and TWO TOTALS for the 2nd and 3rd rows — see below:

This is what a (row form) table
looks like when it's completed:

No. of Sisters	0	1	2	3	4	5	6	Totals	
Frequency	7	15	12	8	3	1	0	46	(People asked)
No. × Freq.	0	15	24	24	12	5	0	80	(Sisters)

"Where does the third row come from?"....I hear you cry!

THE THIRD ROW (or column) is ALWAYS
obtained by MULTIPLYING the numbers
FROM THE FIRST 2 ROWS (or columns).

THIRD ROW = 1ST ROW × 2ND ROW

Once the table is complete, you can easily find the MEAN, MEDIAN, MODE AND RANGE (see P.61)
which is what they usually demand in the Exam:

Mean, Median, Mode and Range:

This is easy enough _if you learn it_. If you don't, you'll drown in a sea of numbers.

1) MEAN = $\dfrac{\text{3rd Row Total}}{\text{2nd Row Total}}$ = $\dfrac{80}{46}$ = 1.74 (Sisters per person)

2) MEDIAN: — imagine the original data SET OUT IN ASCENDING ORDER:

0000000 111111111111111 222222222222 33333333 444 5

and the median is just the middle, which is here between the 23rd and 24th digits, so for this
data THE MEDIAN IS 2. (When you get slick at this you can easily find the middle value straight from the table.)

3) The MODE is _very easy_ — it's just THE GROUP WITH THE MOST ENTRIES: i.e. 1

4) The RANGE is 5 – 0 = 5 The first row tells us there are people with anything from
"no sisters" right up to "five sisters" (but not 6 sisters). (Always give it as a _single number_.)

The Acid Test:

LEARN the 3 IMPORTANT FACTS for Frequency Tables,
and how to find the MEAN, MEDIAN, MODE and RANGE.

Using the methods you've just learnt, and this
frequency table, find the MEAN, MEDIAN, MODE
and RANGE of the no. of phones people have:

No. of Phones	0	1	2	3	4	5	6
Frequency	1	25	53	34	22	5	1

Grouped Frequency Tables

These are a bit trickier than simple frequency tables, but they can still look deceptively simple, like this one which shows the distribution of weights of a bunch of 60 school kids.

Weight (kg)	31 — 40	41 — 50	51 — 60	61 — 70	71 — 80
Frequency	8	16	18	12	6

Class Boundaries and Mid-Interval Values

These are the two little jokers that make Grouped Frequency tables so tricky.

1) THE CLASS BOUNDARIES are the precise values where you'd pass from one group into the next. For the above table the class boundaries would be at 40.5, 50.5, 60.5, etc. It's not difficult to work out what the class boundaries will be, just so long as you're clued up about it — they're nearly always "something.5" anyway, for obvious reasons.

2) THE MID-INTERVAL VALUES are pretty self-explanatory really and usually end up being "something.5" as well. Mind you a bit of care is needed to make sure you get the exact middle!

"Estimating" The Mean using Mid-Interval Values

Just like with ordinary frequency tables you have to *add extra rows and find totals* to be able to work anything out. Also notice you can only "estimate" the mean from grouped data tables — you can't find it exactly unless you know all the original values.

> 1) Add a 3rd row and enter MID-INTERVAL VALUES for each group.
> 2) Add a 4th row and multiply FREQUENCY × MID-INTERVAL VALUE for each group.

Weight (kg)	31 — 40	41 — 50	51 — 60	61 — 70	71 — 80	TOTALS
Frequency	8	16	18	12	6	60
Mid-Interval Value	35.5	45.5	55.5	65.5	75.5	—
Frequency × Mid-Interval Value	284	728	999	786	453	3250

1) ESTIMATING THE MEAN is then the usual thing of DIVIDING THE TOTALS:

$$\text{Mean} = \frac{\text{Overall Total (Final Row)}}{\text{Frequency Total (2nd Row)}} = \frac{3250}{60} = \underline{54.2}$$

2) THE MODE is still nice'n'easy: the modal group is 51 — 60kg (the one with the most entries).

3) THE MEDIAN can't be found exactly but you can at least say which group it's in. If all the data were put in order, the 30th/31st entries would be in the 51 — 60kg group.

The Acid Test:

LEARN all the details on this page, then turn over and write down everything you've learned. Good clean fun.

1) Estimate the mean for this table:
2) Also state the modal group and the approximate value of the median.

Length(cm)	15.5 —	16.5 —	17.5 —	18.5 — 19.5
Frequency	12	18	23	8

Cumulative Frequency Tables

Usually you'll get a half-finished table and they'll ask you to complete it as a cumulative frequency table. This means adding a third row and filling it in (as shown in the example below). Make sure you know these:

FOUR KEY POINTS

1) **CUMULATIVE FREQUENCY** just means **ADDING IT UP AS YOU GO ALONG**.
So each entry in the table for cumulative frequency is just "**THE TOTAL SO FAR**".

2) **You have to ADD A THIRD ROW to the table**
— this is just the **RUNNING TOTAL** of the 2nd row.

3) **If you're plotting a graph**, always plot points **using the HIGHEST VALUE in each group** (of row 1) with the value from **row 3**. (i.e. plot at the *class boundaries*) i.e. for the example below, plot 13 at **160.5**, 33 at **170.5**, etc.

4) **CUMULATIVE FREQUENCY** is always plotted **up the side** of a graph, not across.

Example

"Complete the table below for cumulative frequency:"

Height (cm)	141 – 150	151 – 160	161 – 170	171 – 180	181 – 190	191 – 200	201 – 210
Frequency	4	9	20	33	36	15	3

ANSWER: *Add in the third row* where each entry for row 3 (cumulative frequency) is just "**THE TOTAL SO FAR**" of the numbers for frequency (row 2).

Height (cm)	141 – 150	151 – 160	161 – 170	171 – 180	181 – 190	191 – 200	201 – 210
Frequency	4	9	20	33	36	15	3
Cumulative Frequency	4 (AT 150.5)	13 (AT 160.5)	33 (AT 170.5)	66 (AT 180.5)	102 (AT 190.5)	117 (AT 200.5)	120 (AT 210.5)

The graph is plotted from these pairs: (150.5, 4) (160.5, 13) (170.5, 33) (180.5, 66) etc. because the cumulative frequency has only reached those values (4, 13, 33 etc) by the TOP END of each group, not at the middle of each group, and *150.5* is the actual **CLASS BOUNDARY** between the first group and the next — a tricky detail.

The Acid Test:

LEARN the 4 Key Points,
then turn over and write them down.

1) Complete the table shown here for cumulative frequency.

Weight (kg)	41 – 45	46 – 50	51 – 55	56 – 60	61 – 65	66 – 70	71 – 75
Frequency	2	7	17	25	19	8	2

The Cumulative Frequency Curve

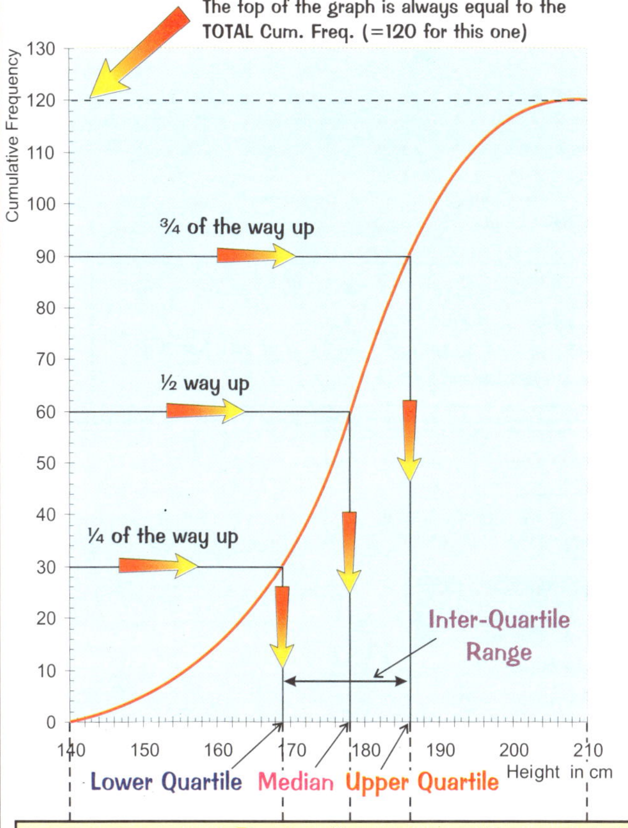

From the cumulative frequency curve you can get **THREE VITAL STATISTICS**:

1) **MEDIAN**
   Exactly halfway UP, then across, then down and *read off the bottom scale*.

2) **LOWER AND UPPER QUARTILES**
   Exactly ¼ and ¾ UP the side, then across, then down and *read off the bottom scale*.

3) **THE INTER-QUARTILE RANGE**
   The distance *on the bottom scale* between the lower and upper quartiles.

So from the above cumulative frequency curve, we can easily get these results:

MEDIAN = **178cm**
LOWER QUARTILE = **169cm**
UPPER QUARTILE = **186cm**
INTER-QUARTILE RANGE = **17cm** (186-169)

A Box plot shows the Inter-Quartile Range as a Box

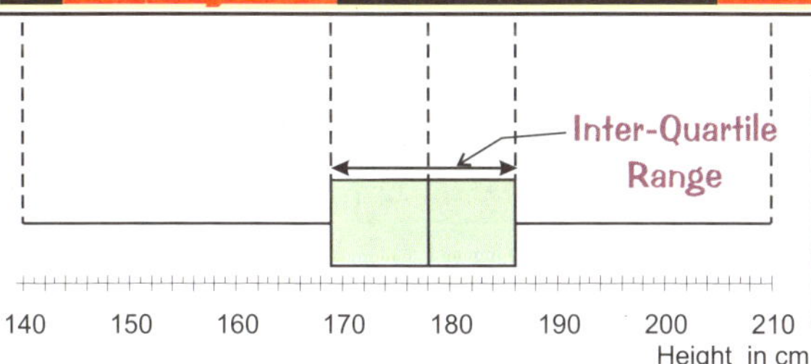

TO CREATE YOUR VERY OWN BOX PLOT:
1) *Draw the scale* along the bottom.
2) *Draw a box* the length of the *inter-quartile range*.
3) *Draw a line* down the box to show the *median*.
4) *Draw "whiskers"* up to the *maximum and minimum*.

(They're sometimes called "Box and Whisker diagrams".)

Interpreting The shape

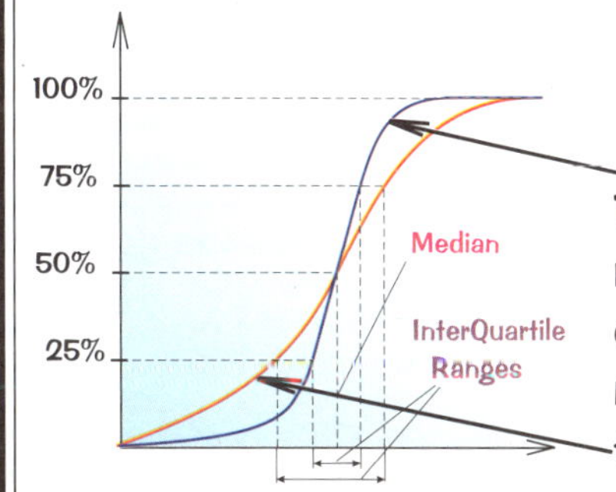

The shape of a CUMULATIVE FREQUENCY CURVE also tells you *how spread out* the data values are.

This 'tighter' distribution (which has a small interquartile range) represents very **CONSISTENT** results, which is usually good — e.g. *lifetimes of batteries or light bulbs* all very close together means a *good product*, compared to the other curve where the lifetimes show *wide variation*, i.e. poor quality product.

The Acid Test:

LEARN THIS PAGE, then cover it up and write down all the important details.

1) Using your completed frequency table from the previous page, draw the cumulative frequency graph and box plot and use them to find the three vital statistics.

Time Series

Time Series — Measure the Same Thing over a Period of Time

A time series is what you get if you measure the same thing at a number of different times.

EXAMPLE: Measuring the temperature in your greenhouse at 12 o'clock each day gives you a time series — other examples might be profit figures, crime figures or rainfall.

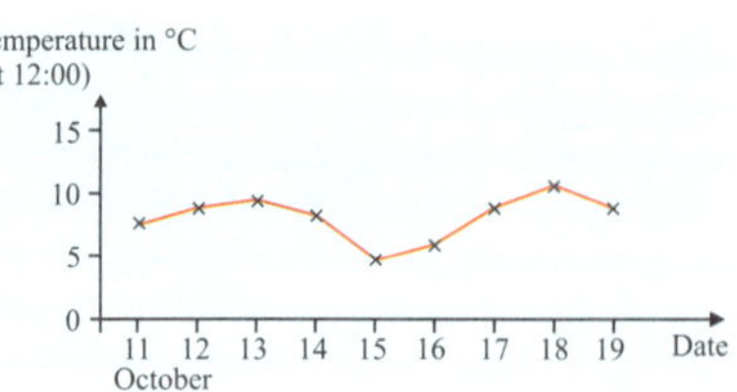

THE RETAIL PRICE INDEX (RPI) IS A TIME SERIES: *Every month, the prices of loads of items (same ones each month) — are combined to get an index number called the RPI, which is a kind of average.*
As goods get more expensive, this index number gets higher and higher. So when you see on TV that inflation this month is 2.5%, what it actually means is that the RPI is increasing at an annual rate of 2.5%.

Seasonality — The Same Basic Pattern

This is when there's a definite pattern that *REPEATS ITSELF* every so often. This is called *SEASONALITY* and the *"so often"* is called the *PERIOD*.

To find the *PERIOD*, measure *PEAK TO PEAK* (or trough to trough).

This series has a *period of 12 months*. There are a few irregularities, so the pattern isn't exactly the same every 12 months, but it's about right.

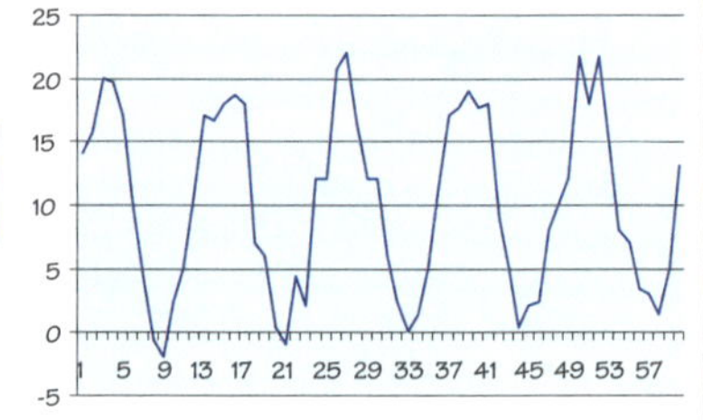

Trend — Ignoring the Wrinkles

This time series has lots of random fluctuations but there's a definite upwards *trend*.

The pink line is the trend line.
It's straight, so this is a linear trend.

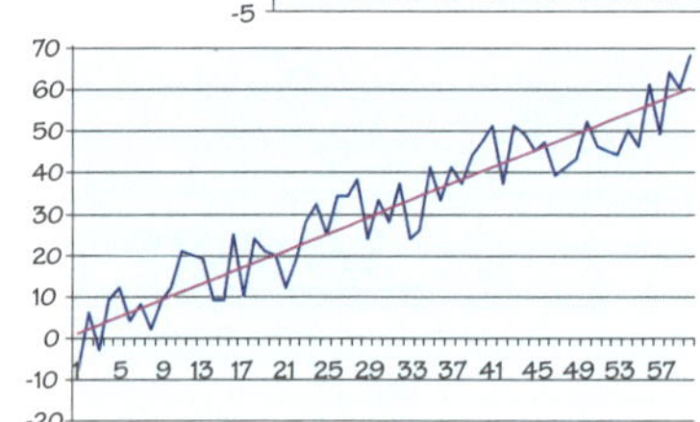

Moving Average — Smooths Out the Seasonality

It's easier to spot a trend if you can 'get rid of' the seasonality and some of the irregularities.

One way to smooth the series is to use a *moving average*.

This is a time series that definitely looks periodic — but it's difficult to tell if there's a trend.

The period is 12, so you use 12 values for the moving average:

... but plot the moving average (in pink — must be pink — that's dead important)...

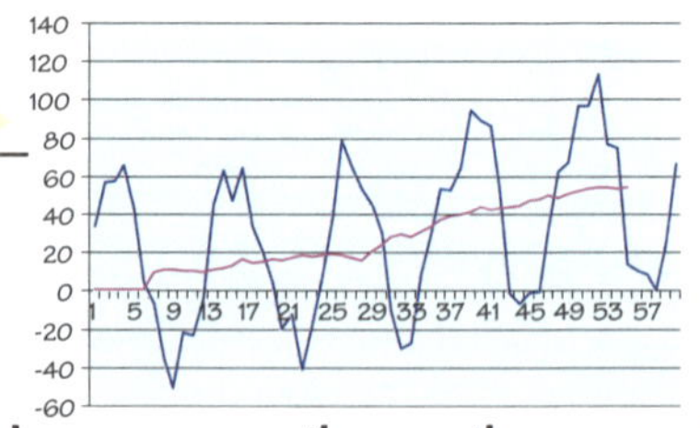

...and you can easily see the *upward trend*.

HOW TO FIND A MOVING AVERAGE:

month	1	2	3	4	5	6	7	8	9	10	11	12	13	14	...
temperature	38.00	42.30	59.00	32.30	25.00	2.00	-5.00	-51.30	-35.00	-45.30	-22.00	1.00	49.00	62.30	...

Find the average of these 12 values...
...then of these...
...then of these, and so on.

The Acid Test:
LEARN the words TIME SERIES, SEASONALITY, PERIOD, TREND, MOVING AVERAGE. Cover the page and write a description of each.

1) My town's rainfall is measured every month for 20 yrs and graphed. There's a rough pattern, which repeats itself every 4 months. a) What is the period of this time series? b) Describe how to calculate a moving average.

Revision Summary for Section Four

Here's the really fun page. The inevitable list of straight-down-the-middle questions to test how much you know. Remember, these questions will sort out quicker than anything else can, exactly what you _know_ and what you _don't_.   And that's exactly what revision is all about, don't forget: <u>finding out what you DON'T know</u> and then learning it <u>until you do</u>. Enjoy.

Keep learning these basic facts until you know them

1) How big or small can a probability be?
2) Draw a line to represent all probabilities with words to describe it.
3) Which two types of number can be used to represent probabilities?
4) How should $P(x) = \frac{1}{2}$ be read?
5) What must the total probability always add up to?
6) Which calculator button is mighty useful for doing probabilities?
7) What is the full significance of "with replacement" or "without replacement"?
8) What are combined probabilities?
9) What can you say about the overall probability of 2 events _both_ happening?
10) Draw a general tree diagram with all the features that all tree diagrams have.
11) Give the names of the four different types of chart for displaying data.
12) Draw 2 examples of each type of chart.
13) When should the bars of a frequency chart touch and not touch?
14) What does correlation mean? Draw graphs showing the 3 different degrees.
15) What are the 3 steps for finding the angles in a pie chart?
16) Sketch the two different extremes of spread for histograms, and explain each one's significance.
17) Here's the results of a survey to find the number of soft toys owned by each member of a class of thirty primary school students. Draw a stem and leaf diagram of the results, using class widths of 5: 1, 9, 13, 20, 21, 29, 17, 13, 3, 32, 25, 27, 44, 31, 19, 7, 37, 24, 21, 43, 11, 23, 35, 27, 33, 17, 24, 26, 15, 22.
18) Give the definitions for mean, median, mode and range.
19) What is The Golden Rule in connection with mean, median etc.?
20) How do you work out the mean and median from a frequency table?
21) How do you find the mode and range from a frequency table?
22) What's the difference between Frequency Tables and _Grouped_ Frequency Tables?
23) What are the 2 things that make Grouped Frequency Tables so tricky?
24) How do you estimate the mean from a grouped frequency table?
25) What are the four key points for cumulative frequency?
26) Do you need to think about *class boundaries* when plotting a cumulative frequency curve from a table of values? Why?
27) Sketch a typical cumulative frequency graph.
28) What are the 3 vital statistics you can obtain from a C. F. graph?
29) Explain exactly how you obtain them, and illustrate on your graph.
30) What would you use a box plot for? Illustrate this on your graph.
31) How do you decide where halfway up the graph is?
32) Which one of these is NOT a time series?
   a) measuring the temperature in 20 different countries at 12:00 today, GMT,
   b) measuring the temperature in Britain at 12:00 every day for 100 days,
   c) the Retail Price Index.
33) How can you find out if a seasonal time series has an overall trend?

X, Y and Z Coordinates

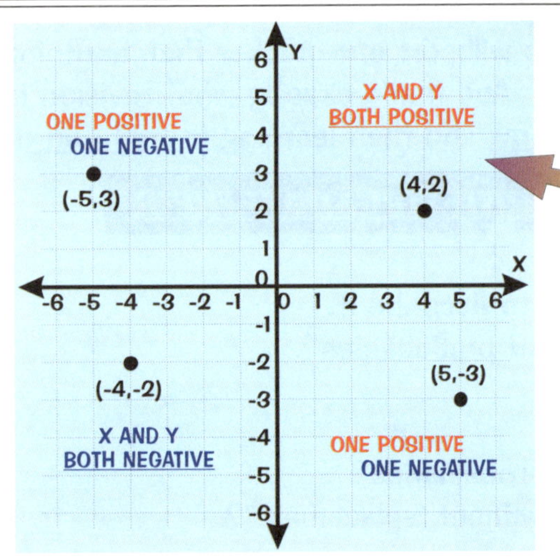

A graph has <u>four different regions</u> where the X- and Y- coordinates are either <u>positive</u> or <u>negative</u>.

This is the easiest region by far because here **ALL THE COORDINATES ARE POSITIVE**.

You have to be *dead careful* in the <u>*OTHER REGIONS*</u> though, because the X- and Y- coordinates could be <u>negative</u>, and that always makes life much more difficult.

X, Y Coordinates — getting them in the right order

You must always give <u>COORDINATES</u> in brackets like this: (x,y)

(x , y)

And you always have to be real careful to get them *the right way round*, X first, then Y. Here are *THREE POINTS* to help you remember:

1) The two coordinates are always in **ALPHABETICAL ORDER, X then Y**.

2) X is always the flat axis going **ACROSS** the page.

   In other words " <u>X is a..cross</u> "   Get it! - x is a "×".   (Hilarious isn't it)

3) Remember it's always **IN THE HOUSE** (→) and then **UP THE STAIRS** (↑),

   so it's **ALONG first** and **then UP**, i.e. X-coordinate first, and then Y-coordinate.

Z Coordinates are for 3-D space

1) All z-coordinates do is *extend* the normal x-y coordinates into a *third direction*, z, so that *all positions then have 3 coordinates*:   (x,y,z)

2) This means you can give the coordinates of the *corners of a box* or any other *3-D SHAPE*.

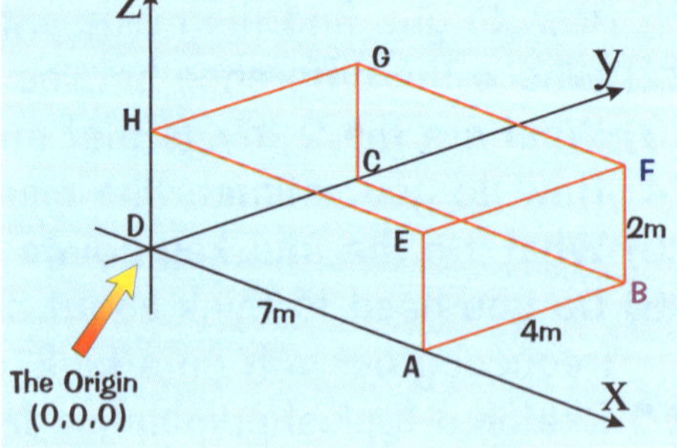

For example in this drawing, the coordinates of B and F are   B(7,4,0)   F(7,4,2)

The Acid Test:

OH — AND DON'T FORGET:
3 COORDINATES = 3-D SPACE
2 COORDINATES = 2-D SPACE

LEARN the *3 Rules for getting X and Y the right way round*.
Then turn over and <u>write it all down</u>.

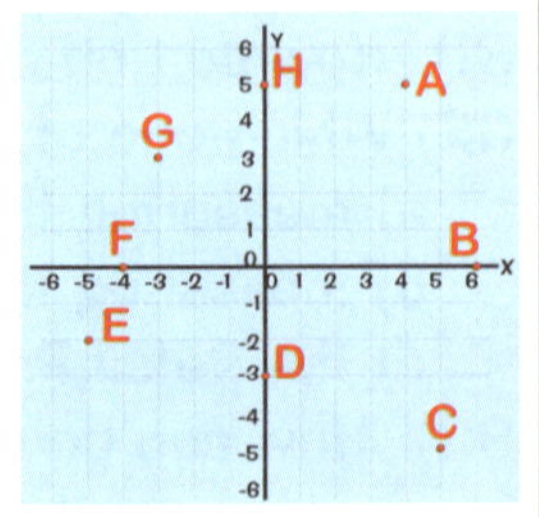

1) Write down the coordinates of the letters A to H on this graph:

Easy Graphs You should Know

If you want to make life easy for yourself, then you _definitely_ need to know a few simple graphs straight off _without even having to blink_.   These are they:

1) "X = a"
VERTICAL Lines

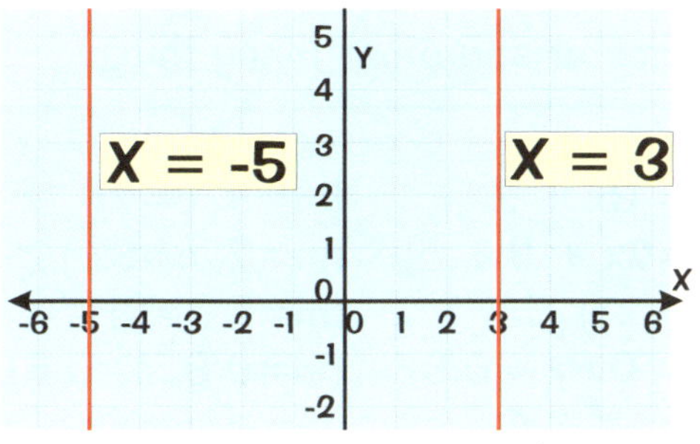

"X = a number"   is a line that goes straight up through that number on the X-axis,   e.g. X = 3 goes straight up through 3 on the X-axis as shown.
Don't forget: the y-axis is also the line "x =0"

2) "Y = a"
HORIZONTAL Lines

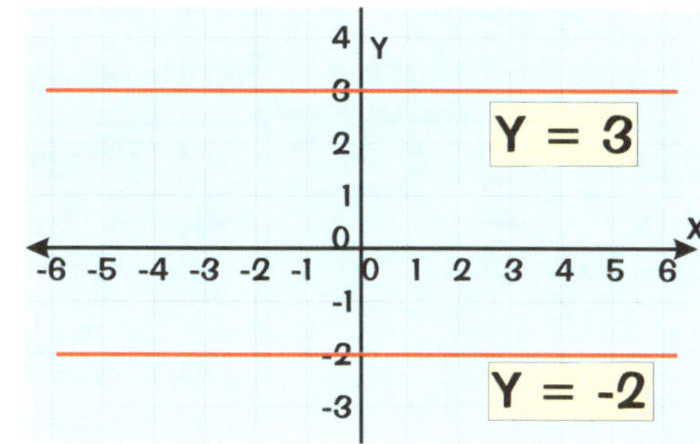

"Y = a number"   is a line that goes straight across through that number on the Y-axis,   e.g. Y = -2 goes straight through -2 on the Y-axis as shown.
Don't forget: the x-axis is also the line "y =0"

3) "Y = X" and "Y = –X"
(The Main Diagonals)

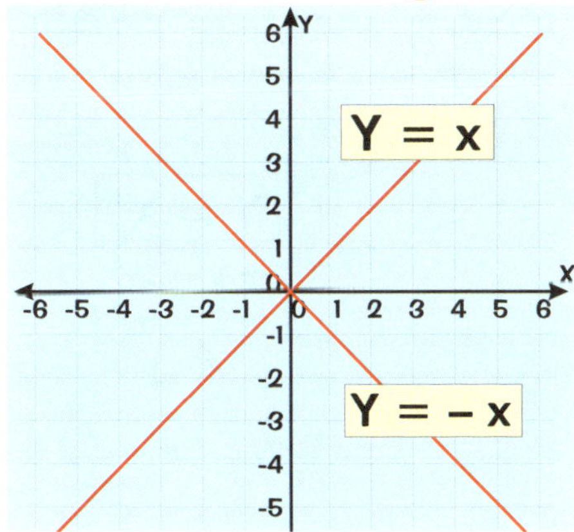

"Y = X" is the main diagonal that goes UPHILL from left to right.

"Y = -X" is the main diagonal that goes DOWNHILL from left to right.

4) "Y = AX" and "Y = –AX"
(Other Sloping Lines)

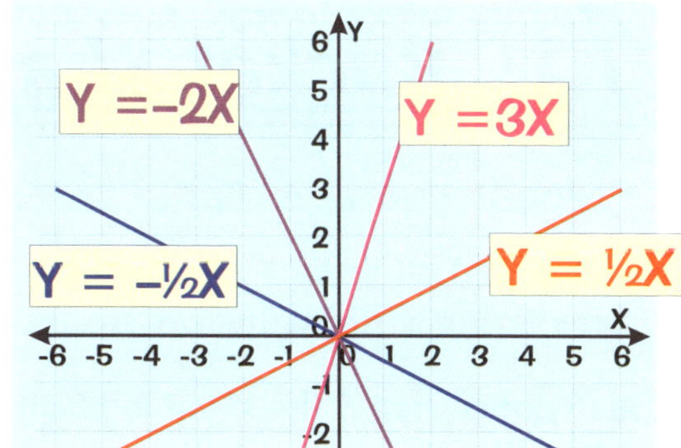

Y = AX and Y = -AX are the equations for A SLOPING LINE THROUGH THE ORIGIN.

The value of A is the _GRADIENT of the line_, so the BIGGER the number the STEEPER the slope, and a MINUS SIGN tells you it slopes DOWNHILL as shown by the ones above.

The Acid Test:
LEARN the FOUR EASY TYPES OF GRAPH, then turn over and WRITE IT ALL DOWN with examples.

Then _cover the page_ and do these:
1) Write down the equations of _the four graphs shown here_:
2) Draw these 6 graphs: X = 3, Y = -4, Y = X,   Y = -X, Y = 0, Y = -½X.

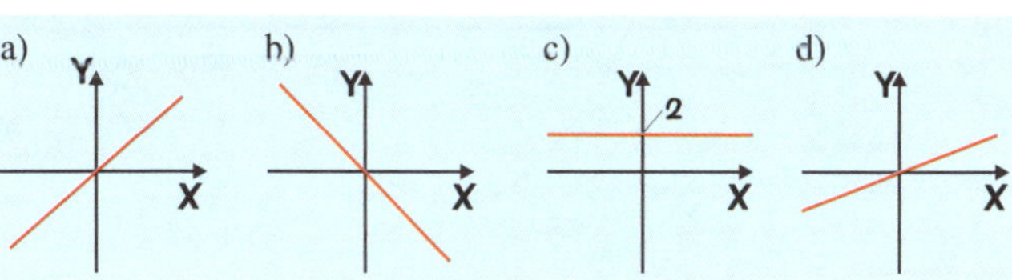

Four Graphs You Should Recognise

There are four types of graph that you should know the basic shape of just from looking at their equations — it really isn't as difficult as it sounds.

1) Straight Line Graphs: "Y = mx + c"

Straight line equations are really quite easy to spot — they have an *x-term*, a *y-term* and *a number* and that's it. There's no x^2 or x^3 or $1/x$ terms or any other fancy things.

NOT straight lines	Straight lines		Rearranged into "y = mx + c"	
$y = x^3 + 3$	$y = 2 + 3x$	$\rightarrow$	$y = 3x + 2$	(m=3, c=2)
$2y - 1/x = 7$	$2y - 4x = 7$	$\rightarrow$	$y = 2x + 3\tfrac{1}{2}$	(m=2, c=3½)
$1/y + 1/x = 2$	$x - y = 0$	$\rightarrow$	$y = x + 0$	(m=1, c=0)
$x^2 = 4 - y$	$4x - 3 = 5y$	$\rightarrow$	$y = 0.8x - 0.6$	(m=0.8, c=0.6)
$xy + 3 = 0$	$3y + 3x = 12$	$\rightarrow$	$y = -x + 4$	(m=-1, c=4)

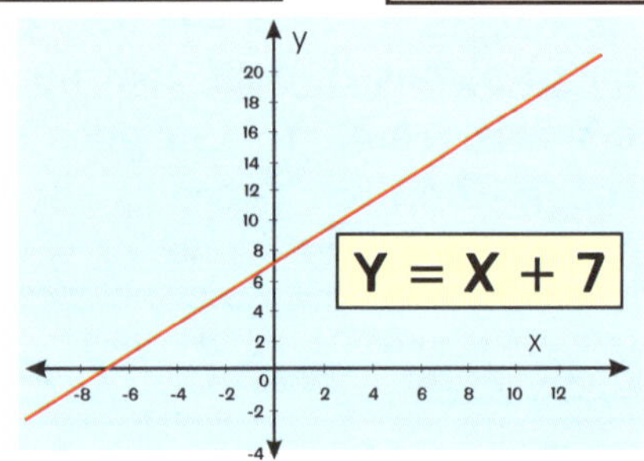

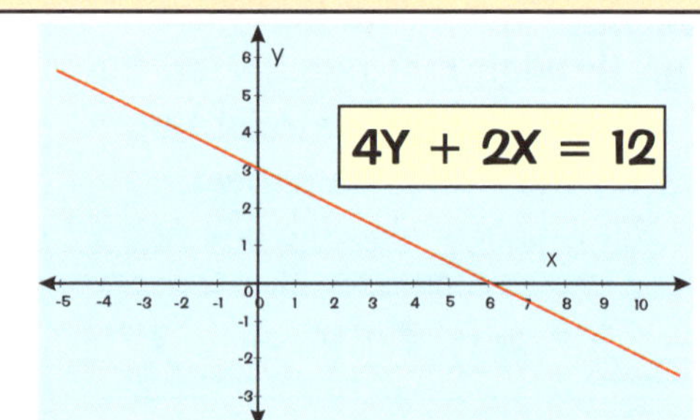

2) X^2 Bucket Shapes:

Y = anything with X^2 in it, but not X^3

Notice that all these X^2 graphs have the same SYMMETRICAL bucket shape.

Also notice that if the X^2 bit is positive (i.e. $+X^2$) then the bucket is the normal way up, but if the X^2 bit has a "minus" in front of it (i.e. $-X^2$) then the bucket is upside down.

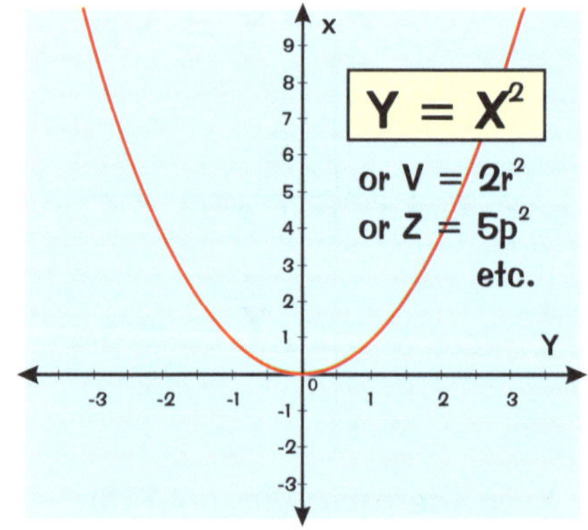

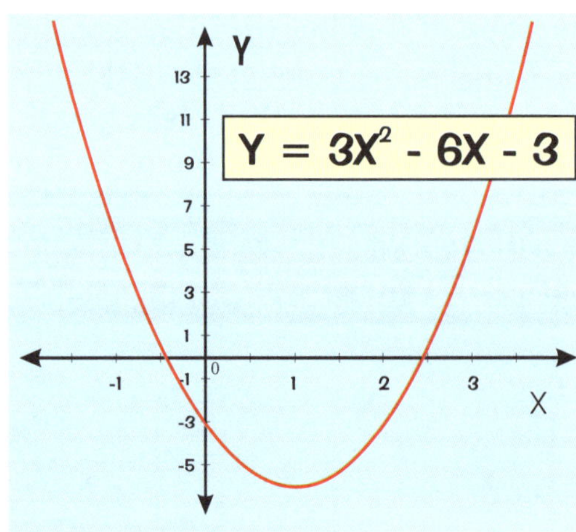

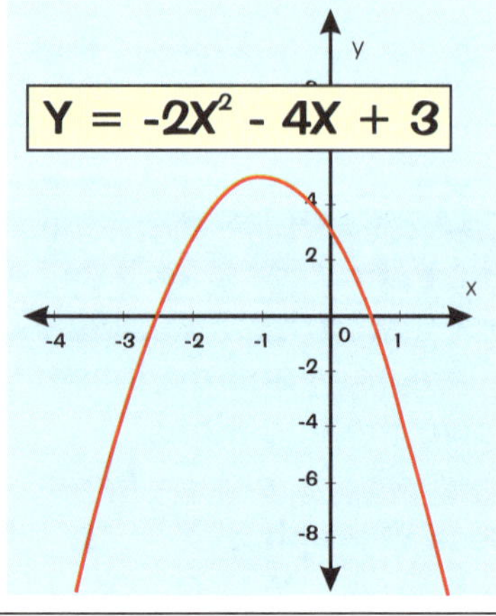

Four Graphs You Should Recognise

3) X^3 Graphs:

$Y =$ "something with X^3 in it"

All X^3 graphs have the same basic _wiggle_ in the middle, but it can be a flat wiggle or a more pronounced wiggle.

Notice that "$-X^3$ graphs" always come _down from top left_ whereas the $+X^3$ ones go _up from bottom left_.

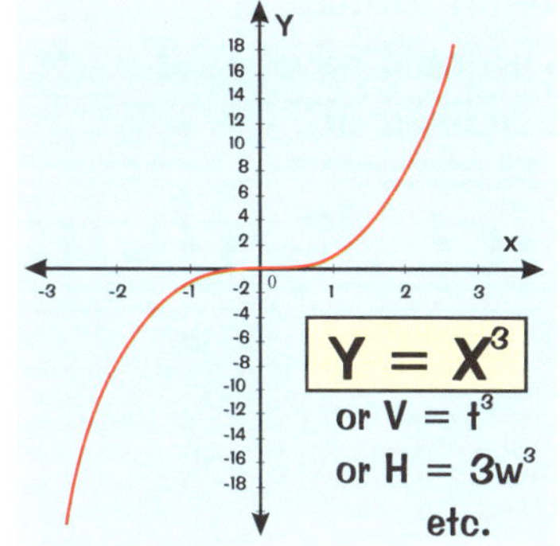

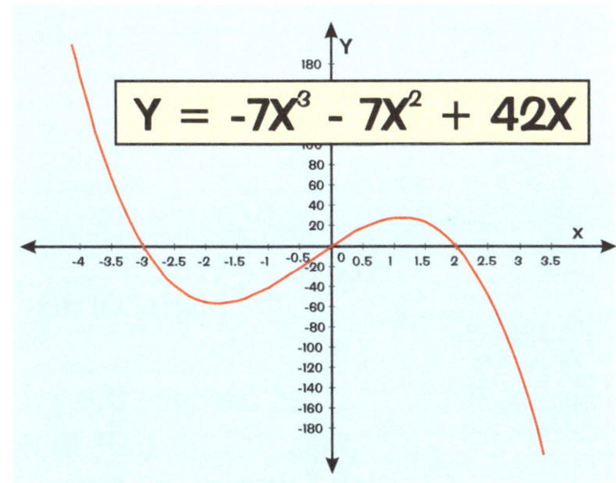

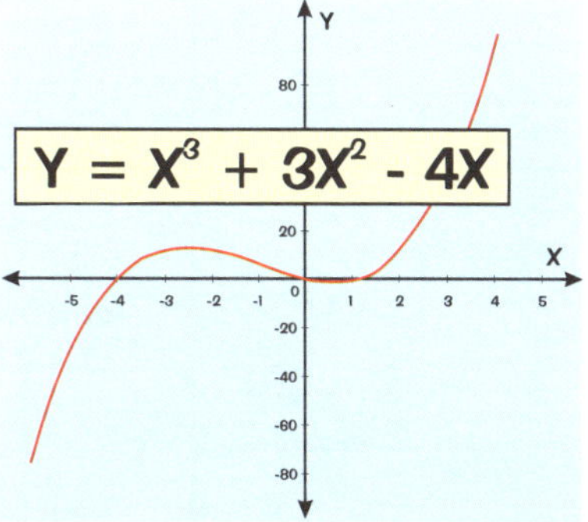

4) 1/X GRAPHS:

$Y = \dfrac{A}{X}$, where A is some number.

These graphs are _all EXACTLY the same shape_, the only difference being how close in they get at the corner. They are all _symmetrical about the line y=x_. This is also the graph you get when x and y are in _inverse proportion_.

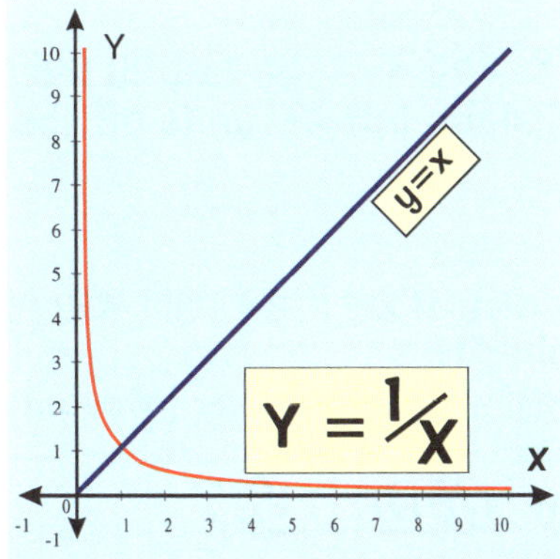

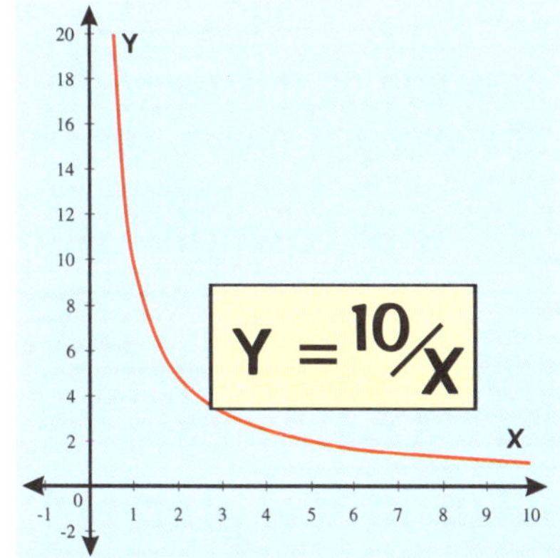

The Acid Test:

LEARN all the details about the 4 Types of Graph, their equations and their shapes.

Then _turn over_ and _sketch three examples_ of each of the _four types_ of graph — and if you can also give some extra details about their equations, _so much the better_.
Remember, if you don't LEARN IT, then it's a waste of time even reading it. This is true for all revision.

Finding The Gradient of a Line

Working out the gradient of a straight line is a slightly involved business, and there are quite a few things that can go wrong.

Once again though, if you *learn and follow the steps below* and treat it as a <u>STRICT METHOD</u>, you'll have a lot more success than if you try and fudge your way through it, like you usually do.

Strict Method For *Finding Gradient*

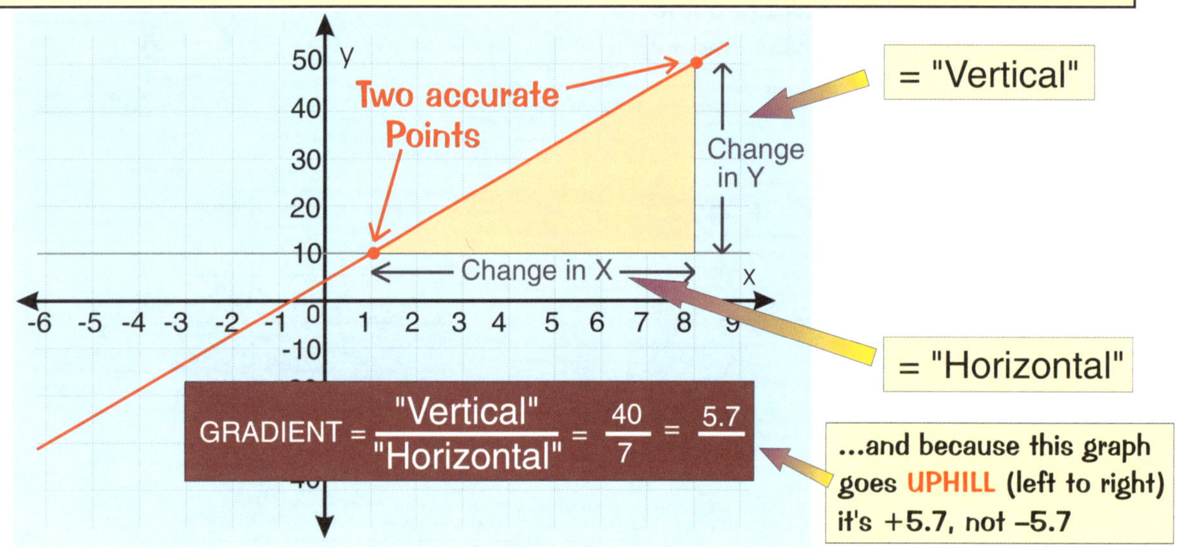

1) Find *TWO ACCURATE POINTS*, reasonably far apart

Both in the *upper right quadrant* if possible, (to keep all the numbers positive and so reduce the chance of errors).

2) *COMPLETE THE TRIANGLE* as shown

3) Find the CHANGE IN Y and the CHANGE IN X

Make sure you do this *using the SCALES on the Y- and X- axes*, <u>not by counting cm</u>! (So in the example shown, the Change in Y is NOT 4cm, but *40 units* off the Y-axis.)

4) *LEARN* this formula, and use it:

$$\text{GRADIENT} = \frac{\text{VERTICAL}}{\text{HORIZONTAL}}$$

Make sure you get it the right way up too!
Remember it's
<u>VER</u>y <u>HO</u>t — <u>VER</u>tical over <u>HO</u>rizontal

5) Finally, is the gradient *POSITIVE* or *NEGATIVE*?

If it slopes <u>UPHILL</u> left → right (↗) <u>then it's +ve</u>

If it slopes <u>DOWNHILL</u> left → right (↘) <u>then it's –ve</u>   (so put a minus(–) in front of it)

The Acid Test:

LEARN the <u>FIVE STEPS</u> for finding a gradient then turn over and <u>WRITE THEM DOWN</u> from memory.

1) Plot these 3 points on a graph: (0,3) (2,0) (5,-4.5) and then join them up with a straight line. Now carefully apply the <u>FIVE STEPS</u> to find the gradient of the line.

Plotting Straight Line Graphs

A lot of people wouldn't know a straight line equation if it ran up and bit them, but they're pretty easy to spot really — they just have *two letters* and *a few numbers*, but with *nothing fancy* like squared or cubed.   (Now that you're inflamed with burning curiosity, look at P.70 to see some examples)

Anyway, in the Exam you'll be expected to draw the graph of a straight line equation.
"y = mx + c" is the hard way of doing it (see P.74). Here's the __EASY WAY__ of doing it:

The "Table of 3 values" method

You can __EASILY__ draw the graph of __ANY EQUATION__ using this __EASY__ method.

Method:

1) Choose __3 VALUES OF X__ and __draw up a table__,

2) __WORK OUT THE VALUE OF Y__ for each value of **X**.

3) __PLOT THE COORDINATES__, and __DRAW THE LINE__.

If it's a straight line equation, the 3 points will be in a dead straight line with each other, which is the usual check you do when you've drawn it.
If they aren't, then it could be a curve and you'll need to do more values in your table to find out what's going on.

Example: *"Draw the graph of Y = 2X – 3".*

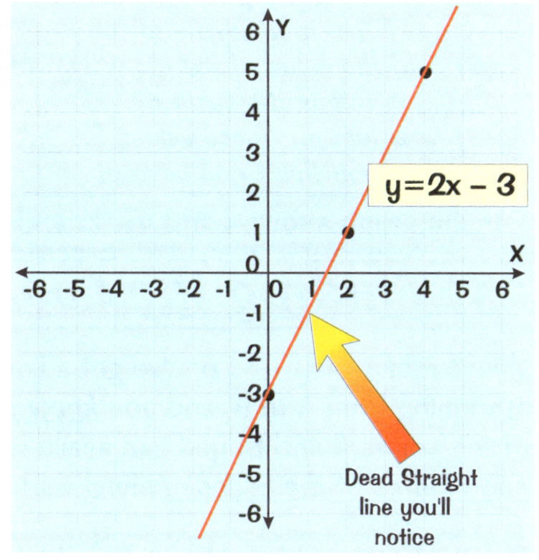

1) __DRAW UP A TABLE__ with some *suitable values* of **X**.
   Choosing X = 0, 2, 4 is usually oool enough.
   i.e.

X	0	2	4
Y			

2) __FIND THE Y-VALUES__
   by putting each
   x-value into the
   equation:

   e.g. When X = 4,
   y = 2X – 3
     = 2×4 – 3
     = 8 – 3   = 5

X	0	2	4
Y	-3	1	5

3) __PLOT THE POINTS__ and __DRAW THE LINE__ *right across the graph (as shown).*

   (The points should always lie in a __DEAD STRAIGHT LINE__. If they don't, do more values in the table to find out what on earth's happening.)

The Acid Test: __LEARN__ the details of this __easy method__ then __turn over and write them all down.__

1) Draw the graphs of   a) y = 4 + x   b) y = 3x + 2   c) y = 6 –2x

Straight Line Graphs: "y = mx + c"

Using y = mx + c

y = mx +c is the general equation for a straight line graph, and you need to remember:

"m" is equal to the GRADIENT of the graph

"c" is the value WHERE IT CROSSES THE Y-AXIS and is called the INTERCEPT.

1) Drawing a Straight Line using "y = mx + c"

The main thing is being able to identify "m" and "c" and knowing what to do with them:
BUT WATCH OUT — people often mix up "m" and "c", especially with say, "y = 5 + 2x"
REMEMBER: "m" is the number IN FRONT OF X and "c" is the number ON ITS OWN.

Method

1) Get the equation into the form "y = mx + c".

2) IDENTIFY "m" and "c" CAREFULLY.

3) PUT A DOT ON THE Y-AXIS at the value of c.

4) Then go ALONG ONE UNIT and up or down by the value of m and make another dot.

5) Repeat the same "step" in both directions as shown:

6) Finally CHECK that the gradient LOOKS RIGHT.

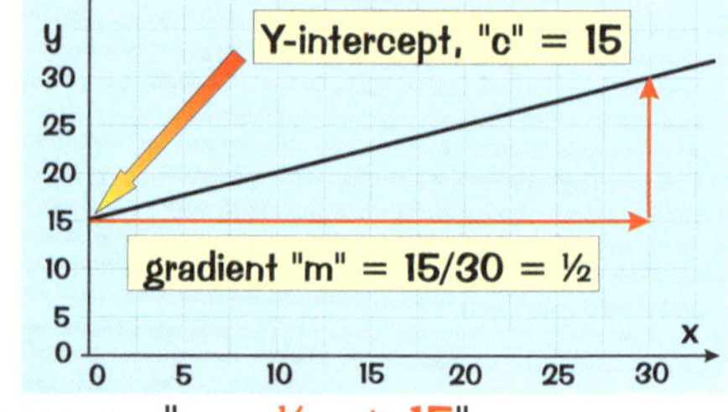

The graph shows the process for the equation "y = 2x + 1":
1) "c" = 1, so put a first dot at y = 1 on the y-axis.
2) Go along 1 unit → and then up by 2 because "m" = +2.
3) Repeat the same step, 1→ 2↑ in both directions. (i.e. 1 ← 2 ↓ the other way)
4) CHECK: a gradient of +2 should be quite steep and uphill left to right — which it is.

2) Finding the Equation Of a Straight Line Graph

THIS IS EASY:
1) Find where the graph CROSSES THE Y-AXIS.
   This is the value of "c".
2) Find the value of the GRADIENT (see P.72).
   This is the value of "m"
3) Now just put these values for "m" and "c" into "y = mx + c"
   ~ and there you have it!

For the graph shown here, m=½ and c = 15 so "y = mx + c" becomes "y = ½x + 15"

3) Finding the Coordinates of the Midpoint

This is really easy — if you've got a line (or part-line) stretching from A to B, and you know the coordinates of the points A and B, you can easily work out the coordinates of the midpoint along that line.

JUST TAKE THE AVERAGE OF THE X-COORDINATES AND THE AVERAGE OF THE Y-COORDINATES AND PLONK THEM IN A PAIR OF BRACKETS.

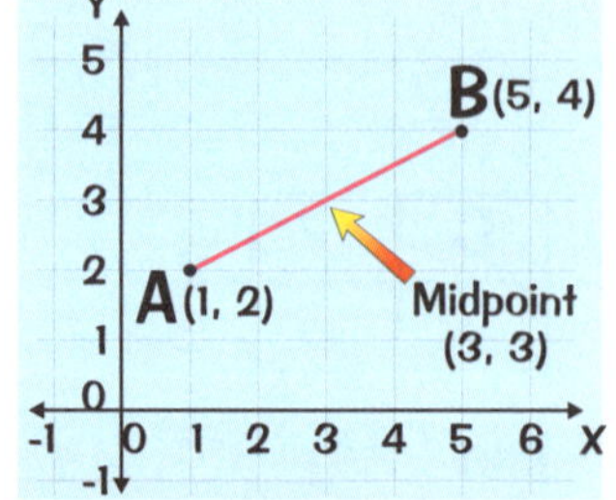

A = (1, 2) ⇒ X=1, Y=2
B = (5, 4) ⇒ X=5, Y=4
Average of X-coordinates = (1 + 5) ÷ 2 = 3
Average of Y-coordinates = (2 + 4) ÷ 2 = 3
PLONK 'EM TOGETHER...
Average coordinates = coordinates of midpoint = (3, 3)

The Acid Test:

LEARN THE DETAILS of the two methods for "y = mx +c".
Then TURN OVER and WRITE IT ALL DOWN.

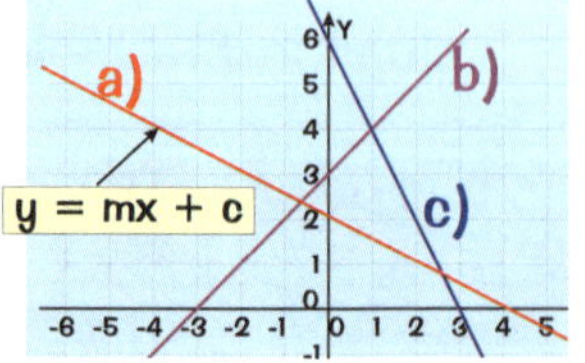

1) Using "y = mx +c" draw the graphs of y=x − 3 and y=4 − 2x.
2) Using "y = mx +c" find the equations of these 3 graphs →
3) Give the coordinates of the midpoint, N, of the line segment from L(16, 12) to M(4, 3).

Typical Graph Questions

There's a lot of fiddly details involved in graph questions: getting the right values in the table; plotting the right points; and getting the final answers from your graph.
If you want to get all these easy marks, then you've got to learn all these little tricks:

Filling in The Table of Values

A typical question: *"Complete the table of values for the equation $y = x^2 - 4x + 3$"*

x	-2	-1	0	1	2	3	4	5	6
y				0			3		15

<u>WHAT YOU DON'T DO</u> is try to punch it all into the calculator in one go. Not good. The rest of the question hinges on this table of values and one silly mistake here could cost you a lot of marks. This might look like a long-winded method but it takes far less time than you think and is the only <u>REALLY SAFE</u> method.

1) For EVERY value in the table you should WRITE THIS OUT:

<u>For x=4</u>: $y = x^2 - 4x + 3$ <u>For x=-1</u>: $y = x^2 - 4x + 3$

$= 4^2 - 4\times4 + 3$ $= (-1\times-1) - (4\times-1) + 3$

$= 16 - 16 + 3$ $= 1 - -4 + 3 = 1 + 4 + 3$

$= \underline{3}$ $= \underline{8}$

2) Make sure you can reproduce the y-values they've already given you...

— *BEFORE you fill in the spaces in the table.*   This is really important to make sure you're doing it right, before you start cheerfully working out a pile of wrong values!

I wouldn't tell you all this without good reason, so ignore it at your peril.

Plotting the Points and Drawing the Curve

Here again there are easy marks to be won and lost — this all matters:

1) <u>GET THE AXES THE RIGHT WAY ROUND</u>: The values from the <u>FIRST row or column</u> are ALWAYS plotted <u>on the X-axis</u>.

2) <u>PLOT THE POINTS CAREFULLY</u>, and don't mix up the x and y values.

3) The points will ALWAYS form a <u>DEAD STRAIGHT LINE</u> or a <u>COMPLETELY SMOOTH CURVE</u>.

If they don't, they're *wrong*.

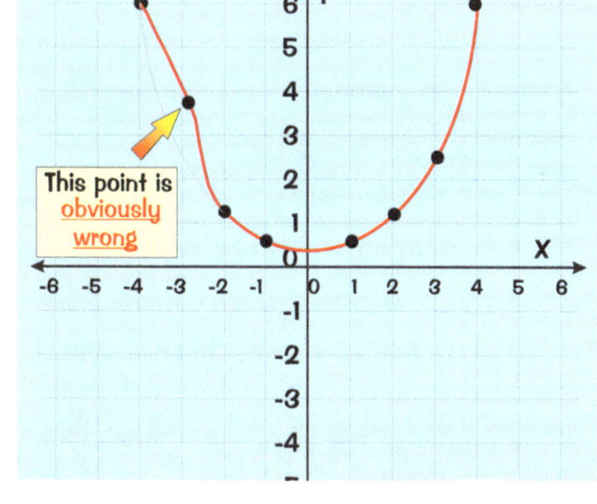

4) A graph from an <u>ALGEBRA EQUATION</u>, must always be drawn as a <u>SMOOTH CURVE</u> (or a dead straight line). You only use lots of short straight line sections to join points in *"Data Handling"* when it's called a "frequency polygon". (See P.58)

<u>NEVER EVER</u> *let one point drag your line off* in some ridiculous direction — if one point seems out of place, *check the value in the table* and then check the position where you've plotted it. When a graph is generated from an equation, *you never get spikes or lumps* — only MISTAKES.

Typical Graph Questions

Getting Answers from Your Graph

1) **FOR A SINGLE CURVE OR LINE**, you **ALWAYS** get the answer by *drawing a straight line to the graph from one axis*, and then *down or across to the other axis*, as shown here:

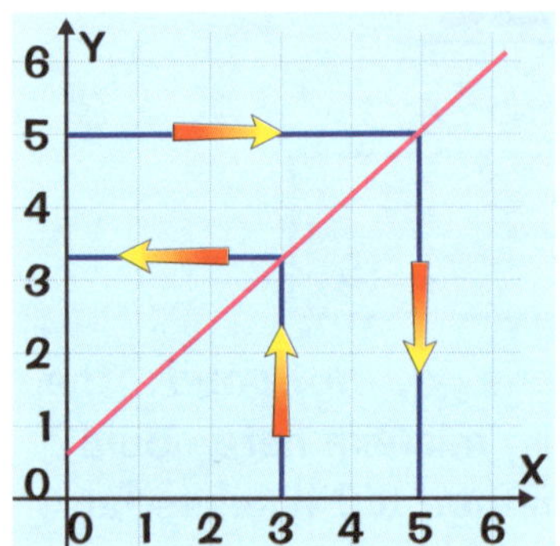

You should be *fully expecting* this to happen so that even if you don't understand the question, you can still have a pretty good stab at it:

If the question said *"Find the value of y when x is equal to 3"*, **ALL YOU DO IS THIS**: *start at 3 on the x-axis, go straight up to the graph, then straight over to the y-axis and read off the value, which in this case is $y = 3.2$* (as shown opposite).

2) **IF TWO LINES CROSS.....**

you can bet your very last fruitcake the answer to one of the questions will simply be:
THE VALUES OF X AND Y WHERE THEY CROSS
and you should be expecting that *before they even ask it!* (See Simultaneous Eqns. P.92).

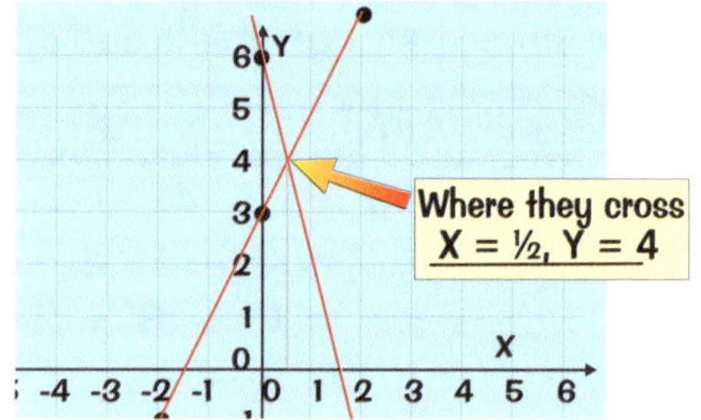

What The Gradient of a Graph MEANS

No matter what the graph, **THE MEANING OF THE GRADIENT** is always simply :

(Y-axis UNITS)   PER   (X-axis UNITS)

EXAMPLES:

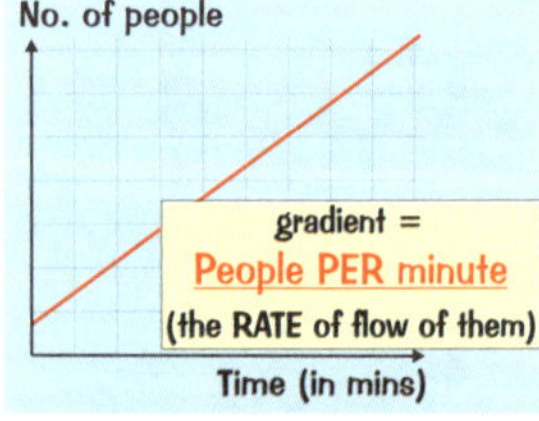

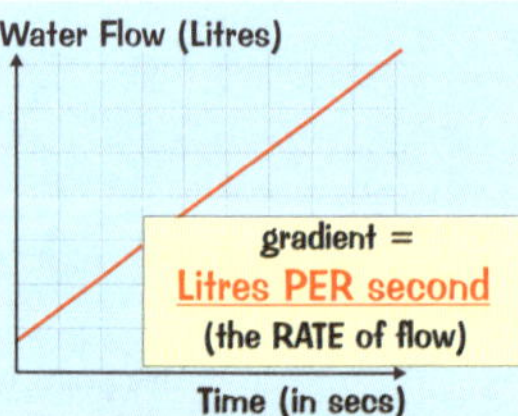

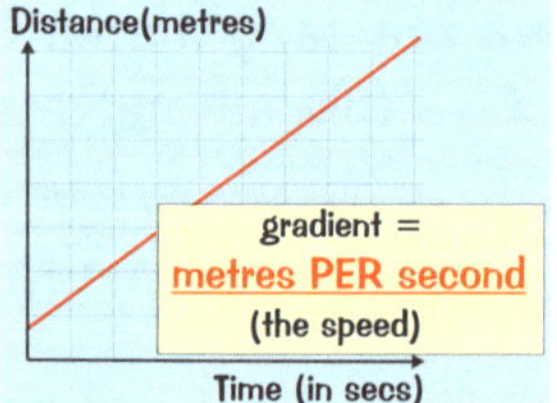

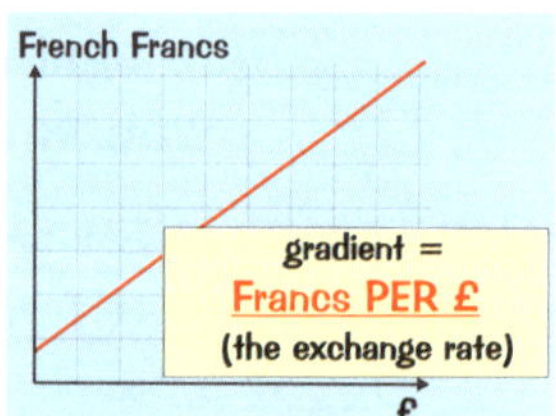

Some gradients have special names like *Exchange Rate* or *Speed*, but once you've written down *"something PER something"* using the Y-axis and X-axis **UNITS**, it's then pretty easy to work out what the gradient represents.

The Acid Test:

LEARN the 2 Rules for doing tables of values, the 4 points for drawing graphs, the 2 simple Rules for getting answers, and the meaning of gradient.

Now turn over and *write it all down from memory*. Then *try again until you can do it*.

1) *Complete the table of values* at the top of the previous page (using the proper methods!), and then *draw the graph* taking note of the Four Points.
2) From your graph *find the value of y when x is 4.2*, and *the values of x when y=12*.
3) If I drew a graph of "miles covered" up the y-axis and "gallons used" along the x-axis, and worked out the gradient, what would the value of it tell me?

Revision Summary for Section Five

Aren't graphs great. I think everyone likes graphs. Anyway, here are the scary questions to find out what you know.   By the way, I hope you haven't started trying to kid yourself that these aren't proper maths questions so you don't have to bother with them.   Oh no. Maths is _packed_ with _facts_ — and you need to know them _to be able to do it_. All these questions do is see how many of the simple facts you've learnt so far. Try it now and scare yourself. Then learn some stuff and try again.

Keep learning these basic facts until you know them

1) Give 3 ways of remembering which way round the x and y coordinates go.
2) Sketch a pair of x and y axes and show on it where the x-coordinates and the y-coordinates are positive and negative in the four different regions.
3) Which way does the z-axis point?
4) What are z-coordinates used for?
5) What type of line is $x = a$?
6) What type of line is $y = b$?
7) What type of line is $y = ax$?
8) What's special about $y = x$ and $y = -x$?
9) What are the 4 different types of graph you should know the basic shape of?
10) What does the graph of inverse proportion look like?
11) What sort of equation produces a bucket shaped graph?
12) What about an upside down bucket?
13) What sort of equation produces a graph with a wiggle in the middle?
14) Do 2 examples of each, giving the equation and sketching the graph.
15) What does the equation of a straight line look like?
16) What makes them different from equations that aren't straight lines?
17) What is the formula for gradient? How do you remember it?
18) Write down the 5 steps of the method for finding gradient.
19) What's the easiest method for drawing or sketching the graph of an equation?
20) What difference is there in this method if it's not a straight line?
21) Explain what "$y = mx + c$" means, including the significance of m and c.
22) Detail the 6 steps for plotting a graph using "$y = mx + c$".
23) Detail the 3 steps for getting the equation of a straight line graph.
24) If a line passes through the two points P(12, 34) and Q(4, 12), find the coordinates of the midpoint of the line segment, PQ.
25) What are the two rules for filling in a table of values?
26) What are the 4 rules for plotting the graph from a table of values?
27) What are the two rules for getting answers from a graph or graphs?
28) How do you determine the _meaning_ of the gradient of a graph?
29) What x- and y-axes would you need if the gradient was going to be equal to speed, in metres per second?
30) What axes would you need if the gradient was going to be the _rate of flow_ of water, in litres per minute?
31) What axes would you have if the gradient was equivalent to an "Exchange Rate"?

Negative Numbers and Letters

Everyone knows RULE 1, but sometimes RULE 2 applies instead, so make sure you know *BOTH* rules AND when to use them.

Rule 1

Only to be used when:

1) Multiplying or dividing

e.g. $-2 \times 3 = -6$, $-8 \div -2 = +4$ $-4p \times -2 = +8p$

2) Two signs appear next to each other

e.g. $5 - {}^-4 = 5 + 4 = 9$ $4 + {}^-6 - {}^-7 = 4 - 6 + 7 = 5$

+	+	makes	+
+	−	makes	−
−	+	makes	−
−	−	makes	+

Rule 2

THE NUMBER LINE

Use this when ADDING OR SUBTRACTING:

e.g. "Simplify $4X - 8X - 3X + 6X$"

+6X   +4X

-10 -9 -8 -7 -6 -5 -4 -3 -2 -1 0 1 2 3 4 5 6 7 8 9 10

-3X   -8X

So $4X - 8X - 3X + 6X = -1X$

Letters Multiplied Together

This is the super-slick notation they like to use in algebra which just ends up making life difficult for folks like you. You've got to remember these five rules:

1) "abc" means "a×b×c"   The ×'s are often left out to make it clearer.

2) "gn² " means "g×n×n"   Note that only the n is squared, not the g as well.

3) "(gn)² " means "g×g×n×n"   The brackets mean that BOTH letters are squared.

4) "p(q − r)³ " means "p×(q − r) × (q − r) × (q − r)"   Only the brackets get cubed.

5) "−3² " is too ambiguous.   It should either be written $(-3)^2 = 9$, or $-(3^2) = -9$.

D.O.T.S. — The Difference Of Two Squares:

$$a^2 - b^2 = (a + b)(a - b)$$

The "difference of two squares" (D.O.T.S. for short) is where you have "one thing squared" minus "another thing squared". In the Exam you're likely to be asked to factorise a D.O.T.S. expression (i.e. put it into two brackets as above). People mess this up because they haven't made enough effort to learn it. Best do it now, eh, before it's too late. Make sure you LEARN this one example:

Factorise $x^2 - 16$.   Answer: $x^2 - 16 = (x + 4)(x - 4)$

The Acid Test:

LEARN the Two Rules for negative N°s. and when each is used, the 5 special cases of Letters Multiplied Together, and the DOTS example above.

Then turn over and write down what you've learned.

1) For each of a) to d), decide where Rule 1 and Rule 2 apply, and then work them out.

a) -4×-3 b) $-4 + {}^-5 + 3$ c) $(3X + {}^-2X - 4X) \div (2 + {}^-5)$ d) $120 \div {}^-40$

2) If $m = 2$ and $n = -3$, work out: a) mn^2 b) $(mn)^3$ c) $m(4+n)^2$ d) n^3 e) $3m^2n^3 + 2mn$

Standard Index Form

Standard Form and **Standard Index Form** are the **SAME THING**.
So remember **both of these names** as well as **what it actually is**:

Ordinary Number: 4,300,000   **In Standard Form**: 4.3×10^6

Standard form is <u>only really useful for writing</u> **VERY BIG** or **VERY SMALL** numbers in a more convenient way, e.g.

56,000,000,000 would be 5.6×10^{10} in standard form.

0.000 000 003 45 would be 3.45×10^{-9} in standard form.

but **ANY NUMBER** can be written in standard form and *you need to know how to do it*:

What it Actually is:

A number written in standard form must <u>ALWAYS</u> be in <u>EXACTLY</u> this form:

$$A \times 10^n$$

This *number* must *always* be <u>BETWEEN 1 AND 10</u>.

(The fancy way of saying this is:

"$1 \leqslant A < 10$" — they sometimes write that in Exam questions — don't let it put you off, just remember what it means).

This number is just the <u>NUMBER OF PLACES</u> *the Decimal Point moves*.

Learn The Three Rules:

1) The <u>front number</u> must always be <u>BETWEEN 1 AND 10</u>

2) The power of 10, n, is purely: <u>HOW FAR THE D.P. MOVES</u>

3) n is <u>+ve</u> for BIG numbers,   n is <u>−ve</u> for SMALL <u>numbers</u>

(This is much better than rules based on which way the D.P. moves.)

Examples:

1) *"Express 35 600 in standard form".*

METHOD:
1) Move the D.P. until 35 600 becomes 3.56 ("$1 \leqslant A < 10$")
2) The D.P. has moved 4 places so n=4, giving: 10^4
3) 35600 is a BIG number so n is +4, not −4

ANSWER:

$3.5600. = \underline{3.56 \times 10^4}$

2) *"Express 8.14×10^{-3} as an ordinary number".*

METHOD:
1) 10^{-3}, tells us that the D.P. must move 3 places...
2) ...and the "−" sign tells us to move the D.P. to make it a SMALL number. (i.e. 0.00814, rather than 8140)

ANSWER:

$8.14 = \underline{0.00814}$

Standard Index Form

Standard Form and The Calculator

People usually manage all that stuff about moving the decimal point OK *(apart from always forgetting that FOR A BIG NUMBER it's "ten to the power +ve something" and FOR A SMALL NUMBER it's "ten to the power –ve something")*, but when it comes to doing standard form on a *calculator* it's invariably a sorry saga of confusion and ineptitude.

But it's not so bad really — you just have to learn it, that's all.....

1) Entering Standard Form Numbers EXP

The button you MUST USE to put standard form numbers into the calculator is the EXP

(or EE) button — but DON'T go pressing X 10 as well, like a lot of people do,

because that makes it WRONG

Example: *"Enter 2.67×10^{15} into the calculator"*

Just press: 2.67 EXP 15 = and the display will be $2.67^{\ 15}$

Note that you ONLY PRESS the EXP (or EE) button — you DON'T press X or 10 at all.

2) Reading Standard Form Numbers:

The big thing you have to remember when you write any standard form number from the calculator display is to put the "×10" in yourself. DON'T just write down what it says on the display.

Example: *"Write down the number $7.986^{\ 05}$ as a finished answer."*

As a finished answer this must be written as 7.986×10^5.

It is NOT 7.986^5 so DON'T write it down like that — YOU have to put the $\times 10^n$ in yourself, even though it isn't shown in the display at all. *That's the bit people forget.*

The Acid Test: LEARN the Three Rules and the Two Calculator Methods, then turn over and write them down.

Now cover up these 2 pages and answer these:
 1) What are the Three Rules for standard form?
 2) Express 958,000 in standard index form.   3) And the same for 0.00018
 4) Express 4.56×10^3 as an ordinary number.
 5) Work this out using your calculator: $3.2 \times 10^{12} \div 1.6 \times 10^{-9}$, and write down the answer, first in standard form and then as an ordinary number.

Powers (or "Indices")

Powers are a very useful shorthand:

$$2\times2\times2\times2\times2\times2\times2 = 2^7 \text{ ("two to the power 7")}$$
$$7\times7 = 7^2 \text{ ("7 squared")}$$
$$6\times6\times6\times6\times6 = 6^5 \text{ (" Six to the power 5")}$$
$$4\times4\times4 = 4^3 \text{ ("four cubed")}$$

That bit is easy to remember. Unfortunately, there are SEVEN SPECIAL RULES for Powers that are not quite so easy, but *you do need to know them for the Exam*:

The Seven Rules

1) When MULTIPLYING, you ADD the powers.

e.g. $3^4 \times 3^6 = 3^{6+4} = 3^{10}$ $8^3 \times 8^5 = 8^{3+5} = 8^8$

2) When DIVIDING, you SUBTRACT the powers.

e.g. $5^4 \div 5^2 = 5^{4-2} = 5^2$ $12^8/12^3 = 12^{8-3} = 12^5$

3) When RAISING one power to another, you MULTIPLY the powers.

e.g. $(3^2)^4 = 3^{2\times4} = 3^8,$ $(5^4)^6 = 5^{24}$

4) $X^1 = X$,   ANYTHING TO THE POWER 1 is just ITSELF

e.g. $3^1 = 3,$ $6 \times 6^3 = 6^4,$ $4^3 \div 4^2 = 4^{3-2} = 4^1 = 4$

5) $X^0 = 1$,   ANYTHING TO THE POWER 0 is just 1

e.g. $5^0 = 1$ $67^0 = 1$ $3^4/3^4 = 3^{4-4} = 3^0 = 1$

6) $1^x = 1$,   1 TO ANY POWER is still just 1

e.g. $1^{23} = 1$ $1^{89} = 1$ $1^2 = 1$ $1^{1012} = 1$

7) FRACTIONAL POWERS mean one thing: ROOTS

The Power ½ means *Square Root*, e.g. $25^{\frac{1}{2}} = \sqrt{25} = 5$
The Power ⅓ means *Cube Root*, e.g. $64^{\frac{1}{3}} = \sqrt[3]{64} = 4$

The Acid Test:
LEARN the Seven Rules for Powers. Then turn over and write it all down. Keep trying until you can do it!

Then cover the page and apply the rules to SIMPLIFY these:
1) a) $3^2 \times 3^6$ b) $4^3 \div 4^2$ c) $(8^3)^4$ d) $(3^2 \times 3^3 \times 1^6)/3^5$ e) $7^3 \times 7 \times 7^2$
2) a) $5^2 \times 5^7 \times 5^3$ b) $1^3 \times 5^0 \times 6^2$ c) $(4^3 \times 4 \times 4^2) \div (2^3 \times 2^4)$
3) If $6\times6\times6 = 216$, what is the value of $216^{\frac{1}{3}}$?

Square Roots and Cube Roots

Square Roots

"Squared" means "times by itself" : $P^2 = P \times P$
— SQUARE ROOT is the reverse process.

The best way to think of it is this:

"Square Root" means "What Number Times by Itself gives..."

Example: "Find the square root of 49" (i.e. " Find $\sqrt{49}$ " or "Find $49^{½}$ ")

To do this you should say it as: "What number TIMES BY ITSELF gives... 49"

Now, if you ever felt inclined to learn the number sequences on P.1 (like you were told to!), then of course you'd know instantly that the answer is 7.

On your calculator, *it's easy to find any positive square root* using the SQUARE ROOT BUTTON: Press  = 7 (See P.17)

Square Roots can be Positive or Negative

If you multiply a negative number by itself, you get a positive one (see P.78):

$(-2)^2 = (-2) \times (-2) = 4$ But $2^2 = 4$ as well. (What's going on...)

It's actually quite simple: $\sqrt{4} = +2 \text{ or } -2$

... and that goes for all square roots —
whenever you get a positive square root, you also get a negative one.

Cube Roots

"Cubed" means "times by itself three times" : $T^3 = T \times T \times T$
— CUBE ROOT is the reverse process.

"Cube Root" means "What Number Times by Itself THREE TIMES gives..."

Well, strictly there are only two × signs, but you know what I mean.

Example: "Find the cube root of 64" (i.e "Find $\sqrt[3]{64}$ " or " Find $64^{\frac{1}{3}}$ ")

You should say: "What number TIMES BY ITSELF THREE TIMES gives... 64"

From your in-depth revision of P.1 you will of course know the answer is 4.

OR on your calculator just use the CUBE ROOT BUTTON:
Press  = 3   (See P.17)

And Don't Forget:

"SOMETHING TO THE POWER ½" is just a different way of asking for a SQUARE ROOT
e.g. $81^{½}$ is the same as $\sqrt{81}$ which is just 9.

"SOMETHING TO THE POWER 1/3" is just a different way of asking for a CUBE ROOT
e.g. $27^{\frac{1}{3}}$ is the same as $\sqrt[3]{27}$ which is just 3.

The Acid Test:

LEARN the 2 statements in the shaded boxes, the best method for finding roots and what fractional powers mean. Then turn the page and write it all down.

1) Use your calculator to find a) $56^{½}$ b) $450^{\frac{1}{3}}$ c) $\sqrt{200}$ d) $\sqrt[3]{8000}$.
    For a) and c), what are the other values that your calculator didn't give?

2) a) If $g^2 = 36$, find g.   b) If $b^3 = 64$, find b.   c) If $4 \times r^2 = 36$, find r.

Substituting Values into Formulas

This topic is a lot easier than you think!

$$C = \frac{5}{9}(F - 32)$$

Generally speaking, algebra is a pretty grim subject, but you should realise that some bits of it are VERY easy, and this is definitely the easiest bit of all, so whatever you do, don't pass up on these easy Exam marks.

Method

If you don't follow this STRICT METHOD you'll just keep getting them wrong — it's as simple as that.

1) **Write out the Formula**   e.g $F = \frac{9}{5}C + 32$

2) **Write it again**, directly underneath, but **substituting numbers for letters** on the **RHS**. $F = \frac{9}{5}15 + 32$
(Right Hand Side)

3) Work it out **IN STAGES**. $F = 27 + 32$
Use **BODMAS** to work things out **IN THE RIGHT ORDER**. $= 59$
WRITE DOWN values for each bit as you go along. $F = 59°$

4) **DO NOT** attempt to do it all in one go on your calculator.
That ridiculous method fails at least 50% of the time!

BODMAS

Brackets, Other, Division, Multiplication, Addition, Subtraction

BODMAS tells you the ORDER in which these operations should be done: Work out brackets first, then Other things like squaring, then multiply / divide groups of numbers before adding or subtracting them. This set of rules works really well for simple cases, so remember the word: BODMAS   (See P.18)

Example

A mysterious quantity T, is given by: $T = (P - 7)^2 + 4R/Q$
Find the value of T when P = 4, Q = -2 and R = 3

ANSWER:

1) Write down the formula: $T = (P - 7)^2 + 4R/Q$
2) Put the numbers in: $T = (4 - 7)^2 + 4\times3/-2$
3) Then work it out in stages : $= (-3)^2 + 12/-2$
$= 9 + -6$
$= 9 - 6 \; = \; 3$

Note BODMAS in operation:

Brackets worked out first, then squared. Multiplications and divisions done before finally adding and subtracting.

The Acid Test:

LEARN the 4 Steps of the Substitution Method and the full meaning of BODMAS. Then turn over.....

… and write it all down from memory.   1) Practise the above example until you can do it easily without help.   2) If $C = \frac{5}{9}(F - 32)$, find the value of C when F = 77.

Basic Algebra

1) Terms

Before you can do anything else, you **MUST** understand what a **TERM** is:

1) **A TERM IS A COLLECTION OF NUMBERS, LETTERS AND BRACKETS, ALL MULTIPLIED/DIVIDED TOGETHER.**

2) **TERMS are SEPARATED BY + AND − SIGNS**   e.g. $4x^2 - 3py - 5 + 3p$

3) **TERMS** always have a + or − **ATTACHED TO THE FRONT OF THEM**

4) e.g. $4xy + 5x^2 - 2y + 6y^2 + 4$

Invisible + sign   "xy" term   "x²" term   "y" term   "y²" term   "number" term

2) Simplifying "Collecting Like Terms"

EXAMPLE: "Simplify $2x - 4 + 5x + 6$"

$2x \quad -4 \quad +5x \quad +6 \quad = \quad +2x \quad +5x \quad -4 \quad +6$

x-terms   number terms

$= \quad 7x \quad +2 \quad = \quad 7X + 2$

1) <u>Put bubbles round each term</u>, — be sure you *capture the +/− sign* IN FRONT *of each*.

2) Then you can *move the bubbles into the best order* so that **LIKE TERMS** *are together*.

3) "**LIKE TERMS**" have exactly the same combination of letters, e.g. "x-terms" or "xy-terms".

4) <u>Combine LIKE TERMS</u> using the <u>NUMBER LINE</u> (not the other rule for negative numbers).

3) Multiplying out Brackets

1) The thing <u>OUTSIDE</u> the brackets <u>multiplies each separate term INSIDE the brackets</u>.

2) When letters are <u>multiplied together</u>, they are just <u>written next to each other</u>, pq.

3) Remember, $R \times R = R^2$, and TY^2 means $T \times Y \times Y$, whilst $(TY)^2$ means $T \times T \times Y \times Y$.

4) Remember <u>a minus outside the bracket REVERSES ALL THE SIGNS when you multiply</u>.

Examples:

1) $3(2x + 5) = 6x + 15$ 2) $4p(3r - 2t) = 12pr - 8pt$

3) $-4(3p^2 - 7q^3) = -12p^2 + 28q^3$ (note both signs have been *reversed* — Rule 4)

4) Cancelling Algebraic Fractions

This is <u>exactly the same</u> as cancelling ordinary fractions.

1) Look for any bits that look the same (common factors) that are on *both the top and the bottom*.

2) Cancel them.

Examples:

1) Simplify: $\dfrac{2x(x-1)}{(x-1)}$ Answer: $\dfrac{2x(x-1)}{(x-1)} = 2x$

Cross out each term that's on both the top and the bottom.

2) Simplify: $\dfrac{6x(x+4)(x-1)}{3x(x-1)}$ Answer: $\dfrac{\overset{2}{6x}(x+4)(x-1)}{3x(x-1)} = 2(x+4)$

Basic Algebra

5) *Expanding* and *Simplifying*

a) With DOUBLE BRACKETS
— you get <u>4 terms</u> after multiplying them out and usually <u>2 of them combine</u> to leave <u>3 terms</u>, like this:

$$(2P - 4)(3P + 1) = (2P \times 3P) + (2P \times 1) + (-4 \times 3P) + (-4 \times 1)$$
$$= 6P^2 + 2P - 12P - 4$$
$$= \underline{6P^2 - 10P - 4} \qquad \text{(these 2 combine together)}$$

b) SQUARED BRACKETS:
e.g. $(3d + 5)^2$ ALWAYS write these out as two brackets: $(3d + 5)(3d + 5)$ and work them out CAREFULLY like this:

$$(3d + 5)(3d + 5) = 9d^2 + 15d + 15d + 25 = \underline{9d^2 + 30d + 25}$$

YOU SHOULD ALWAYS GET <u>FOUR</u> TERMS from squared brackets, and inevitably *two of these* will combine together to leave <u>THREE TERMS IN THE END</u>, as shown above.

(The usual <u>WRONG ANSWER</u>, by the way, is $(3d + 5)^2 = 9d^2 + 25$ — eeek!)

6) *Factorising*   — putting brackets <u>in</u>

This is the *exact reverse* of multiplying-out brackets. Here's the method to follow:

> 1) Take out the <u>biggest NUMBER</u> that goes into all the terms.
> 2) <u>Take each letter in turn</u> and take out the <u>highest power</u> (e.g. x, x^2 etc) that will go into EVERY term.
> 3) Open the brackets and <u>fill in all the bits needed to reproduce each term.</u>

EXAMPLE: Factorise $15x^4y + 20x^2y^3z - 35x^3yz^2$

Answer: $5x^2y(3x^2 + 4y^2z - 7xz^2)$

Biggest number that'll divide into 15, 20 and 35

Highest powers of X and Y that will go into <u>all three terms</u>

Z wasn't in ALL terms so it can't come out as a <u>common factor</u>

REMEMBER:

> 1) The bits *taken out* and put at the front are the *COMMON FACTORS*.
> 2) The bits *inside the brackets* are *what's needed to get back to the original terms* if you were to multiply the brackets out again.

The Acid Test:
LEARN the <u>important details</u> for <u>each of the 6 sections</u> on these 2 pages, then <u>turn over</u> and <u>write it all down.</u>

Then apply the methods to these:
1) Simplify: a) $5x + 3y - 4 - 2y - x$ b) $4k + 3y^2 - 6k + y^2 + 2$ c) $\dfrac{2(x+1)^2}{(x+1)}$
2) Expand: a) $2pq(3p - 4q^2)$ b) $(2g+5)(4g-2)$ c) $(4 - 3h)^2$
3) Factorise: a) $14x^2y^3 + 21xy^2 - 35x^3y^4$ b) $12h^2j^3 + 6h^4j^2k - 36h^3jk$

Quadratics

Factorising a Quadratic

"Factorising a quadratic" means *"putting it into 2 brackets"* — you'll need to remember that. There are several different methods for doing this, so stick with the one you're happiest with. If you have no preference then learn this one. The standard format for any quadratic equations is:

$$x^2 + bx + c = 0$$

(e.g. $x^2 + 3x + 2 = 0$)

Factorising Method

1) **ALWAYS** rearrange into the **STANDARD FORMAT**: $x^2 + bx + c = 0$.

2) Write down the **TWO BRACKETS** with the x's in: $(x\ \ \ )(x\ \ \ ) = 0$.

3) Then <u>find 2 numbers</u> that **MULTIPLY to give "c"** (the end number) but also **ADD/SUBTRACT to give "b"** (the coefficient of x).

4) Put them in and check that the +/− signs work out properly.

Example

"Solve $x^2 - x = 12$ by factorising."

ANSWER: 1) <u>First rearrange it</u> (into the standard format): $\quad x^2 - x - 12 = 0$

2) The initial brackets are (as ever): $\quad (x\ \ \ )(x\ \ \ ) = 0$

3) We now want to look at <u>all pairs of numbers</u> that <u>multiply to give "c"</u> (=12), but which also <u>add or subtract to give the value of b</u>: (-1)

1×12	*Add/subtract to give:*	13 or 11
2×6	*Add/subtract to give:*	8 or 4 this is what we're after
3×4	*Add/subtract to give:*	7 or ①← (1 is "b", within ±)

4) So 3 and 4 will give b = ±1, so put them in: $\quad (x\ \ \ 3)(x\ \ \ 4) = 0$

5) <u>Now fill in the +/− signs</u> so that the 3 and 4 add/subtract to give -1 (=b), Clearly it must be +3 and − 4 so we'll have: $\quad (x + 3)(x - 4) = 0$

6) <u>As an ESSENTIAL check, EXPAND the brackets</u> out again to make sure they give the original equation:
$(x + 3)(x - 4) = x^2 + 3x - 4x - 12 = x^2 - x - 12$

<u>We're not finished yet mind</u>, because $(x + 3)(x - 4) = 0$ is only the <u>factorised form of the equation</u> — we have yet to give the actual **SOLUTIONS**. This is very easy:

7) **THE SOLUTIONS** are simply <u>the two numbers in the brackets</u>, but with **OPPOSITE +/− SIGNS**: i.e. $\quad x = -3 \text{ or } +4$

*Make sure you remember that last step. <u>It's the difference</u> between **SOLVING THE EQUATION** and merely <u>factorising it</u>.*

The Acid Test:

LEARN the <u>7 steps</u> for solving quadratics by <u>factorising</u>.

1) Solve these <u>by the factor method</u>:   a) $x^2 + 5x + 6 = 0$ b) $x^2 + 8x + 12 = 0$
                                                  c) $x^2 + 5x - 24 = 0$ d) $x^2 - 6x + 9 = 16$

Trial and Improvement

In principle, this is an easy way to find approximate answers to quite complicated equations, especially "cubics" (ones with x^3 in). BUT... you have to make an effort to LEARN THE FINER DETAILS of this method, otherwise you'll never get the hang of it.

Method

1) SUBSTITUTE TWO INITIAL VALUES into the equation that give OPPOSITE CASES. These are usually suggested in the question. If not, you'll have to think of your own. Opposite cases means one answer too big, one too small, or one +ve, one −ve, for example. If they don't give opposite cases try again.

2) Now CHOOSE YOUR NEXT VALUE IN BETWEEN THE PREVIOUS TWO, and SUBSTITUTE it into the equation.
   Continue this process, always choosing a new value between the two closest opposite cases, (and preferably nearer to the one which is closest to the answer you want).

3) AFTER ONLY 3 OR 4 STEPS you should have 2 numbers which are to the right degree of accuracy but DIFFER BY 1 IN THE LAST DIGIT.
   For example if you had to get your answer to 2 DP then you'd eventually end up with say 5.43 and 5.44, with these giving OPPOSITE results of course.

4) At this point you ALWAYS take the Exact Middle Value to decide which is the answer you want.   e.g. for 5.43 and 5.44, you'd try 5.435 to see if the real answer was between 5.43 and 5.435 or between 5.435 and 5.44 (see below).

Example

"The equation $X^3 + X = 40$ has a solution between 3 and 3.5. Find this solution to 1 DP"

Try X = 3	$3^3 + 3 = 30$	(Too small)	← (2 opposite cases)
Try X = 3.5	$3.5^3 + 3.5 = 46.375$	(Too big)	

40 is what we want and it's closer to 46.375 than it is to 30 so we'll choose our next value for X closer to 3.5 than 3

Try X = 3.3	$3.3^3 + 3.3 = 39.237$	(Too small)

Good, this is very close, but we need to see if 3.4 is still too big or too small:

Try X = 3.4	$3.4^3 + 3.4 = 42.704$	(Too big)

Good, now we know that the answer must be between 3.3 and 3.4. To find out which one it's nearest to, we have to try the EXACT MIDDLE VALUE: 3.35

Try X = 3.35	$3.35^3 + 3.35 = 40.945$ (Too big)

This tells us with certainty that the solution must be between 3.3 (too small) and 3.35 (too big), and so to 1 DP it must round down to 3.3.   ANSWER = 3.3

The Acid Test:
"LEARN and TURN" — if you don't actually commit it to memory, then you've wasted your time even reading it.

To succeed with this method you must LEARN the 4 steps above. Do it now, and practise until you can write them down without having to look back at them.
It's not as difficult as you think.

   1) The equation $X^3 - 2X = 1$ has a solution between 1 and 2. Find it to 1 DP.

Solving Equations The Easy Way

The "proper" way to solve equations is shown on P.89. In practise the "proper way" can be pretty difficult so there's a lot to be said for the much easier methods shown below.

The drawback with these is that you can't always use them on very complicated equations. In most Exam questions though, they do just fine.

1) THE "COMMON SENSE" APPROACH

The trick here is to realise that the unknown quantity "X" is after all just a number and the "equation" is just a cryptic clue to help you find it

Example: *"Solve this equation: 3X + 4 = 46"*

(i.e. find what number X is)

Answer: *This is what you should say to yourself:*

> "<u>Something + 4 = 46</u>"   hmm, so that "something" must be 42.
>
> So that means 3X = 42, which means "3 times something = 42"
>
> So it must be 42 ÷ 3 which is 14   so <u>X = 14</u> "

In other words don't think of it as algebra, but as "<u>Find the mystery number</u>".

2) THE TRIAL AND ERROR METHOD

This is a perfectly good method, and although it won't work every time, it usually does, especially if the answer is a *whole number*.

The *big secret of trial and error* methods is to <u>find TWO OPPOSITE CASES</u> and keep taking values <u>IN BETWEEN</u> them.
  In other words, find a number that makes the <u>RHS bigger</u>, and then one that makes the <u>LHS bigger</u>, and then try values *in between them*. (See P.87)

Example: *"Solve for X: 3X + 5 = 21 – 5X"*

(i.e. find the number X)

Answer:

> Try X=1:   3+5 = 21 – 5,   8 = 16 — no good, <u>RHS too big</u>
>
> Try X=3:   9 + 5 = 21 – 15,   14 = 6 — no good, <u>now LHS too big</u>

<u>SO TRY IN BETWEEN</u>: X = 2:   6 + 5 = 21 – 10, 11 = 11,   YES, so <u>X = 2</u>.

The Acid Test:
LEARN these two methods until you can <u>turn the page and write them down</u> with an example for each.

1) Solve: 4x – 12 = 20   2) Solve: 3x + 5 = 5x – 9

Solving Equations

Solving Equations means finding the value of x from something like: $3x + 5 = 4 - 5x$.
Now, not a lot of people know this, but *exactly the same method applies* to both
solving equations and *rearranging formulas*, as illustrated on these two pages.

1)   EXACTLY THE SAME METHOD APPLIES TO BOTH FORMULAS AND EQUATIONS.
2)   THE SAME SEQUENCE OF STEPS APPLIES EVERY TIME.

To illustrate the sequence of steps we'll use this equation: $\sqrt{2 - \dfrac{x+4}{2x+5}} = 3$

The *Six Steps* Applied to *Equations*

1) Get rid of any square root signs by <u>squaring both sides</u>: $2 - \dfrac{x+4}{2x+5} = 9$

2) Get everything off the bottom by
   <u>cross-multiplying up to **EVERY OTHER TERM**</u>:

$$2 - \frac{x+4}{2x+5} = 9 \quad \Rightarrow \quad 2(2x+5) - (x+4) = 9(2x+5)$$

3) Multiply out any brackets: $4x + 10 - x - 4 = 18x + 45$

4) Collect all <u>subject terms</u> on one side of the "=" and all <u>non-subject terms</u>
   on the other side, <u>remembering to reverse the +/– sign of any term that</u>
   <u>crosses the "="</u> :

+18x moves across the "=" and becomes -18x
+10 moves across the "=" and becomes -10
-4 moves across the "=" and becomes +4

$$4x - x - 18x = 45 - 10 + 4$$

5) <u>Combine together like terms</u> on each side of the equation, and reduce it to
   the form "<u>Ax = B</u>", where A and B are just numbers (or bunches of letters
   in the case of formulas):

$$-15x = 39$$
("Ax = B":   A = -15,   B = 39,   x is the subject)

6) Finally <u>slide the A underneath the B</u> to give "X = $\frac{B}{A}$",
   divide, and that's your answer:

$$x = \frac{39}{-15} = -2.6 \qquad \text{So } \underline{x = -2.6}$$

The Acid Test:
LEARN the <u>6 STEPS</u> for <u>solving equations</u> and
<u>rearranging formulas</u>. Turn over and write them down.

1) Solve the following equations: a) $5(x + 2) = 8 + 4(5 - x)$ b) $\dfrac{4}{x+3} = \dfrac{6}{4-x}$

Rearranging Formulas

Rearranging Formulas means making one letter the subject, e.g. getting "y= " from something like $2x + z = 3(y + 2p)$. Generally speaking "solving equations" is easier, but don't forget:

1) EXACTLY THE SAME METHOD APPLIES TO BOTH FORMULAS AND EQUATIONS.
2) THE SAME SEQUENCE OF STEPS APPLIES EVERY TIME.

We'll illustrate this by making "y" the subject of this formula: $M = \sqrt{2K - \dfrac{K^2}{2y + 1}}$

The _Six Steps_ Applied to _Formulas_

1) Get rid of any square root signs by <u>squaring both sides</u>: $M^2 = 2K - \dfrac{K^2}{2y + 1}$

2) Get everything off the bottom by <u>cross-multiplying up to</u> **EVERY OTHER TERM**:

$$M^2 = 2K - \dfrac{K^2}{2y + 1} \quad \Rightarrow \quad M^2(2y + 1) = 2K(2y + 1) - K^2$$

3) Multiply out any brackets: $2yM^2 + M^2 = 4Ky + 2K - K^2$

4) Collect all <u>subject terms</u> on one side of the "="
and all <u>non-subject terms</u> on the other side,
<u>remembering to reverse the +/− sign of any term that crosses the "=":</u>

+4Ky moves across the "=" and becomes −4Ky
+M^2 moves across the "=" and becomes −M^2

$$2yM^2 - 4Ky = -M^2 + 2K - K^2$$

5) <u>Combine together like terms</u> on each side of the equation, and reduce it to
the form "<u>Ax = B</u>", where A and B are just bunches of letters which DON'T
include the subject (y). Note that the LHS has to be **FACTORISED**:

$$(2M^2 - 4K)y = 2K - K^2 - M^2$$

("Ax = B" i.e. $A = (2M^2 - 4K)$, $B = 2K - K^2 - M^2$, y is the subject)

6) Finally <u>slide the A underneath the B</u> to give "X = $^B\!/_A$",
(cancel if possible) and that's your answer: So $y = \dfrac{2K - K^2 - M^2}{(2M^2 - 4K)}$

And One _Extra Thing..._

If you find yourself having to solve for a
<u>squared coefficient</u> then treat it just like
normal (i.e. put x^2 = a random variable,
say 'P') then at the end, just take the
<u>square root</u> of the other side — simple!
Try and follow this example through:

Solve for x:

$$y = 3K + \frac{2x^2 - 3L}{2}$$

$$\Rightarrow y = 3K + \frac{2P - 3L}{2}$$

$$\Rightarrow P = \frac{2(y - 3K) + 3L}{2} = x^2 \Rightarrow x = \sqrt{\frac{2(y - 3K) + 3L}{2}}$$

I've missed out a load of steps here, but you should be able to work out what I did by looking through the stuff above.

The Acid Test:

LEARN the <u>6 STEPS</u> for <u>solving equations</u> and
<u>rearranging formulas</u>. Turn over and write them down.

1) Rearrange " $F = \frac{9}{5}C + 32$ " from "F= ", to "C= " and then back the other way.
2) Make p the subject of these: a) $\dfrac{p}{p + y} = 4$ b) $\dfrac{1}{p} = \dfrac{1}{q} + \dfrac{1}{r}$ c) $y = x^2p^2 - 3p^2$

Compound Growth and Decay

This can also be called "Exponential" Growth or Decay. But you don't want to know that.

You want to know this:

The Formula

This topic is simple if you LEARN THIS FORMULA. If you don't, it's pretty well impossible:

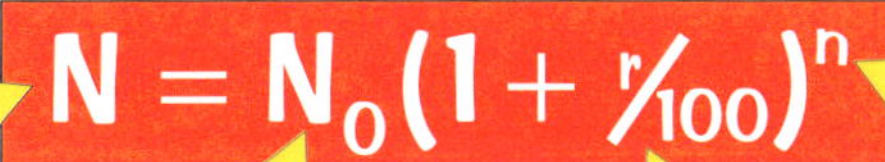

$$N = N_0 \left(1 + \tfrac{r}{100}\right)^n$$

Existing amount at this time

Initial amount

Percentage change per day/hour/year

Number of days/hrs/yrs

Percentage Increase and Decrease

The $(1 + r/100)$ bit might look a bit confusing in the formula but in practice it's really easy:

E.g   5% increase will be 1.05   5% decrease will be 0.95 $(= 1 - 0.05)$
      26% increase will be 1.26   26% decrease will be 0.74 $(= 1 - 0.26)$

3 Examples to show you how EASY it is:

1) *"A man invests £1000 in a savings account which pays 8% per annum. How much will there be after 6 years?"*

ANSWER: Usual formula (as above):   Amount $= 1000 \times (1.08)^6 =$ £1586.87

Initial amount   8% increase   6 years

2) *"The activity of a radio-isotope falls by 12% every hour. If the initial activity is 800 counts per minute, what will it be after 7 hours?"*

ANSWER: Same old formula:

$$\text{Activity} = \text{Initial value}(1 - 12/100)^n$$

$$\text{Activity} = 800(1 - 0.12)^7 = 800 \times (0.88)^7 = \underline{327 \text{ cpm}}$$

3) *"In a sample of bacteria, there are initially 500 cells and they increase in number by 15% each day. Find the formula relating the number of cells, n, and the number of days, d."*

ANSWER: Well stone me, it's the same old easy-peasy compound increase formula again:

$$n = n_0(1 + 0.15)^d \quad \text{or finished off:} \quad \underline{n = 500 \times (1.15)^d}$$

The Acid Test:

LEARN THE FORMULA. Also learn the 3 Examples.
Then turn over and write it all down.

1) A colony of stick insects increases by 4% per week. Initially there are 30. How many will there be after 12 weeks?

2) The speed of a tennis ball rolled along a smooth floor falls by 16% every second. If the initial speed was 5m/s find the speed after 20 seconds. How long will it take to stop?

Simultaneous Equations

These are OK as long as you learn these **SIX STEPS** in every meticulous detail.

There are Six Steps here too:

We'll use these two equations for this example: $2x = 6 - 4y$ and $-3 - 3y = 4x$

1) REARRANGE BOTH EQUATIONS INTO THE FORM: $ax + by = c$
where a,b,c are numbers,   (which can be negative).
Also **LABEL THE TWO EQUATIONS** —① and —②

$$2x + 4y = 6 \qquad —①$$
$$-4x - 3y = 3 \qquad —②$$

2) You need to **MATCH UP THE NUMBERS IN FRONT** (the "coefficients")
of either the x's or y's in **BOTH EQUATIONS**.
To do this you may need to **MULTIPLY** one or both equations by a
suitable number. You should then **RELABEL** them: —③ and —④

$$①×2: \quad 4x + 8y = 12 \qquad —③$$
$$-4x - 3y = 3 \qquad —④$$

(This gives us +4x in equation —③ to match the –4x in equation —②, now called —④)

3) ADD OR SUBTRACT THE TWO EQUATIONS ...
...to eliminate the terms with the same coefficient.
If the coefficients are the **SAME** (both +ve or both –ve) then **SUBTRACT**.
If the coefficients are **OPPOSITE** (one +ve and one –ve) then **ADD**.

$$③ + ④ \qquad 0x + 5y = 15$$

(In this case we have +4x and –4x so we ADD)

4) SOLVE THE RESULTING EQUATION to find whichever letter is left in it.

$$5y = 15 \Rightarrow y = 3$$

5) SUB THIS BACK into equation ① and solve it to find the other quantity.

Sub in ①: $2x + 4×3 = 6 \Rightarrow 2x + 12 = 6 \Rightarrow 2x = -6 \Rightarrow x = -3$

6) Then **SUBSTITUTE BOTH THESE VALUES INTO EQUATION** ② to make
sure it works out properly. If it doesn't then you've done
something wrong and you'll have to do it all again!

Sub x and y in ②: $-4×-3 - 3×3 = 12 - 9 = 3$

which is right, so it's worked.

So the solutions are: $x = -3$, $y = 3$

The Acid Test: LEARN the _6 Steps_ for solving _Simultaneous Equations_.

Remember, you only know them when you can write them all out from memory, so
turn over the page and try it. Then apply the 6 steps to find F and G given that
$$2F - 10 = 4G \quad \text{and} \quad 3G = 4F - 15$$

Simultaneous Equations With Graphs

On the opposite page is the *tricky algebra method* for solving simultaneous equations.
On this page is the *nice easy graph method* for solving them.
You could be asked to do *either* method in the Exam so make sure you *learn them both*.

Solving Simultaneous Equations Using Graphs

This is a very easy way to find the x- and y- solutions to two simultaneous equations.
Here's the simple rule:

> **THE SOLUTION** OF TWO **SIMULTANEOUS EQUATIONS** IS SIMPLY THE **X** AND **Y** VALUES **WHERE THEIR GRAPHS CROSS**

Three Step Method

1) Do a **"TABLE OF 3 VALUES"** for both equations.

2) Draw the Two **GRAPHS**.

3) Find the X- and Y-values **WHERE THEY CROSS**.

Easy Peasy.

Example

"Draw the graphs for "Y = 2X + 3" and "Y = 6 – 4X" and then use your graphs to solve them."

1) <u>TABLE OF 3 VALUES</u> (see P.73)
   for both equations:

X	0	2	-2
Y	3	7	-1

X	0	2	3
Y	6	-2	-6

2) <u>DRAW THE GRAPHS</u>:

3) <u>WHERE THEY CROSS</u>,
   <u>x = ½, y = 4</u>.
   And that's the answer!

$x = ½$ and $y = 4$

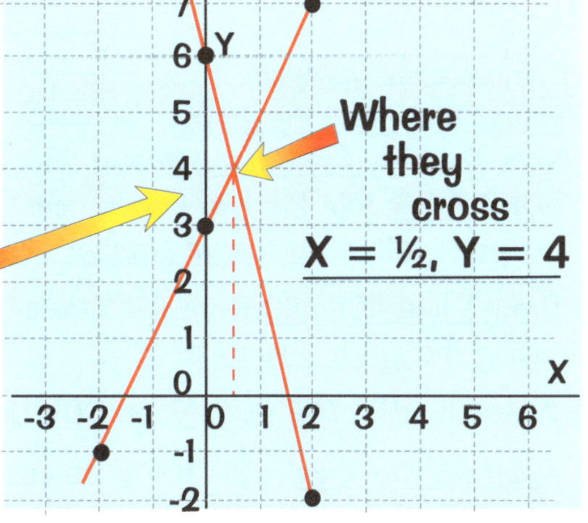

The Acid Test:

LEARN the Simple Rule and the <u>3 step method</u> for solving simultaneous equations using **GRAPHS**.

1) Cover the page and write down the Simple Rule and the 3 step method.
2) Use graphs to find the solutions to these pairs of equations:
   a) Y = 4x - 4 and Y = 6 - X   b) Y = 2x   and   Y = 6 - 2x

Solving Equations Using Graphs

In your Exam you might get a question asking you to solve an equation using a graph.
These aren't too bad, so long as you know how to tackle them.   Learn all this stuff:

The _Answers_ are where The _Y-value_ Hits the _Graph_

The typical question will have a _nasty-looking equation_ a
bit like this: $y = x^3 + 2x^2 + 4$ and a _graph_ already drawn
(or mostly done for you anyway).
Then they'll ask you something like this:
"From the graph, find the value of x which makes y = 8."
This is how you do it:

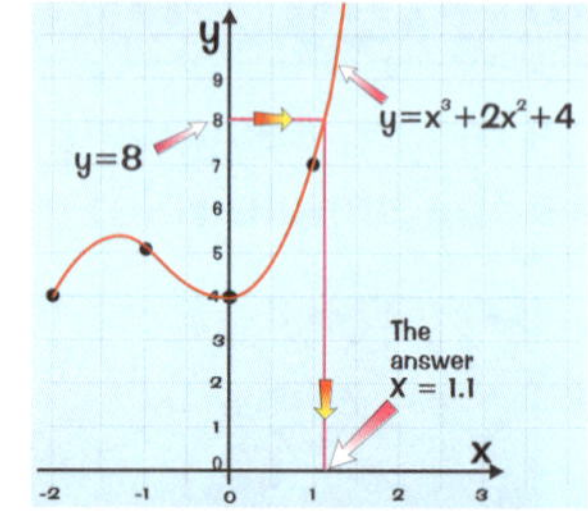

The Easy Peasy _Four-Step Method_

1) Draw (or finish off) the _GRAPH_ from a _TABLE OF VALUES_. (See P.72)

2) Draw a line _ACROSS_ from the _Y-AXIS_ at the value _GIVEN_.

3) Where it _crosses the graph_, draw a line (or lines)
                    DOWN to the _X-AXIS_.

4) _READ OFF_ the _X-VALUES_ — they're the _ANSWERS_.

Example

_"Complete the table of values shown
for the equation $y = 25x - 5x^2$._
Plot the points and draw the graph.
Use the graph to find the values of x when y = 25."

X	0	1	2	3	4	5
Y		20				0

Answer

1) Complete the _table of
values_ and _draw the graph_.
Note the _nice smooth curve_ and the _curved peak_.
DON'T EVER join the two points near
the peak with a _ridiculous straight line_.

X	0	1	2	3	4	5
Y	0	20	30	30	20	0

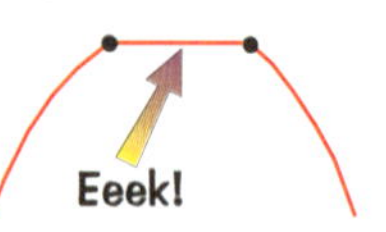

2) _Draw a line ACROSS_ from the Y-axis
(using the _given y-value_ of _25_).

3) Where it _HITS THE CURVE_, go _DOWN_ to the _X-axis_.

4) _Read off the X-values_.   It's as easy as that.

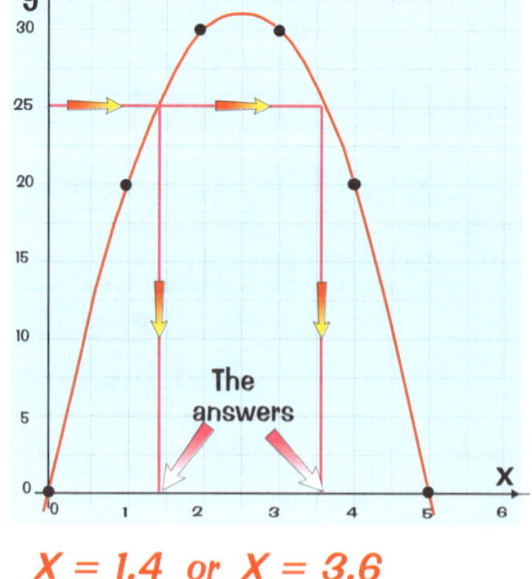

So from the graph we get the _ANSWERS_ to be   _X = 1.4 or X = 3.6_

The Acid Test:

LEARN the first big _coloured heading_, the _Four
Step Method_ and all the _details_ on _both graphs_.

Cover the page and write down everything you've learnt.

1) Using the above graph for $y = 25x - 5x^2$, find the values of x which give y = 15.
2) Do a table of values and a graph for $y = 2x^3 - 3x$. Find the value of x when y = 12.

Travel Graphs

A nice easy page for you, to help relieve the stress of extremely grisly Section Six.

Travel Graphs — *Always the same and always Easy*

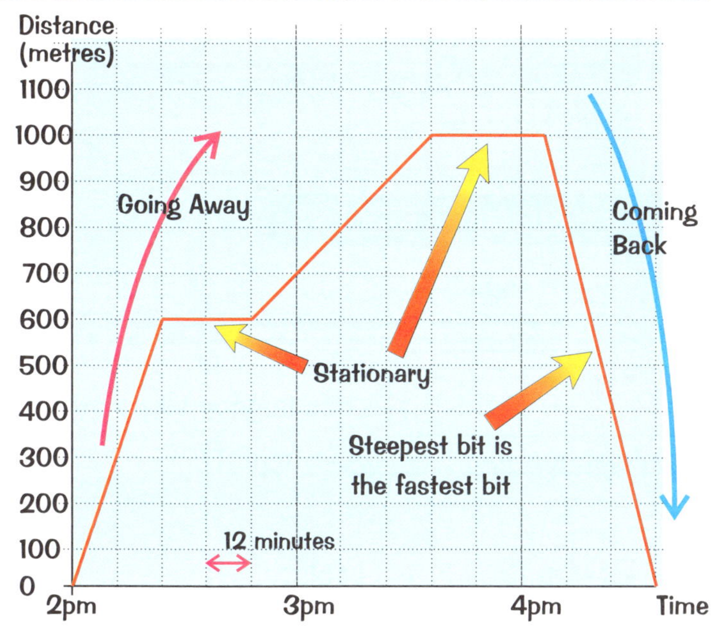

1) Make sure you know *all these details* about travel graphs.

2) Also, always make sure you know exactly *how much time* each interval on the Time axis actually is. On this graph there are *5 divisions* for each *hour*, so each one must be *12 minutes* (60÷5).

THE SIX KEY POINTS ABOUT TRAVEL GRAPHS

1) A TRAVEL GRAPH is always DISTANCE ($\uparrow$) against TIME ($\rightarrow$).

2) For any section, SLOPE (gradient) = SPEED, but watch out for the UNITS.

3) FLAT SECTIONS are where it's STOPPED.

4) The STEEPER the graph the FASTER it's going.

5) UPHILL SECTIONS mean it's TRAVELLING AWAY from its starting point.

6) DOWNHILL SECTIONS means it's COMING BACK towards its starting point.

A Typical Tricky Question:

"What's the speed of the return section on the graph shown above?"

ANSWER Speed = gradient

= 1000m/30mins = 33.33 m/min (metres per minute)

or   1km ÷ ½hr = 2 km/h (kilometres per hour)

or   1000m ÷ 1800s = 0.56 m/s (metres per second)

(See P.54 on Units)

Note that the answer (and its units) depends very much on what units you use to work it out.

The Acid Test:

LEARN all the details on the graph above and then the Six Key Points for Travel Graphs.

Now cover the page and write down everything you've learnt.

1) For the travel graph above, work out the speed of the middle section, in km/h.

2) Also, describe the whole sequence of events between 2pm and 4:36pm.

Inequalities

This is basically quite difficult, but it's still worth learning the easy bits in case they ask a very easy question on it, as well they might. Here are the easy bits:

The 4 Inequality Symbols:

> means "Greater than"   ≥ means "Greater than or equal to"
< means "Less than"   ≤ means "Less than or equal to"

REMEMBER, the one at the BIG end is BIGGEST

so   "X > 4"   and   "4 < X"   BOTH say: "X is greater than 4"

Algebra With Inequalities — this is generally a bit tricky

The thing to remember here is that inequalities are just like regular equations:

$$5X < X + 2$$
$$5X = X + 2$$

in the sense that all the normal rules of algebra (See P.84) apply...

...BUT WITH ONE BIG EXCEPTION:

Whenever you MULTIPLY OR DIVIDE BY A NEGATIVE NUMBER,
you must FLIP THE INEQUALITY SIGN.

Example: "Solve $5X < 6X + 2$"

ANS: First move the 6X over the "=" : $5X - 6X < 2$

combining the X-terms gives: $-X < 2$

To get rid of the "−" in front of X you need to divide both sides by -1 — but
remember that means the "<" has to be flipped as well, which gives:

$X > -2$ i.e. "X is greater than -2" is the answer

(The < has flipped around into a >, because we divided by a −ve number)

This answer, $X > -2$, can be displayed as a shaded region on a number line like this:

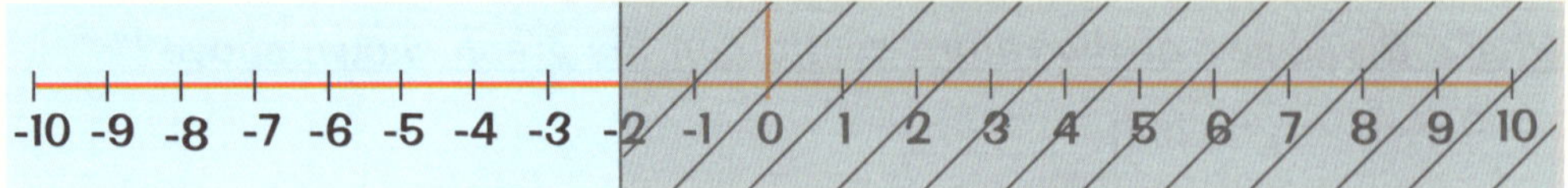

The main thing you should realise, is that MOST OF THE TIME you just treat the "<" or ">" as though it was an "=" and do all the usual algebra that you would for a regular equation.   The "Big Exception" doesn't actually come up very often at all.

The Acid Test:

LEARN: The 4 Inequality Signs, the similarity with EQUATIONS and the One Big Exception.

Now turn over and write down what you've learned.

1) Solve this inequality: $4X + 3 \leq 6X + 7$.

2) Find all the integer values of X which satisfy both $2X + 9 \geq 1$ and $4X < 6 + X$

Graphical Inequalities

This is easy so long as you remember the easy method for drawing graphs — i.e. a table of 3 values (see P.73).

The questions always involve <u>**SHADING A REGION ON A GRAPH**</u>, which is actually easy but it's always presented as some really horrid-looking algebra that puts most people right off before they even start.

The thing is, once you realise that the horrid-looking algebra just means something really simple then the whole thing becomes quite mind-numbingly simple.   (!)

Method

1) <u>CONVERT each INEQUALITY to an EQUATION</u>

by simply putting an "=" in place of the "<"

2) <u>DO A TABLE OF 3 VALUES FOR EACH EQUATION</u> (See P.73)

and then <u>draw the lines</u> on the graph.

3) <u>SHADE THE ENCLOSED REGION</u>

The lines you've drawn will always enclose the region that you're after — and they nearly always ask you to <u>shade it</u>.

Example

"Shade the region represented by : $y < x + 2$, $x + y < 5$ and $y > 0$ *"*

(See what I mean about the horrid-looking algebra)

<u>*ANSWER*</u>:

1) <u>CONVERT EACH INEQUALITY TO AN *EQUATION*</u>:

$y < x + 2$ becomes $y = x + 2$,
$x + y < 5$ becomes $x + y = 5$,
$y > 0$ becomes $y = 0$

2) <u>DO A TABLE OF 3 VALUES</u> for each equation, and draw the lines on a graph.
e.g. for $y = x + 2$:

X	0	2	4
Y	2	4	6

3) <u>SHADE THE ENCLOSED REGION</u>,
and Bob's your Uncle, it's done.

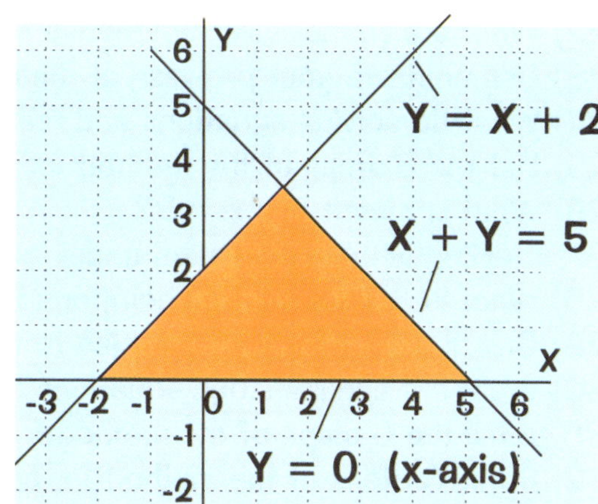

The Acid Test:

LEARN the <u>Three Steps</u> for doing <u>graphical inequalities</u>, then <u>turn over</u> and <u>write them down</u>.

1) Show on a graph the region enclosed by the following three conditions:
$X + Y < 6$, $Y > 0.5$, $Y < 2X - 2$

Revision Summary for Section Six

Section Six is the really nasty one — grisly grimsdike algebra. But grisly or not, you still have to learn it. Here's the last set of questions to test what you know. Don't forget, you've got to keep trying these *over and over again*. Making sure that you can do these questions is the *best revision* you can possibly do.

Just keep practising till you can glide through them all like a turtle or something.

Keep learning these basic facts until you know them

1) Give the 2 rules for negative numbers and say when each should be used.
2) List 5 combinations of letters that cause confusion in algebra, e.g. mn^2.
3) What is the general format of a number expressed in standard form?
4) What are the three rules for expressing a number in standard form?
5) Which calculator button is used for entering numbers in standard form?
6) What's the trick for writing down a number given in standard form on the calculator display?
7) What are the 3 rules for combining powers?
8) What are the other 4 rules for powers?
9) Explain what the square root of a number is. Explain what the cube root is.
10) What are the 4 steps of the method for substituting numbers into formulas?
11) What has BODMAS got to do with putting numbers into formulas?
12) In algebra, what is a *term*?
13) List the 4 steps for simplifying (collecting like terms).
14) List the 4 most important details relating to multiplying out brackets.

15) Cancel this equation down to its simplest form: $2(y+1) = \dfrac{3x\big((x-2)\times(12x^2+6)\big)}{9x(x-2)}$

16) What happens with double and squared brackets?
17) What are the 3 steps of the method for factorising?
18) What does factorising a Quadratic mean you have to do?
19) What check should you do to make sure you've done it right?
20) How exactly do you get solutions to a Quadratic once you've factorised it?
21) List the 4 steps for solving an equation by trial and improvement.
22) What are the 2 easier alternative methods for tackling simple equations?
23) Demonstrate your prowess at these methods by doing an example of each.
24) What do solving equations and rearranging formulas have in common?
25) List the 6 steps of the method for doing equations and formulas.
26) What is meant by $Ax = B$?
27) Starting with the equation under 'one extra thing' on P.90, solve it for x showing *every* step.
28) What is the formula for compound growth and decay?
29) Give three important examples to show how the method is always the same.
30) What are simultaneous equations? Give an example.
31) Detail the 6 steps of the method for solving simultaneous equations.
32) Detail 3 steps of the method for solving simultaneous equations using graphs.
33) Give the four step method for solving equations using graphs.
34) Give the six main details concerning travel graphs.
35) What happens with units when you work out the speed from a travel graph?
36) What are the four inequality symbols and what do they mean?
37) What are the rules of algebra for inequalities?
38) What is the big exception?
39) What are the 3 steps for doing graphical inequalities?
40) What is the meaning of *life*?   Why are we here?   And why do we have to do so much algebra?

<u>Answers</u>

<u>SECTION ONE</u>

P1   Special Number Sequences:
1) a) EVENS: 2,4,6,8,10,12,14,16,18,20,22,24,26,28,30   b) ODDS: 1,3,5,7,9,11,13,15,17,19,21,23,25,27,29
c) SQUARES: 1,4,9,16,25,36,49,64,81,100,121,144,169,196,225   d) CUBES:1,8,27,64,125,216,343,512,729,1000,1331,
1728,2197,2744,3375   e) POWERS OF 2: 2, 4, 8, 16, 32, 64, 128, 256, 512, 1024, 2048, 4096, 8192, 16384, 32768;
POWERS OF 10: 10, 100, 1000, 10 000, 100 000, 1 000 000, 10 000 000, 100 000 000, 1 000 000 000, 10 000 000
000, 100 000 000 000, 1 000 000 000 000, 10 000 000 000 000, 100 000 000 000 000, 1 000 000 000 000 000 hmm...
f) TRIANGLE Nos: 1,3,6,10,15,21,28,36,45,55,66,78,91,105,120   2) a) 56, 134, 156, 36, 64   b) 23, 45, 81, 25, 97,
125, 1   c) 81, 25, 36, 1, 64   d) 125, 1, 64   e) 64   f) 45, 36, 1

P2   Multiples, Factors, Prime Factors: 1)   7,14,21,28,35,42,49,56,63,70   and   9,18,27,36,45,54,63,72,81,90
2) 1,2,3,4,6,9,12,18,36 and 1,2,3,4,6,7,12,14,21,28,42,84   3)   990 = 2×3×3×5×11, 160 = 2×2×2×2×2×5

P3 LCM and HCF: 1) 8,16,24,32,40,48,56,64,72,80   and   9,18,27,36,45,54,63,72,81,90   LCM = 72
2) 1,2,4,7,8,14,28,56 and 1,2,4,8,13,26,52,104   HCF = 8   3) 63   4) 12

P4 Prime numbers: 1)   2,3,5,7,11,13,17,19,23,29,31,37,41,43,47
2) 97, 101, 103, 107, 109

P5   Fractions, Decimals, Percentages: See table to right:

Fraction	Decimal	Percentage
1/5	0.2	20%
7/20	0.35	35%
9/20	0.45	45%
3/25	0.12	12%
1/8	0.125	12.5%
77/100	0.77	77%

P6 Rounding Off: 1) 3.57   2) 0.05   3) 12.910   4) 3546.1
P7 Rounding Off: 1) a) 3.41   b) 1.05   c) 0.07   d) 3.60
2 a) 568 (Rule3)   b) 23400 (Rule 3) c) 0.0456 (Rules 1 and 3)
d) 0.909 (Rules 1, 2 and 3)   3) 16 feet 6 in. to 17 feet 6 in.

P9 Accuracy: 1) a) 35g   b) 134 mph   c) 850g   d) 76cm   2) a) Approx 600 miles × 150 miles = 90,000
sq. miles   b) Approx 7cm × 7cm × 12cm high = 590cm^3 3) a) Actual answer = 5.831. Accept anything from
5.5 to 5.9   b) 2.236. Accept 2.1 to 2.5   c) 7.810. Accept 7.5 to 7.99   d) 4.690. Accept 4.5 to 4.9

P10   Conversion Factors: 1) 2,300m   2) £34   3) 3.2cm
P11 Metric and Imperial Units: 1) 15.75 litres   2) 200 or 220 yards   3)115 cm   4) 62.9p per litre   5) 104 km/h
P13   Fractions: 1 a) 3/8   b) 2 $^7/_{10}$ c) 11/15   d) x = 13   e) y = 1   f) 0.375   g) 35/1000 = 7/200
2 a) 8/15   b) 8/3 = 2 $^2/_3$ c) 1/2   d) 3/7   e) 84   f) 84 $^{12}/_{19}$
P15   Percentages: 1) Type 2, profit=£2, 40% 2) Type 1, £42.30 3) Type 3, £20,500

P19 Calculator Buttons: 1) See P.17   2) [17] [X²] [=]   3) [(−)][5][×][(−)][8][=] or [5][⁺⁄₋][×][8][⁺⁄₋][=]
4) See P.17   5) Fractions   6) [6][xʸ][8][=]   7) [6][EXP][8][=]   8) DEG (or D)
P20 Number Patterns: 2 a) 162, 486   b) 18, 29   c) 23, 30   d) 16, 8
P21 Finding the nth Term: 1 a)   3n + 1   b)   5n − 2   c) ½n(n+1)   d) n^2 − 2n + 4

<u>SECTION TWO</u>

P23 Regular Polygons:1)–4) See P.23   5) Ext. angle = 72°, Int. angle = 108°   6) Ext. angle = 30°, Int. angle − 150°
P25   Symmetry:
   H : 2 lines of symmetry, Rot^{nl}. symmetry Order 2,   N: 0 lines of symmetry, Rot^{nl}. symmetry Order 2
   E : 1 line of symmetry, no Rotational symmetry,   Y: 1 line of symmetry, no Rot^{nl}. symmetry
   M : 1 line of symmetry, no Rotational symmetry,   O: 2 lines of symmetry, Rot^{nl}. symmetry Order 2
   S : 0 lines of symmetry, Rot^{nl}. symmetry Order 2,   T: 1 line of symmetry, no Rot^{nl}. symmetry

P28 Circle Questions: 1) Area = 154cm^2 Circumference = 44.0 cm   2) A = 113m^2 ,   C = 37.7m
P29 Perimeters and Areas: 2) Perimeter = 49.7cm   Area = 129.3cm^2
P30 Volume or Capacity: a) Trapezoidal Prism, V = 148.5 cm^3 b) Cylinder, V = 0.70 m^3
P31 Solids and Nets: 1) 128.8cm^2 2) 294cm^2 3) 174cm^2 4) 96cm^2
P32 Length, Area and Volume: 1) πr^2 = Area,   Lwh = Volume, πd = Perimeter,
½bh = Area,   2bh + 4lp = Area, $4r^2p + 3\pi d^3$ = Volume,   2πr(3L + 5T) = Area
P34 Transformations: A→B,   Rotation of 90° clockwise about the origin.
        B→C,   Reflection in the line Y = X   C→A, Reflection in the Y-axis.   A→D, Translation of $\binom{-9}{7}$

P35   Combinations of Transformations:
1)   C→D, Reflection in the Y-axis, and an enlargement SF 2, centre the origin
D→C, Reflection in the Y-axis, and an enlargement SF ½, centre the origin.
2) A'→B,   Rotation of 180° clockwise or anticlockwise about the point (0,3).
P37   Geometry: 1) z = 65°   2) 360° 3) 540°   4) 120° and 60° all round
P40   Three-Letter Angle Notation: 1) BAC = 35° a) DAC = 30° b) BAD = 65°
P41 Projections, Congruence and Similarity: 1) See P.41 and check it looks right.
2) a) i, ii and iv are similar.   b) i and ii are congruent.

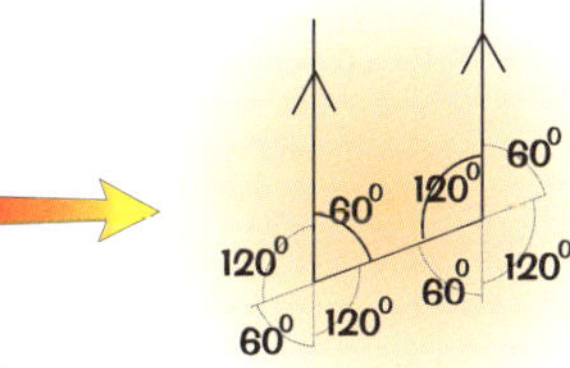

Answers

SECTION THREE

P43 Bearings: 1) 118° 2) 298°   P45 Pythagoras: 1) BC = 8m, 2) 5m, 12m, 13m is a right angled triangle because $a^2 + b^2 = h^2$ *works.*   P47 Trigonometry: 1) X = 26.5m 2) 23.6° 3) 32.60° (both)

P51 Ratio: 1a) 5:7 b) 2:3 c) 3:5 2) 17½ bowls of porridge 3) £3500 : £2100 : £2800

P53 Density and Speed: 1) See P.50 2) 16.5 g/cm³ 3) 603g 4) P.50 5) Time = 7½ hrs   Dist = 11.2km

P54 2 Hints When Using Formulas: 1) 1hr 37mins 51secs

SECTION FOUR

P56 Probability: 1) ¾   P57 Probability – Tree diagrams: 2) 8/15

P59 Graphs and Charts: 2) Guinea Pigs 68°, Rabbits 60°, Ducks 104°, Stick insects 48°

3) That they are not related to each other in any way. i.e. no correlation.

P60 Stem and Leaf Diagrams and Distribution: 1) Sample too small, motorways not representative of average motorist, only done at one time of day and in one place, not easy to get accurate age from registration letter. Better approach: A more detailed survey which deals with all the above problems — surveying people emerging from various Post Offices with new tax discs might be good. Stratified or quota sampling would be essential in choosing the Post Offices.

P61 Mean, Median, Mode and Range: First, do this: -14, -12, -5, -5, 0, 1, 3, 6, 7, 8, 10, 14, 18, 23, 25

Mean = 5.27, Median = 6,   Mode = -5, Range = 39

P62 Frequency Tables:

No. of Phones	0	1	2	3	4	5	6	TOTALS
Frequency	1	25	53	34	22	5	1	141
No. × Frequency	0	25	106	102	88	25	6	352

Mean = 2.5, Median = 2, Mode = 2, Range = 6

P63 Grouped Frequency Tables:

Length(cm)	15.5 —	16.5 —	17.5 —	18.5 — 19.5	TOTALS
Frequency	12	18	23	8	61
Mid-Interval Value	16	17	18	19	—
Freq × M I V	192	306	414	152	1064

Mean = 17.4, Modal Group = 17.5 — 18.5, Median ≈ 17.5

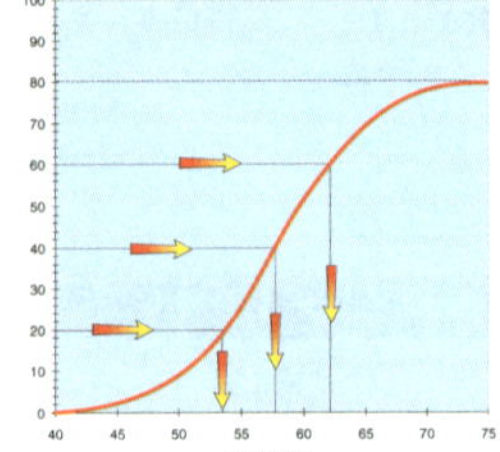

P64/65 Cumulative Frequency:

Weight (kg)	41 – 45	46 – 50	51 – 55	56 – 60	61 – 65	66 – 70	71 – 75
Frequency	2	7	17	25	19	8	2
Cum. Freq.	2	9	26	51	70	78	80

Median = 58 kg,
Lower Quartile = 53 kg
Upper Quartile = 62 kg
Inter-quartile range 9 kg

P66 TIME SERIES: 1) a) period = 4 months b) Find the average of the readings from months 1-4, then the average from months 2-5, then from months 3-6, etc. (& you could plot these on a graph to see the trend.)

SECTION FIVE

P72 Finding The Gradient of a Line: Gradient = -1½

P68 X and Y Coordinates: 1) A(4,5) B(6,0) C(5,-5) D(0,-3) E(-5,-2) F(-4,0) G(-3,3) H(0,5)

P69 Easy Graphs You Should Know: 1) a) y = x b) y = –x c) y = 2 d) y = ½x   2)

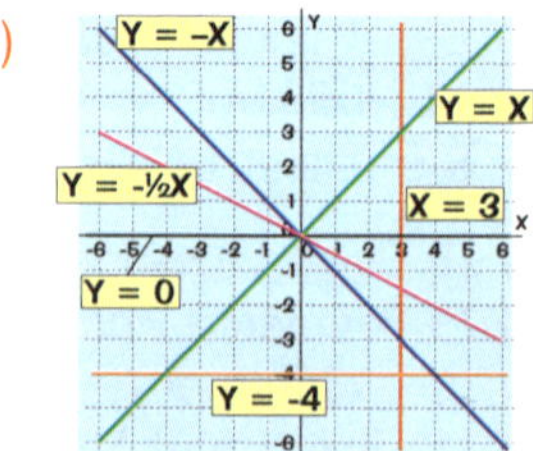

P73 Plotting S/L Graphs: P74 Plotting Straight Line Graphs:

1)

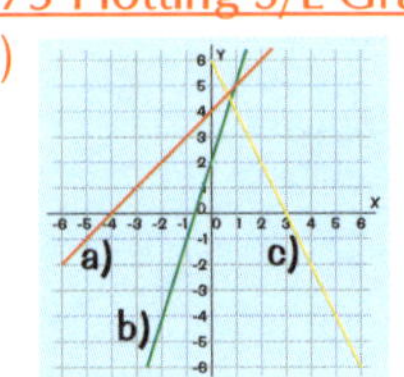

1)

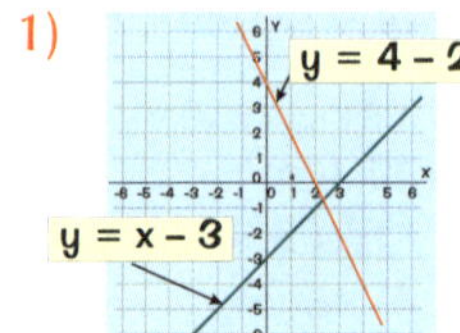

2)

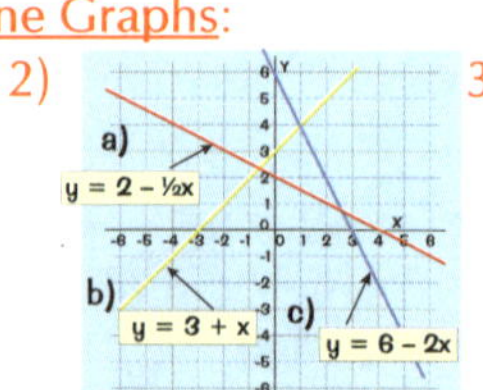

3) N = (10, 7.5)

P76 Typical Graph Questions:

1)	x	-2	-1	0	1	2	3	4	5	6
	y	15	8	3	0	-1	0	3	8	15

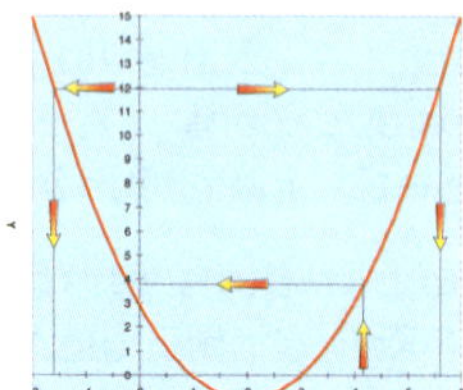

2) Y = 3.8, X = -1.6 and 5.6   3) Miles per Gallon, ie. fuel consumption

SECTION SIX

P78 Negative Numbers: 1a) +12 (Rule 1)   b) -6 (Rule1/Rule 2)   c) X (Rule 2, then Rule 1)   d) -3 (Rule 1)

2a) +18 (Rule 1)   b) -216 (Rule 1)   c) 2 (Rule 2)   d) -27 (Rule 1)   e) -336 (Rule 1 then Rule 2)

P80 Standard Form: 1) See P.79 2) 9.58×10^5 3) 1.8×10^{-4} 4) 4560 5) 2×10^{21} , 2,000,00.....(21 zeros!)

P81 Powers: 1) a) 3^8 b) 4 c) 8^{12} d) 1 e) 7^6 2) a) 5^{12} b) 36 or 6^2 c) 2^5 3) 6

Answers

P82 Square and Cube Roots: 1) a) 7.48 and -7.48 b) 7.66 c) 14.14 and -14.14 d) 20   2 a) g = 6 or -6 b) b = 4
c) r = 3 or -3   **P83 Substitution:** 2) 25° C   **P85 Basic Algebra:** 1)   a) 4x + y – 4   b) 4y^2 – 2k + 2   c) 2x + 2
2) a) 6p^{2}q – 8pq^3 b) 8g^2 + 16g – 10   c) 16 – 24h +9h^2 3) a) 7xy^2(2xy + 3 – 5x^{2}y^2)   b) 6h^{2}j(2j^2 + h^{2}jk – 6hk)

P86 Quadratics: 1) a) X = -2 or -3   b) x = -6 or -2   c) x = 3 or -8   d) x = 7 or -1

P87 Trial and Improvement: 1) X = 1.6   **P88 Easy Equations:** 1) x = 8   2) x = 7

P89 Solving Equations: 1) a) X = 2   b) X = -0.2

P90 Formulae: 1) C = $\frac{5}{9}$ (F – 32), F = $\frac{9}{5}$C + 32   2) a) p = -4y/3   b) p = rq/(r +q)   c) p = $\sqrt{\dfrac{y}{x^2 - 3}}$

P91 Compound Growth and Decay: 1) 48 stick insects   2) 0.15m/s. Forever.

P92 Simultaneous Equations: F = 3 G = -1   **P93 Sim. Eq's With Graphs:** 2) a) x=2, y=4   b) x=1½, y=3

P94 Solving Equations With Graphs: 1) x = 0.7 or 4.3   2) x=2.1

P95 Travel Graphs: 1) 0.5 km/h   2) Phew. Ask your teacher.

P96 Inequalities: 1) X ≥ -2   2) -4, -3, -2 , -1, 0, 1

P97 Graphical Inequalities:
2)

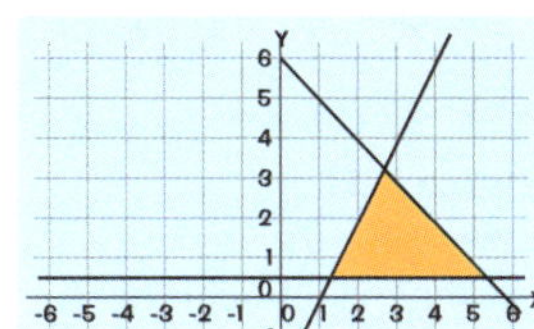
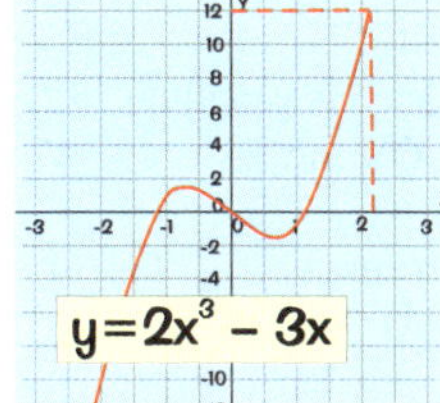

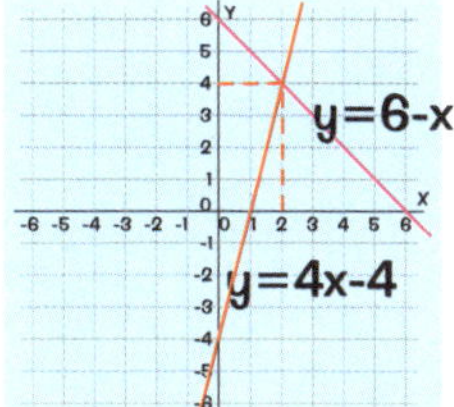

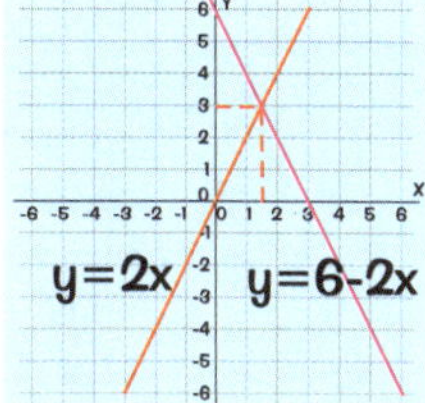

Index

A

absolutely essential 18
accuracy 8
accurate 60° and 90° angles 49
acute angles 32
adjacent side 46
algebra 78, 83, 84, 85, 96, 97
algebraic fractions 84
angle in a semicircle 38-39
angle of depression 47
angle of elevation 47
angles 23, 36-41, 32
arc 28
area of cross-section 30
areas 29, 41
average 61
  moving average 66
"Ax = B", 89, 90

B

bar charts 58
bar-line graph 58
basic algebra 84, 85
bearings 43
BODMAS 18, 83
box and whisker diagrams 65
box plots 65
brackets 78, 83, 84, 85, 89, 90
brackets buttons 18
bucket shapes 70

C

calculator 16-19
cancel button 16
cancelling algebraic fractions 84
cancelling fractions 12
centre of enlargement 33, 34

centre of rotation 34
charts 58, 59
chord 28, 38-39
circles 27, 28, 38-39, 40
circle formulas 27, 28
circle geometry 38-39, 40
circumference 27, 28
class boundaries 63
clockwise 43
coefficients 86, 92
collecting like terms 84
column vectors 44
common difference 20
common sense 10, 88
compasses, using them 48, 49
complicated shapes 29
compound growth/interest 91
congruence 41
constant area of cross-section 30
constructions 48, 49
conversion factors 10, 11
converting F-D-P 5
converting decimals to fractions 5
converting time 54
coordinates 68, 73, 74
coordinates of midpoint 74
correlation 58
COS, cosine 46, 47
cross-multiplying 89, 90
cross-section, prisms 30
cube 31
cube numbers 1
cube roots 17, 81, 82
cube root button 82
cubed 78
cuboid 9, 31

cumulative frequency 64, 65
cumulative frequency curve 65

D

data 61, 62
decimals 5, 14, 53
decimal places, rounding off 6
decimal point 79
density 53
depression, angle of 47
diameter 27, 28, 38-39
diamond shape 26
difference of two squares 78
differences, number patterns 20
distribution 60
DOTS 78
D.P. 79

E

Easy Peasy 93
edge 31
elevation, angle of 47
elevation, views 41
enlargements 33, 35
equations 88, 89, 92
equation of straight line graph
  74
equilateral triangle 23, 26, 49
estimating 8, 9
estimating areas and volumes 9
estimating square roots 9
even numbers 1
exchange rate 10, 76
exponential growth/decay 91
exterior angles 23, 36, 37

F

face 31
factors 2, 3
factor tree 2
factorising 85, 86, 90
feet 11
finding the nth term 21
formula triangles 33, 46, 47,
         52, 53, 54, 53
formulas 90
fractions 5, 12, 13, 14, 53
fraction button 13, 18, 53, 56
fractional powers 81
French francs 10
frequency 58, 62-65
frequency polygons 58
frequency tables 62-64

G

gallons 11
geometry 36-40
Golden Rule 61
gradient 72, 74, 76
graphs 72-75, 93-97
graphical inequalities 97
grouped frequency tables 63

H

HCF, highest common factor
  3
height, of triangles 27
heptagon 23
hexagon 23
horizontal 72
horribly wrong 19
horrid-looking algebra 97
hypotenuse 46

Index

I

imperial units 11
inches 11
indices 81
integer 4
inequalities 96, 97
interest – compound 91
interior angles 23, 37
inter-quartile range 65
inverse button 46
inverse proportion 71
invisible + sign 84
irregular polygons 37
isometric projections 41
isosceles triangles 23, 26, 36,
      38-39

K

kilograms, kg 11
kite, a shape 26
kilometre, km 11

L

LCM, lowest common multiple 3
leaves 60
like it or lump it 40
line graphs 58
line symmetry 24
litres 11
locus/loci 48, 49
lower quartile 65

M

manipulating algebraic
      expressions 84-85, 89, 90
map 10
mass 53
mean 61, 62
meaning of gradient 76
median 61, 62, 65
memory buttons 17
metric-imperial conversions 11
mid-interval values 63
midpoint of a line segment 74
mildly entertaining 2
miles 11
mirror line 24, 34
millimetres, mm 11
mode 61, 62
modes, calculator 19
moving averages 66
multiples 2, 3
multiplier, number patterns 20

N

negative numbers 78, 96
negative square roots 82
nets 31
northline, bearings 43
n^{th} term 21
number line 78
number patterns 20

O

obtuse angles 32
octagon 23
odd numbers 1
opposite, trigonometry 46
order of rotational symmetry 25
origin 69
original value, percentages 15
ounces 11

P

pi, π 27, 28, 29, 32
parallel lines 37
parallelograms 27, 32
pentagon 23
percentages 5, 14, 15
perimeter 29
period, of a time series 66
pie charts 59
pints 11
plan 41
plane symmetry 24
plotting 64, 75
plus/minus button 17
polygons, 23, 37
porridge 51
possible error of half a unit 7
pounds 11
power ½, roots 82
powers 1, 18, 81, 82
prime factors 2
prime numbers 4
prisms 30, 31
probability 56, 57
product of prime factors 2
projections 41
proportion 5
proportional division 51
pyramid 31
Pythagoras' theorem 45

Q

quadratic equations 86
quadrilaterals 36, 32
quartiles 65

R

radius, radii 27, 28, 38-39
range 61, 62
ratios 53, 51
rearranging formulas 90
rectangles 9, 27, 32
rectangular block 30
reflections 24, 34, 35
reflex angles 32
retail price index 66
ridiculous 10, 41, 48,
      75, 83, 94
right-angled triangles 26, 46, 45
roots 81, 82
rotations 34
rotational symmetry 25
rounding off 9
Russian agent 53

S

sample size 60
sampling methods 60
scale factors 33, 34
scatter graphs 58, 59
seasonality 66
second function Button 16
sector 27
segment 27, 38, 39
sensible 11, 14, 46, 47, 45
sequences 1
shading a region 97
shapes 26
significant figures, 6, 7, 8
similarity 41
simultaneous equations 92, 93
SIN, COS and TAN 46, 47, 45
sisters 62
smooth curves 75, 94
SOCKATOA! 46
SOH CAH TOA 46
solids 26, 30, 31
solving equations 88, 89, 92, 94
solving for squared coefficients 90
speed 11, 53, 76, 95
speed, distance and time 53
splodge 9
'spread' 60
squares 17, 23, 26, 32
square numbers 1
square roots 17, 45, 81-82, 89-90
square root button 82
squared 78, 85
squared coefficients 90
standard (index) form 19, 79
standard form button 19
stem and leaf diagrams 60
stones 11
straight line graphs 70, 73, 74
substituting 83, 87, 92
surface area 31
surprise surprise 35
symmetry 23, 24, 25, 26, 70

T

table of three values 73, 75, 93
TAN 46, 47
tangent 28, 38-39, 46, 47
tarantulas 57
terms 85, 89, 90
TERRY 34
theta, θ 46
three-letter angle notation 40
time series 66
tonnes, tons   11
transformations 34, 35
translations 34, 35
trapezium 26, 27
travel graphs 95
tree diagrams 57
trends, in a time series 66
trial and error method 88
trial and improvement 87

triangles 26, 27, 36, 37, 47
triangle numbers 1
triangular pyramid 31
trigonometry 46, 47

U

units 11, 54, 76
upper quartile 65

V

vectors 34, 44
vertex 31
vertical 72
vertical height of triangles 27
VERy HOt 72
volumes 11, 30, 41

W

weight 11
whiskers 65
with/without replacement 56
wrong 8, 15, 16, 18, 19, 72,
      83, 85, 92

X

x-axis 68
x = a and y = a, lines 69
x- and y-axis units 76
x^2 bucket shapes 70
x^3 graphs 71

Y

y-axis 68
"y = mx + c" 70, 74
yards 11

Z

"Z", "C" and "U" shapes 37
z-axis 68
zeros 7